Hall *for* Cornwall

A MONTAGE OF MEMORIES

Written and compiled by

Chris Warner & Sarah Smith

With a Foreword and Insightful Contributions by

Benjamin Luxon CBE

To all those who helped to realise a dream

Table of Contents

Foreword by Benjamin Luxon CBE

Ben Luxon backstage in Duchy Opera's Die Fledermaus

There is an ancient philosophy which states that for any undertaking to have lasting success it must have three basic ingredients: right time, right place, right people.

This book tells the story of how over a period of ten years these ingredients were constantly at work until Cornwall had its first multi-purpose, thousand-seat, truly versatile hall, in fact, exactly what it needed! It tells you how it all happened. It's an honest account and a truly inspiring one.

As a Cornishman, and incidentally a Cousin Jack, (having resided in America for the last twenty years), and as a major player in our story, I would like to give you a simple background portrait of musical Cornwall in my lifetime. Born in 1937 in Camborne, my musical career began at the age of nine immediately after the war. As I had an exceptional soprano voice, I was in constant demand for the next four years at the numerous concerts up and down the county involving choirs and a huge range of soloists, mainly singers. The venues - chapels and occasionally town halls and cinemas. This was the pattern established well before I was born.

After singing at most of the world's leading opera houses and with nearly all of the great symphony orchestras, I came back to the Duchy in the late 1980s - and I found all the same venues I had sung in as a boy, nothing more and nothing less. When I eventually became seriously involved in the quest for a hall and would be expounding the need in my favourite pub, the Pendarves Arms at Carnhell Green, the typical and genuine reaction was, "What do 'ee need a 'all for boy? We got Centenary Chapel up Redruth, Camborne Wesley and St. John's 'all down Penzance." To put it broadly and kindly it was a case of what you don't know you don't miss!

Out of the blue, Chris Warner, who I did not know at the time, invited me to become involved with Duchy Opera. I agreed on the condition that Duchy Opera should draw its singers from around the Duchy and would tour extensively within the Duchy. Chris and I soon recognised that we were "birds of a feather" and within a year we had a company that included many of the best amateur singers in the county, who really wanted to sing opera as well as musicals and operetta, and who were more than up to the task. In 1987 we toured our fledgling company from north to south of Cornwall.

For Chris and me it was the big wake-up call because we discovered first-hand how badly Cornwall needed a decent venue. We became determined that Cornwall should have somewhere which could do justice not only to the work of our great amateur opera company but a venue which could showcase the work of other Cornish companies as well as attracting regional and national tours. After our tour of inadequate town halls and sports centres, the dye was cast and for the next three years we did everything in our power to publicise the need for a decent venue.

Back to the ancient philosophy: the time and place were already established, and now so were the people, one a die-hard Cornishman (come to think of it, what Cornishman isn't?) and the other a "foreigner" living in Cornwall and involved with Cornish theatre and music. We were both successful, versatile and experienced practitioners with much the same sense of humour.

One of Chris's greatest talents was his ability to engage people with his ideas. This, accompanied by his ability to listen, remain positive and adaptable, and his theatre experience, would lead the campaign to its ultimate success. However, soon after Chris became responsible for running Truro City Hall - not only the various daytime markets, but also trying to revive and build the place up as a performance venue of sorts while at the same time looking for the funding for its replacement — it became clear that he could not do this alone. He was a creative, not a finance wizard or a business person. This very real problem was solved when Sarah Smith agreed to join Chris at City Hall as General Manager, responsible for turning the loss-making City Hall operation into a profitable business and for finding the funds to build the new venue.

From 1991 to 1996 when it closed down for the construction to begin, Truro City Hall became a pretty lively place in spite of its limitations and dilapidated state. The number of people who joined in to help make the "dream come true" was countless. Some lured in by Chris and Sarah's endless enthusiasm, faith and hard work, and many who just "showed up" because they saw the need and wanted in some way to be involved in this project which seemed to be continually gathering momentum. They were volunteers and professional people, all of whom contributed to the ultimate success of the story of what can happen when the right people come together at the right time and in the right place. I am proud that I was one of those people, and that I was able to contribute to something so tangible for the welfare of my fellow Cornishmen and women.

So much that happened wasn't planned and had a wonderfully organic feel to it. The final twist of fate that gave us the funds to physically build the new Hall was something that no one could have foreseen. But more of that later. This is Chris Warner's and Sarah Smith's story, and although aided and abetted by so many, theirs became the guiding hands that steered this venture to its remarkable conclusion.

Introduction

Choosing where to end our account was easy - we chose to stop at curtain up; choosing where to begin was much harder because there was no obvious nice tidy beginning. It's not a straightforward linear tale; events often overlapped and, to make matters worse, it is told by several people who all have slightly different perspectives and sometimes conflicting recollections. We have tried to record how it felt to be involved.

SS: When Chris and I first started writing this book, we constantly interrupted each other to share a new memory or to disagree about a detail. Gradually the book evolved into a conversation between the two of us.

CW: When we invited others to contribute their memories, it turned into a conversation with cherished old friends.

SS: By using everyone's initials to identify each new voice as it joins in, hopefully you, dear reader, will be able keep track of who is interrupting.

CW: So, if you're sitting comfortably, we'll begin.

SS: Not at the beginning obviously.

Chris and Sarah

Chapter 1

Chris Learns his Trade

CW: The Hall for Cornwall story began for me when, dressed in blue silk "pyjamas," my voice broke on stage while playing a Chinese nurse in a school play.

Like a cat, since then I have thoroughly enjoyed several lives. The twists and turns at the time seemed to have no apparent pattern, but it occurs to me now as I sit down with Sarah to tell the Hall for Cornwall story at the ripe age of Seventy-seven – how did that happen? – that each life contributed skills and knowledge which later informed how the Hall for Cornwall got itself built.

When I was a teenager, I hadn't the slightest idea what I would like to do with my life. This was largely due to the fact that I didn't have a role model in my father – he had never been engaged in any form of gainful employment. Kids at prep school kept asking me what my dad "did", and I really didn't know. When pressed as to how he could afford to pay the school fees, I pretended that he was a cat burglar.

I had to leave Stowe just before my seventeenth birthday because Father wouldn't pay the fees any more. I knew this was coming, so I had a bash – with mixed success - at French and German A level and S level English in one year.

The careers department offered me the standard choices – the Army, the Church or the Law. The Army was quite attractive because I had really enjoyed the Combined Cadet Force (CCF), becoming a member of the elite Demonstration Platoon. Once again, Father put the kibosh on that plan by saying I would never be able to live on my Army pay. He couldn't/wouldn't supplement my pay in order for me to join "a decent regiment". The Church had little appeal even though a distant ancestor had been the Bishop of Rochester and had paid for the font in Canterbury Cathedral. I had been one of a group of bolshie boys who had refused to be confirmed, and although I rather admired the story of a priest who lost his faith but carried on working for the sake of his parishioners, I knew the Church was not for me. And I couldn't hack what, as a priggish lad, I saw as the amorality of the Law, whereby a QC might either prosecute or defend a person depending on who was paying.

I was due to leave school at the end of the summer term in 1961, and when I came home at Easter, we had a rather difficult conversation about my future. I could have gone to Cambridge to read English, but Father wouldn't pay for that either because he "couldn't see the point of it". We had quite a row. "What are you going to do when you graduate?" he asked, "How are you going to earn a living?" I replied that I'd quite like to be a poet. I should have known better, not least because when he had found a poem of mine entitled "On Wearing Glasses" (a spoof of Milton's "On Going Blind"), he had threatened to cart me off to a psychiatrist in order to find out "what was the matter with me".

At this point my mother stepped in to prevent blows being exchanged – I was taller than Father and was very tempted. She took me off to Southwold, where we sat on the promenade swinging our legs and gazing disconsolately at an inhospitable brown Windsor soup of a sea. For once she had a gentler and more sympathetic approach and she tried to tease out what it was that I might want to do with my life.

I told her how much I had enjoyed playing the Chinese nurse at my prep school. It was my first taste of what it felt like to control an audience and make them laugh. The laughter was even more enjoyable because it was unplanned. Mid song, my voice started to break and the audience laughed. So my silk-clad nurse growled occasionally on purpose for the rest of the song. I had loved it.

At Stowe I had somehow got involved in the production side of things. I helped on an open-air Shakespeare play and my task was to get a horse and rider to appear on stage on the South Front on cue after starting over a mile away. The audience and the actors could hear it coming and they all knew that it was bringing bad news. I can't remember the

The South Front at Stowe School – the setting of the open air Shakespeare play

name of the play but I remember the rider slipping out of the saddle and breathlessly delivering his lines bang on time.

The next year we did an obscure show called *The Strong Are Lonely* by Fritz Hochwaelder. One scene involved the prayers for the dying in Latin – ab omni malo, libera nos, etc. I was asked to find out how to pronounce the Latin properly and then to coach the actors. I found a Catholic priest and got him to come to rehearsals. This went very well and I ended up staging the whole scene.

I told Mother that I was constantly in trouble because I was a good mimic. When I confessed to her that I was nearly expelled because I had dressed up as the Headmaster and had been observed riding round the grounds wearing a top hat, she reckoned that a career in the theatre beckoned. This unexpectedly turned out to be acceptable to the careers department on the grounds that Ralph Richardson's son was a pupil. My friends and I were more impressed by Ralph's enormous motorbike than his illustrious career.

Then came Serendipity One – I discovered that the father of a boy in my house "worked in the theatre" in London. At the next Exeat I chased this guy down the study corridor and asked him for a job. "I'll give you a job if you can get into a theatre school," was the reply. What I didn't realise was that "the guy" who made the offer was Donald Albery and that his family owned and ran four West End theatres, including the New, where the first production of *Oliver!* would soon be playing to full houses.

On the strength of this offer, my mother was able to persuade my father to pay for one year at a drama school and we eventually settled on the Bristol Old Vic Theatre School (BOVTS), largely because it ran a one-year technical course.

At the start of the interview with BOVTS, the principal explained that they were not prepared to take anyone unless they had a realistic chance of a job at the end of the course. Like a conjuror producing a white rabbit out of the Headmaster's top hat, I announced that Mr. Albery had offered me a job if I could get into a theatre school. I was in!

Father actually seemed quite pleased even though one of his friends had warned him that I would "never be the same again". Shades of Noel Coward's *"Don't Put Your Daughter On The Stage, Mrs. Worthington."*

So in the autumn of 1960, just turned seventeen, I set out for Bristol. I found myself a room and a landlady who offered some cooking and a laundry service.

I loved my year at the BOVTS and the stuff I learnt was a basic toolkit for a life in theatre. We had to do stage management, stage design, props, lighting, wardrobe, set building, set painting and flying (hanging scenery). We ran BOVTS productions for both year 1 and year 2 in the studio theatre which we shared with the University of Bristol's drama department. If we wanted to borrow anything from the department, I would simply impersonate the BOVTS principal and ring up and bellow, "Hellooooo there, Uncle Glynne (the department Professor). Uncle Richard here. Could one of my young luvvies come down and pick up …" whatever prop or costume we needed. Magic.

But the bees' knees was working shows at the prestigious Bristol Old Vic, a repertory theatre, which produced a new play every three weeks. It was the real McCoy! I worked loads of fit-ups and get-outs, becoming in the process a useful flyman thanks to a friendly Pole – called Frank because no one could pronounce his real name. And I trod those illustrious boards with no less than five walk-on parts in *War and Peace!* One role was a medical orderly, and every night me and another walk-on secretly took Paul Eddington's trousers down while pretending to tend his wounds. He was supposed to be near to death so he couldn't protest or giggle. Not all bad behaviour, though – eight times a week I had to throw a champagne bottle the full width of the stage to a fellow officer, who had to catch it by the neck and use it to parry a sword thrust. That's discipline. I got to see a lot of shows and to work with a lot of theatre people. And I got to go to some pretty wild onstage parties after first nights. Now that's real networking …

At the end of the course, Donald Albery kept his word and took me on as a management trainee. The plan was that I should work a few months in every side of the business, and I was set to work in the box office at the Criterion Theatre in Piccadilly Circus. I bought a suit and became a box office clerk. My biggest disaster was somehow managing to sell the whole of the second row of the stalls twice in a full house …

The "Cri" was a very ornate building with a posh restaurant in the basement, but it was also home to loads of rats, which occasionally crept into the theatre to feast on the chocolates left by audiences under the seats. After the interval one night, a lady in the audience reached under her seat and felt something furry. God, how she screamed!

More importantly than experiencing the ratty underbelly of the West End, suddenly I had access to any show I fancied because box offices all over the West End swapped complimentary tickets. Better even than that, we often got free tickets to first nights. I set out to go to every first night, and particularly every first night party. I went to so many that after a bit I was greeted by other bona fide regular party "faces" as one of them. I fell in with a well-known comedian called Jimmy Edwards (who like me had no real reason to be there) and we used to have a fine old time at least once a week. It was schmoozing at its finest. More useful "networking".

Next, I was put to work as a stage electrician, again based at the "Cri" but also working on other Wyndham Theatres productions. For this I was obliged to join the National Association of Theatrical and Kine Employees, (NATKE), which was the union for non-acting people in the theatre and film industry. I was a bit churlish about paying my 6d a week union subs, because as a greenhorn I had no idea how many doors my NATKE card would open for me in the future. In those days it was really tough getting started. Whoever made the rules might well have read *Catch 22* – you needed a card to work and you couldn't get a card unless you were working. Equity, the actors' union, worked on the same principle.

In the mornings we did theatre maintenance, which included rewiring Donald's motorboat on the river at Marlow, and in the evenings we ran the shows. My job was to operate the lighting board while the Chief checked out the next day's horseracing. The first show that I worked starred Wilfred Hyde-White and a young Richard Briers. Wilfred's chauffeur used to give the Chief lots of hot racing tips and I was included in this favour because each night my Mini, with the addition of a few crates, was used to reserve a space for Wilfred's Roller. When Wilfred wanted to go to the races, he simply arranged for his understudy to cover the matinee! The next show lacked this glamour but it featured a very young Michael Caine fresh out of RADA.

Next up, I was a stagehand working mainly matinees in almost every West End theatre and doing fit-ups and end-of-run breakdowns and get-outs. What a fantastic grounding that was – I got to see how these big shows worked and what top designers could do. The show that really inspired me was *Blitz*, which had, amongst other amazing effects, two huge towers on wheels joined by a bridge. The towers could move up and down stage while the bridge, with actors on it, could be raised or lowered at the same time. There was also a wonderful theatrical sleight of hand which Kneehigh would have been proud of. The illusion of a tube train leaving a station was achieved by a very long cloth on rollers. The actors remained stationary while the background cloth flashed past them.

It was a very thorough no-nonsense old-fashioned bottom-up apprenticeship learning the mechanics of the theatre. As well as all the technical stuff, I was also allowed to attend the occasional rehearsal. After I'd worked in the West End for several months, two shows transferred from the Bristol Old Vic to Albery theatres and I felt very chuffed because I knew the casts and the crews; but seeing all the Bristol Old Vic people again made me realise that I was increasingly missing being around actors.

One day, Serendipity 2 found me working at the Haymarket while the theatre was being used for a Goon Show rehearsal. I was mesmerised. Gradually, everyone in the building stopped whatever they were doing and crept into the auditorium to watch the rehearsal. This was a lightbulb moment. From then on, I wangled my way into as many rehearsals as possible, but it was perfectly clear that Donald was never going to let a nineteen-year-old loose on one of his West End shows. So I resolved to go to a university where I would be able to do some directing using student actors. I chose a three-year degree course at Bristol University which covered radio, film and television as well as theatre. I think they let me in partly because on the application form I had put Bristol, Bristol, Bristol for all of my three choices.

As well as three hours of improvisation every Friday afternoon for three years, I did get to both act and direct. One show I directed featured a young Tim Piggot-Smith in *Next Time I'll Sing To You* – which was the show with Michael Caine which I'd watched every night for three months at the "Cri". A bit of a cheat?

As a drama student, I found all the practical things I had learnt in my three years of real theatre work gave me insights into how to get the texts we studied academically from page to stage. I became particularly interested in the staging of the *Ordinalia*, the wonderful mediaeval Cornish cycle of Mystery Plays. More of those later, because they belong to Serendipities 7 and 8.

Just before going back to three years of student life studying theatre, radio and television at Bristol University, Wendy, the girl I had met at Bristol Old Vic Theatre School, and I got married. It seemed a good idea at the time, not least because my wonderful grandmother had offered me three years' living money, in advance, in one lump.

It seemed a lot of money to spend on living, so I used it to buy a tiny cottage (with a chemical toilet!) for £2,200 at Webb's Heath, just outside Bristol.

My new wife was a designer and she managed to get a job doing props at Bristol Old Vic – so we could eat. And here's another not so small serendipity – she was my introduction to Cornwall, because her father had recently moved his optician business to Truro. Which was where we had got married.

Chris as a toddler practising his tea making skills with his lovely Granny

I was also able to pick up casual work at Bristol Old Vic and managed to wangle one spectacularly well-paid day a week working as an assistant floor manager on two children's serials at Westward TV. One day, I was in the office when the director's PA came in and shouted, "Can anyone ride a horse?" I put my hand up and ended up with several days filming on Children of the New Forest. I was a New Model Army Puritan on a pony and had to have a sword fight on horseback with a member of the Household Cavalry mounted on a 16.3 hand charger. I had to wheel my pony round and round a static camera, "attacking" it as if it was my opponent. My sword was so heavy that I nearly took my pony's ears off and I certainly scared the hell out of the cameraman! Then I had to flee the field, galloping off followed by my comrades, thus causing the Battle of Gloucester to be won by the Royalists. Well paid fun – which was to prove useful later.

After graduation, I found it hard to find creative work. My wife had given birth to our son in Bristol, so I badly needed to do something.

Chapter 2

Piran Round and the Ordinalia

CW: Serendipity 5 was the fact that Peter Hall's father shared a barber with my father and they often chatted while having their monthly haircuts. On the strength of this, I wrote to Peter Hall at the Royal Shakespeare Company asking if he had any work going. I had a nice reply along the lines of "No, I don't, but I know a man who does." The man was RSC actor Tony Church, recently appointed Director of the newly built Northcott Theatre in Exeter.

Northcott Auditorium – photograph by Nick Toyne

It was a three-weekly repertory theatre, which was pretty classy in those days, but I had to swallow my pride because all he could offer me was a job as Deputy Stage Manager (DSM). However, a DSM sits next to the director during rehearsals and was a traditional route to becoming a director. It worked for me, and after a couple of years I started directing at the Northcott.

My first production was the world premiere – for one night only – of *Wrung for All* by a talented Devon playwright called Marjerie St Hill. I must have passed this extended audition because I went on to direct several shows which ran for the normal three weeks in the main repertoire.

A highlight for me was my production of John Osborne's *Look Back in Anger,* which had caused such a rumpus at the Royal Court in 1956. The two leads at the Northcott were two young actors who later became very successful – Eve Best and John Nettles. I bet those two never had an inkling of how their careers would develop, although you could clearly see "the mark upon them". I certainly had no idea that I would eventually work at the Royal Court.

Serendipity 6 was as yet unknown to me – the style of the Northcott auditorium was to be a big influence on the design of Hall for Cornwall. It seated just under 500 in a Greek amphitheatre style, with a very wide proscenium opening and a flat floor stage at the same level as the front row.

Northcott Auditorium – photograph by Nick Toyne

It bore a remarkable resemblance to the future 400-seat mode in Hall for Cornwall and it was a joy to work, offering audiences both intimacy and a very shared experience. Two enduring memories of great theatre: one was the beheading of Monmouth in *The Bastard King*. Monmouth knelt at the block, the axe was raised, the lights turned to red. Monmouth got up, and a sack with a large turnip attached by a thick rope was substituted. The axe fell and the severed turnip rolled slowly towards the feet of people in the front row, who screamed as they tried to get away from the rolling "head".

The other was in *A Day in the Life of Edmund Dew Nevitt*. I was the DSM on this show, which involved me in a particularly tricky bit of cueing for a daring but dangerous stunt. At the back of the stage, hidden in the scenery dock behind slashed black curtains, was a car – a white Sunbeam Alpine – and on the bridge over the dock opening was a hidden swing with very long ropes. A tricycle for two crossed the stage, following the curve of the front row. An engine revved and the hidden car burst through the slashed curtains, lights blazing, driving straight at the tricycle down centre. The car stopped inches from the knees of the people in the front row. The car backed up then chased the tricycle around the stage, following it into the back dock. Just before the car went back under the bridge, an actress on the hidden swing was launched towards the oncoming car. She went out over the front rows in a wedding dress with a twenty-foot silk train trailing behind her. It was stunning! Provided that she didn't go through the car's windscreen.

There is, however, nearly always a fly in the ointment. And the Northcott's fly was that it was invisible. It sat on a hill on the university campus above the town. No-one ever popped in. The town did not feel a sense of ownership. Every night I had to organise a bus from the City Centre up to the theatre and the bus was often empty. It was a grim experience that I was not to forget. The breakthrough came when we opened a city centre box office with a shop window full of production photographs and posters.

Years later, the Hall for Cornwall Campaign was offered a site beside a big roundabout on Carn Brea. This had its attractions – a wild landscape with a very Cornish identity in tin-mining country, good communications, the possibility of an exciting new building unconstrained by neighbours. But no one would have popped in for a coffee or to buy a ticket. Because of Exeter, I knew that we should not accept the Carn Brea offer and that we had to find a town-centre site for the Hall. Sure, there would be other problems with that, but it would be worth it. Ironically, the fierce sense of ownership felt by people in Truro for their beloved – but neglected – town-centre City Hall jolly nearly scuppered us.

Serendipity 7 was the arrival in the UK of an American waving a fairly ghastly English translation of the *Ordinalia*, which was originally written in Cornish. A good example of its ghastliness would be Adam's attempt to prevent the Fall of Man with the words, "Oh, gee, Eve, don't eat the apple." The Bristol University drama department commissioned a more sympathetic version and decided to make this a student project, involving all three years in the production.

Having completed my drama degree at Bristol, and with my newly acquired knowledge of Cornwall, the department asked me to be their man in Cornwall. It was now my job to find a suitable open-air performance space and to get it ready for a production of all three plays, which had not been performed in 500 years!

The Chairman of Cornwall County Council at that time was a guy called Alderman Foster, nick-named "the Gauleiter". He swanned down to Truro each day in an immaculate Rolls-Royce, allegedly making notes about litter on the verges. Somehow or other I managed to get to him and bless him, he took me and the project under his wing. Which made people realise that it was seriously going to happen. I was given an office in what is now Old County Hall (all there was in 1969), a secretary, use of printing and postal services, Highways' personnel and diggers, and financial services from Treasurers, all for free. We also had a generous grant, and I was paid enough to live well for a whole year for doing four months' work. On the strength of all this I rented a little cottage behind the Punchbowl and Ladle pub in Penelewey – handy for Truro and for a pint after work.

It was like Christmas come early! If you remember, as a drama student I had been particularly interested in the Cornish Cycle, which consists of three full-length plays – *The Origin of the World*, which covered the Old Testament, *The Passion*, and *The Resurrection*. It was probably written by someone in Glasney College in Penryn in the early 15th century. The baddies all speak English, the goodies all speak Cornish, and it is one of Cornwall's national treasures. Like Shakespeare, the Cycle has a creative mix of comedy, tragedy and redemption. But the really important thing is that, unlike the English cycles, which were staged on moving wagons, the Cornish Cycle was written for production in the round, which allowed for simultaneous and intercut action both in the central circle and behind the audience, who sat on the slopes of an earthwork bowl.

I therefore needed to find or build a large circular open-air auditorium. And of course, Cornwall actually has several rounds – called a plen-an-gwarry (or playing place). I had to find one which could cope with the installation of seating, loos and of course a car park. Sadly, this ruled out Penryn Church, whose west end looks onto a round (now a graveyard) where the cycle might originally have been performed. The hunt led me to a lovely man called Nigel Holman who owned Piran Round near Goonhavern. It was isolated, overgrown and until recent times had been used for tea treats and various other open-air social events. Nigel generously offered it to us free of charge as our venue and threw in the use of estate staff and a lorry.

First take your Earthwork

by Chris Warner

FIRST take your earthwork, remove the growth of gorse and the accumulation of broken glass, bedsteads and old prams, install some seating, flag poles and fencing, dressing room, tents and lavatory accommodation. Find a donkey for Christ and some pigeons for Noah to release. Keep these in a handy place as you will need them later.

Next take the text of the Cornish Cycle of Mystery plays and translate steadily from the beginning to the end of all three plays. This may take some time. You will discover that there are some 200 speaking parts.

Next take 70 students from Bristol University Drama Department and rehearse them in Bristol over a period of about six weeks. When approaching setting point transport them to your earthwork a week before the first night. Feed thrice daily and stir well into a Cornish Mediaeval mood, while continuing to rehearse vigorously. Allow short breaks for surfing.

Chris Warner praying for fine weather — *Nicholas Toyne*

This light-hearted "recipe" for the project appeared in a Northcott Theatre programme. The real-life challenge of creating a fully functional 2,000-seat theatre with all the usual facilities for audiences and performers in a field should not be underestimated.

Alderman Foster gave commands and Highways JCBs cleared the gorse and we started to put in services – electricity, sewerage, water and the phone. Road signs had to be erected because without them no one would ever have found the round. We built a tiered scaffolding auditorium which could seat 2,000 on the slopes of the newly revealed amphitheatre. It became a vast tented encampment – there were marquees for the box office, bars, catering facilities for the large cast, loos, dressing rooms, storage for the costumes and props for three plays, a stage door and security office, and of course car parks. An army of volunteers made it all function. County Council officers from Treasurers escaped from their offices to man the box office.

Somehow the project caught everyone's imagination and people came literally from all over the world as well as from the UK and of course from Cornwall. We sold out for a fortnight. Not only had the project demonstrated a hunger in Cornwall for theatre with a Cornish identity, it had given me the chance to learn how to move a project from an idea to a bums-on-seats reality. And I learnt what a valuable tool a model could be in persuading people to get behind a project.

Piran Round – completed – photograph by Nick Toyne

Serendipity 8 was learning about the worldwide Cornish diaspora and the large number of Cornish societies who were prepared to help with the marketing – and who, twenty years later, would support the Hall for Cornwall Campaign.

I learnt such a lot about Cornish people and what made Cornwall tick. An abiding memory is calling on a local farmer who was just about to eat a pasty for his tea. He asked me if I had eaten, and when I said no, he solemnly cut his pasty in half and invited me to sit down with him.

Another sharp memory concerns a very special moment from *The Passion.* When Christ was crucified, we cleared the stage, leaving the three crosses isolated in the huge auditorium. And we left them there. And we left them there some more. We left them for what felt like five minutes and gradually people in the audience began to cry. First of all, they hid their tears but gradually the sobs became more audible until the whole audience was overwhelmed. Typing, I'm sniffling again – fifty years later.

The Piran Round production of the *Ordinalia* was one of the most memorable theatrical events in Cornwall, never to be forgotten. On the Sunday of the middle weekend of the two-week run, the three plays were presented in one long, gloriously sunny day. A seed had been sown …

At the end of a subsequent Northcott programme article about Piran Round, I wrote, "I sincerely hope that … this [production] will provide … the inspiration for the building of a "County Arts Centre and Theatre". It's a bit of a shock to discover that a "County Arts Centre and Theatre" was a preoccupation as long ago as 1970!

One evening towards the end of the run, I was called to answer the box-office phone. I asked who was on the line. "Sam Wannamaker," was the reply. All through my student years, my friends and I would joke that there was a call for them from Sam Wannamaker, who wanted to offer them the career break of their lives. He was a distinguished American actor and director, a friend of Yul Brynner, who, fearing the blacklisting in the McCarthy era, had settled in the UK. But Hollywood had left its mark on him – "dig it up and move it three feet to the left" could have been his motto. Much later, he demanded that I "ring Reggie Marsh, you know, the goddam Chairman of British Rail" and demand that Marsh stop the mainline trains running into London through Southwark because the noise was spoiling a Wannamaker pageant production on a horse-drawn wagon.

I didn't believe it was Wannamaker on the line and promptly told the caller to "naff off". But it was him – for real. Apparently, he had woken up one morning and decided to rebuild Shakespeare's Globe on its original site in Southwark. Serendipity 9 was the fact that he had somehow formed the impression that I was a professor of Elizabethan Theatre. He was so excited that I didn't get the chance to tell him I wasn't, and I soon found myself working on his kitchen table as General Manager for his embryonic Globe Playhouse project. His daughter Zoe was about thirteen and used to help, rather reluctantly, with the filing.

It wasn't long before Sam managed to get a substantial grant from Players, the cigarette people, and then persuaded someone to allow us to occupy an unused builder's yard overlooking the Thames on Bankside, very close to the bridge. In Elizabethan times, Southwark was a haven for all sorts of rough and licentious entertainment which, as well as dozens of brothels, also featured numerous cock-fighting and bear-baiting pits, some of which were adapted by the theatre companies moving across the Thames in order to be free of the City of London licensing laws. Three hundred years later, when we arrived, Southwark was very run down. Everywhere seemed derelict – housing, warehouses, wharves, even the people. There was massive unemployment caused by the closure of the wharves and docks. Housing was scarce and of poor quality.

There were, however, plans for a £300m redevelopment, which proved to be both a bonus and a problem. We moved into the old builder's offices and registered our address as 40 Bankside, Liberty of the Clink, Southwark. It was a romantic address but the truth was that Southwark's social problems were so pressing that neither the locals nor the government really wanted our project. People wanted housing and work, not a theatre. Although they owned the site, English Heritage actually refused to divulge the dimensions of the original Globe! While there were many Globe replicas in the USA, the only sign of the Globe in the UK was a dirty plaque on a disused brewery. "You goddam Brits ..." was a constant cry. For Sam just couldn't understand why no one in England had thought to rebuild the Globe and why so many had set their faces against his plans. Later, the local opposition so enraged him that, on camera, he punched a Southwark councillor. Not a good PR move! His response was to frustrate the developers by buying the site of another famous Elizabethan theatre, the foundations of which had to be preserved. His new acquisition sat at the centre of the £300m Hay's Wharf development. Sam was playing Monopoly on a truly grand scale!

It was a foretaste of the kind of resistance which we would meet when we launched the Hall for Cornwall Campaign. "Pie in the sky, boy," said Councillor Cockle on Radio Cornwall, "pie in the sky". But more of that later.

Sam's family and I helped to paint the old builder's office and Sam scrounged carpets from Gamages and desks etc. from elsewhere. We took on two PAs each and we were off. You could run an empire with four talented PAs – and we did. In nine months, we got planning permission for a temporary theatre, erected it, put in services, appointed theatre staff, marketed the first season, and cast and produced our own Hamlet with Keith Michell.

We converted a warehouse, where we presented an exhibition called *In the Clink*, with not one but two first folio editions (which had to be guarded night and day); built and programmed a cinema, which opened with the Russian Lear; and built and staffed a pub, which I made sure had moussaka on the menu. I can still feel the thrill of seeing our posters on the walls of the London Underground.

I was burnt out after that big push and retreated to Cornwall to recover. Sam pursued his vision but sadly died before his dream of the Globe came true. Every now and again I talk to his bust in the Globe foyer and, when no one is looking, I tweak his nose affectionately. As Kipling observed, you can't create a garden by sitting dreaming under a tree.

Perhaps the most important thing I learnt from Sam was the American concept of "the Asking Power", which is now commonly employed in marketing and fundraising. If you want to borrow a fiver off the Queen, it's no good asking her yourself – you've got to get HRH The Duke of Cornwall to ask for you. And so we had produced a wonderful brochure complete with sketches of our proposed new Globe and loads of written endorsements by celebrity "Vice Presidents", who were mostly Sam's personal friends from Hollywood.

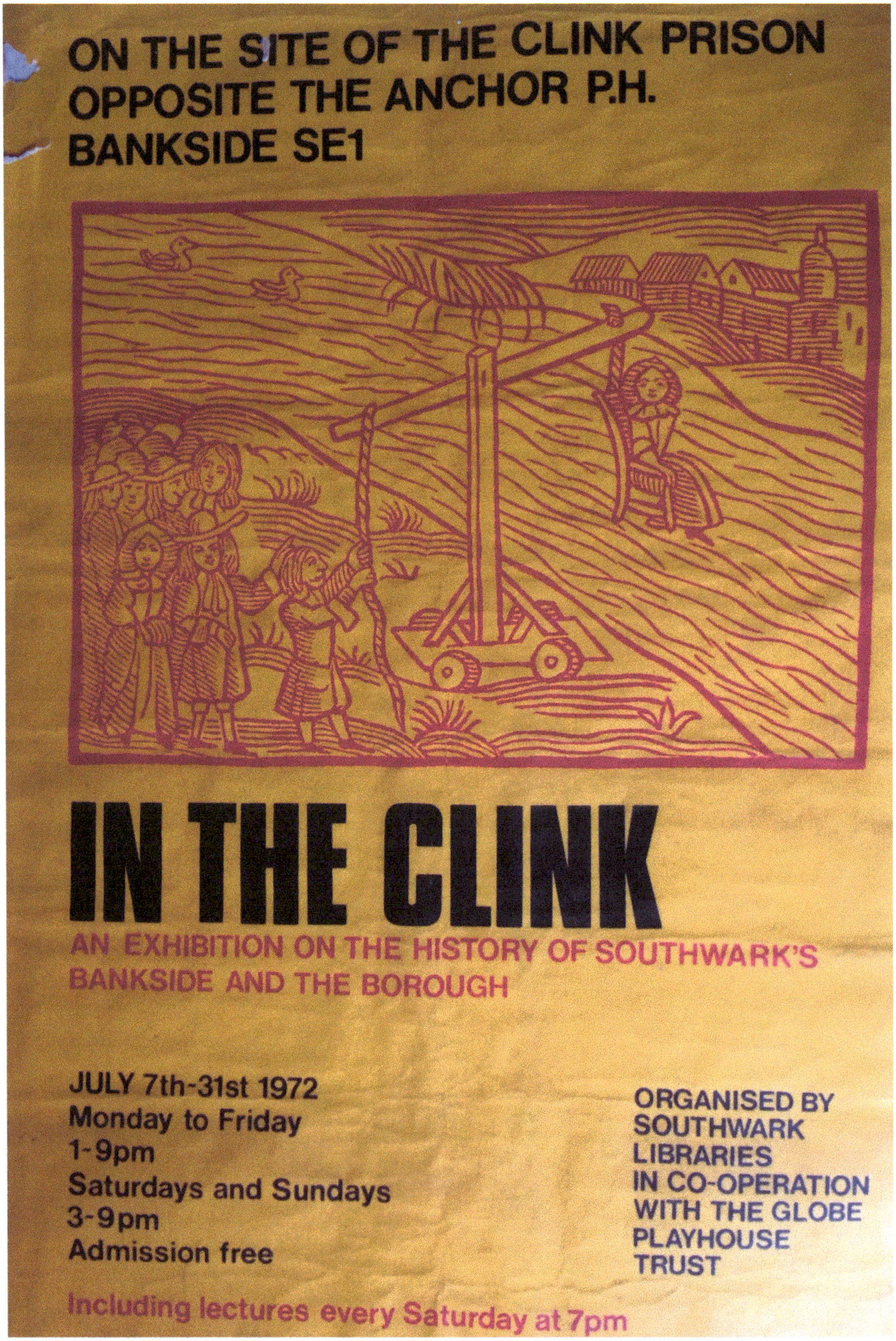
ON THE SITE OF THE CLINK PRISON
OPPOSITE THE ANCHOR P.H.
BANKSIDE SE1
IN THE CLINK
AN EXHIBITION ON THE HISTORY OF SOUTHWARK'S
BANKSIDE AND THE BOROUGH
JULY 7th-31st 1972
Monday to Friday
1-9pm
Saturdays and Sundays
3-9pm
Admission free
ORGANISED BY
SOUTHWARK
LIBRARIES
IN CO-OPERATION
WITH THE GLOBE
PLAYHOUSE
TRUST
Including lectures every Saturday at 7pm

Chapter 3

Meeting Ben Luxon

I was offered a second season choosing and running the programme at Piran Round. On the strength of this I bought a cottage, a barn and five acres near Come to Good. My eldest boy needed to go school the following autumn and it seemed to make sense to base the family in Cornwall, where I had a well-paid summer job at Piran and where my wife could enjoy the support of her parents while I gallivanted off in the winter pursuing my career. Wendy Shier (WS) takes up the tale:

WS: The Mystery Plays had proved that Piran Round could offer an alternative venue for the companies who wanted to bring a production to Cornwall but couldn't find a slot at the oversubscribed Minack Theatre. So the following year Chris had arranged a short programme of visiting productions, which included one of his own. This had a cast of actors drawn from the Northcott Theatre company who we accommodated in our very scruffy farmhouse and even in the barn! What a lot of fun that was; the cast included John Nettles, who brought his wife and their new baby. Because the house, as Chris put it, "wasn't quite finished", the baby was bathed each evening in our huge farmhouse sink.

CW: So there I was, at the ripe old age of twenty-six, directing my own company in my own theatre – even if it did actually belong to Nigel Holman. Heady stuff. But never count your chickens before your eggs have hatched – the County Council pulled the funding after the second season. After all sorts of odd jobs, I eventually managed to secure a proper job as Assistant Director at the Royal Court Theatre, Sloane Square. It was a heady time! Lindsay Anderson, who had recently directed *If*, took a shine to me at the interview and I became Bill Gaskill's assistant. *The Contractor* was playing, with Ralph Richardson and John Gielgud on the main stage. Other assistants included David Hare, Bill Bryden and Christopher Hampton. You never knew what you were going to be asked to do from one minute to the next and one day I was given a list of actors to whom I was to offer the lead in Osborne's *The Entertainer.* I remember ringing up Peter Finch in Rome, Richard Burton, who was staying at the Dorchester, Gielgud and various other "names". Bizarrely, I was once asked by a distinguished actress, "Do I know you? Or have we had" – theatrical pause to assume husky voice – "a relationship?" On another occasion

I found myself hosting Germaine Greer (of *The Female Eunuch* fame) because mostly men ran the theatres in those days and they were absolutely terrified of her! And I got to transfer a production of *Lulu* into the Apollo after its six-week run at the Court.

The "Court" was a wonderfully organic – not to say chaotic – place to work. I vividly remember rewrites in taxis on the way to rehearsals, and to find out what was going on you had to hang around in the upper-circle bar after curtain down. I remember being quite shocked by overhearing someone exclaim, "Oh God, what the hell are we going to do next?" And it could well be that anyone who happened to be standing around might get to work with the next Penguin Playwright or a theatrical knight of the realm. And standing around with a drink in my hand was how I got my big break. A fairly well-known actress wanted to do a one-woman show about her life and she wanted an unknown to direct her. Someone suggested, "Chris could do that for you!" I didn't feel it was really my sort of show, and anyway by this time Cornwall was a-tugging, so I turned it down. I often wonder where it might have led – but hey, sometimes you should ignore your head and go with your heart.

Years of being away from home and spending more than I could afford on the sleeper had taken its toll on my marriage. The spell at the Court had finished us off. My wife wanted a life and a career of her own. So we hatched a plan whereby I would spend yet another year away in order to qualify as a teacher. After which she would be free to pursue her own career and I would become the primary carer of our two boys.

WS: As Chris's dream faded, so did our marriage. However, although going our separate ways we still had two young boys to bring up, we still lived in the same parish, we both turned to teaching as a more sustainable career, and I think it's fair to say that we continued to respect each other's talents in theatre and retained a similar sense of humour about life. We had been a good team!

CW: It had been a great privilege to be around distinguished actors and four distinguished directors, especially Bill Gaskill and Lindsey Anderson (who had recently won an Oscar), to learn to allow the rehearsal process to be a journey of discovery, that rehearsals were also about defining the journeys of the individual actors, to value excellence over expense, to dare, and to be very clear about what you wanted the audience to feel at any given moment.

APOLLO
THEATRE
Under the direction of Prince Littler
Shaftesbury Avenue, London W1. Tel: 01-437 2663
Lewenstein-Delfont Productions Ltd
and the Royal Court Theatre presents
JULIA
FOSTER
in the Nottingham Playhouse Production of
LULU
Frank
Wedekind
adapted by
Peter Barnes

What was the most valuable thing I learnt? Bill's mantra, "Just say the words, dear, just say the words." Think Hamlet's request to the travelling players. It's the hardest thing in the world for some actors, and I saw distinguished people reduced to tears because they just couldn't do it. Ben Luxon had a similar mantra: "Just sing the notes, stop all that acting and let the music do the work, just sing the notes."

It had been a bit of a contrast to working as a barman at the Pandora Inn, driving a lorry and being an oyster fisherman in a hundred-year-old sailing boat with no engine! But far more important for Hall for Cornwall (HfC) than the Royal Court was Serendipity 8: a gentleman who ran a sailing school in Flushing dropped a car battery on his foot. The significance of the smashed toes for HfC cannot be over-estimated, for it led to the establishment of my very own Loe Beach Sailing School. What on earth has that got to do with HfC? you may well ask. The answer is that many key figures in our story of the HfC campaign and the eventual building of Hall for Cornwall were pupils or related to pupils who learnt to sail at Loe Beach – particularly Leon Lovett the conductor – who introduced me to Benjamin Luxon – and Sarah Smith, who offered free office accommodation and secretarial services at Smith and Reed and who went on to play such a crucial role as General Manager and Fundraiser. Pupils including John de la Cour (the South West Arts Music Officer), the MP Matthew Taylor's girlfriend, Annette Penhaligon and her children, and Lord Falmouth's grandchildren come to mind. People talk in boats. But more of that later. Ben caused quite a stir at Loe Beach in breaks from *The Magic Flute* rehearsals. We should have sold tickets for people to watch him learning to windsurf.

Another pupil was a guy called John Wooldridge who, with his wife, ran a freelance film crew working mainly for the BBC. When his wife hurt her back and could no longer carry the heavy tape machine, I became his sound recordist. My NATKE ticket allowed me to join him and we had a fun-filled and very lucrative few years before everything went digital and he decided to retire. He was a lovely man who always ploughed his own furrow, and he taught me how a thirty-second news item should be delivered. He died too young, doing the Twist.

Armed with my shiny Cert Ed from Birmingham University, I had got a job teaching English and Drama at Redruth Grammar School. After a year or so, Redruth secondary and grammar schools were merged into a single comprehensive. It was huge – 1,200 pupils and over 100 staff. And I became Head of Drama, working in a fabulous new state-of-the-art studio. But sadly, the school saw drama as a bit of a dustbin subject, suitable for the less able pupils. After three years I'd had enough. I had come to realise that teaching was way down the list of all the other things teachers are obliged to do (dinner money, registers, reports, exams, child-minding, etc.). What finished me was the loss of my lovely studio to exams each summer term. Young people with low reading ages, whose personal and social development thrived in the studio, were relegated to a hot Elliott hut where they were obliged to "read" plays. I told the Head that if it happened again, I would leave. Sure enough, he booked my studio as an exam hall the following summer. I realised that I loved teaching but hated schools. The Head was astonished when I resigned.

By the time I started at Redruth, I had got together with a lovely lady who, like me, was looking after her own two children. During the half term of what became my last summer term at Redruth, I was towing my step-daughter's Mirror dinghy down to our local beach when I was serendipitously flagged down by a couple who wanted to know where they could find someone to teach their daughter to sail. The guy with the crushed toes had given me a couple of months work and I knew that it was really hard to find sailing lessons on the Fal. Quick as a flash I said that I could do that, and we fixed a price and a start date. I went on down to the beach and asked the owner if he would allow me to teach sailing from his beach. It was perfect, facing south at the Feock end of the Carrick Roads. He was up for it. Serendipity 9 was a blank (literally) cheque from a university friend which enabled me to buy a Wayfarer and so began a very happy – and productive – part of my life.

Serendipity 10 manifested itself as a loud knock on my door. It was not the Gestapo but a shortish Welshman in need of a shave. He enquired as to whether I was Chris Warner and asked if I had ever directed any operas. He went on to explain that he was from a company called Duchy Opera which had parted with its director in mid rehearsal, and that they were in urgent need of a replacement. I told him that I found opera quite ludicrous, whereupon he reached into his jacket pocket. I wondered if he was going to shoot me for my blasphemy, but instead of a gun he produced a chequebook. I decided that opera might have its attractions after all.

So I found myself directing a production of *Rigoletto* in the 100-seat Falmouth Arts Centre, with a piano and four hands as the orchestra. Sure enough the heroine was stabbed, chained up in a sack, thrown in a river, rescued half dead from the river – and could still manage to sing a hefty aria before she finally expired.

WS: In 1979 Chris was asked to direct Duchy's first production of *The Magic Flute* and he asked me to design a simple set for it. This was the first of seven Duchy productions which we worked on together.

CW: Serendipity 11 was Leon Lovett entering stage left in a Wayfarer. Leon had bought a holiday cottage near Feock and he came for sailing lessons. Unexpectedly becalmed one day nearer Black Rock than Loe Beach, it emerged that he was a successful conductor who worked with two distinguished choirs and various orchestras in London. He was amazed to discover that his sailing instructor directed operas. We chatted, and what seemed a very cunning plan emerged. Leon knew that the BBC was looking for a ready-made production of Britten's *Curlew River* to be part of the next Proms season at the Albert Hall.

We decided to set up a production with Duchy Opera, using professional Cornish singers conducted by Leon, directed by you-know-who, and then offer it to the Beeb. Leon knew Ben Luxon, who had been an early member of Britten's company in Aldeburgh, and Leon thought Ben would be up for it. Leon went back to London – a familiar HfC scenario, as we shall discover – and I set to work.

I got positive responses from the agents representing Richard Jackson, Benjamin Luxon, John Trelevean and Alan Opie. John de la Cour, the Music Officer at South West Arts, was amenable partly because it was a cracking idea and partly because he too had been a pupil at Loe Beach. But he was doubtful that we'd ever get Ben – the first Cornishman to sing at La Scala – to take time out from his humongous career. How wrong he was!

The budget of course was eye-watering, but the real difficulty was finding dates which worked for the singers, some of whom had five-year diaries. I'm not sure we ever owned up to the Duchy Opera management, but it didn't matter because Auntie changed her mind and without the Proms fee we couldn't make it work financially.

There were two consequences of our attempted scam. Firstly, we appeared on the radar of some of the most respected Cornish singers, who did eventually come to sing with Duchy; and secondly, Leon was invited to conduct *Carmen*, the next Duchy production, and his appointment would lead to new developments for Duchy. It was agreed that Leon would recruit some young professional singers, the leader of the orchestra and possibly some additional players. Rehearsals were to take place in London and later in Cornwall. All very exciting.

I decided to set the production in South America with Carmen running guns, and once again, probably against her better judgement, I persuaded Wendy to be the designer.

Costume designs by Wendy Shier for Carmen

The garrison troops, of which Don Jose was a member, would be bored GIs. Shades of Vietnam. Like a real-life South American presidential candidate, Escamillo would sing in a football stadium supported by armed guards and American-style cheerleaders complete with pompoms. Luckily, this concept turned out not to be completely barmy because a fortnight before curtain-up President Regan invaded Grenada. Talk about serendipity …

Where to do it, had been the problem! Leon couldn't believe it when he discovered that lots of Cornish towns had small arts theatres but that neither Truro nor indeed Cornwall had a suitable middle-scale venue with an orchestra pit. In the end we opted for the old cinema in Falmouth. It was still used periodically by the Falmouth Operatic Society and so had retained its rudimentary flying and lighting, and there was room for a small pit.

Serendipity 12 – Ben Luxon's mother persuaded her boy to take her to see our *Carmen*. He hated the South American setting but was apparently surprised and impressed by what had been achieved by the company. At the time, neither Ben nor I had an inkling of how important his trip to the opera would become. If he had not happened to be in Cornwall at that time, or if he had turned down his mother's request to see the production, I might never have met him and he might not have played such a crucial role in getting the Hall for Cornwall Campaign off the ground.

Fast-forward to Leon's sitting room in Barnet, where I was introduced to a slightly defensive Ben. Those blue eyes fixed on me like lasers. "What do you want?" he demanded. "I want you to come and sing in Cornwall," I said. "And so does everyone else. You haven't sung at home for ages."

I'm ashamed to say that I didn't really know much about Ben, so, dear reader, in case you don't, here in his own words is what he has to say about his life up to the fatal moment when he agreed to get involved with Duchy Opera:

BL: I'm a Camborne boy, born 1937 in a Cornwall that before the advent of television was alive with music-making and regular concerts featuring soloists of all kinds, and both male-voice and ladies' choirs. As a boy, I participated in so many of these concerts, and of course eisteddfods, and was known throughout the county as Benny Luxon, the Boy Soprano.

At age twelve, I sang on BBC Children's Hour just before my voice broke, but I was back at age fourteen singing tenor in the Camborne Wesley Chapel choir. After a year of leaving out all the high notes, I was sent to join the baritones and basses where I belonged.

Singing, as with so many Cornish people at that time, was second nature to me. Aged fifteen, I went and had some lessons in Redruth with Kenneth Ellis and learned some songs. Won the baritone section at the county music festival when I was sixteen, and when I was eighteen, although given the lead in *Perchance to Dream* [Ivor Novello] with Redruth Operatic Society, I was called up for National Service instead!

And that was the last Cornwall saw of me for a while, except short visits home to see my parents.

After my two years in the RAF as a pay accountant, I went to teacher training college at Westminster College in the heart of London on a [then] two-year course. And now in London for the first time, I heard all the major symphony orchestras, and opera at the old Sadler's Wells and Covent Garden. I couldn't get enough of it, but still did not realise that these musicians were doing this for a living. Talk about naïve! And although I was a singer, at the College, in pubs, I just didn't identify with these people. There was no one in my Cornish background who had ever done such a thing, so I suppose it wasn't surprising.

And now fast-forward. After Westminster College, someone heard me sing and I ended up at the Guildhall School of Music and Drama. On my first lesson there, I was confronted by my new teacher, Walther Gruner. He told me he was sure I could have a career as a professional singer and he needed to know my decision then and there. I was startled and embarrassed, but I instantly knew I only wanted to sing and that I had only ever wanted to sing. That was in 1959.

Four years later, in 1963, after periods of supply teaching and study at the Guildhall, I won the School's Gold Medal, and was hired by The English Opera Group [Benjamin Britten's company] to sing major roles on a tour of Russia. My life as a professional singer had begun!

In the next few years things moved very fast – I was working regularly with the BBC and singing with all the major British orchestras.

What I really wanted was to somehow let my fellow Cornishmen and women know that one of their kind was making history – that such a career was possible, and that, if I could do it, so could others. So, on one of my trips home, I walked into Westward Television in Plymouth and asked to talk to someone. I was ushered into a Mr. Lewenhak's office. He listened to my story and said simply, "Are you as good as you say you are?" I said, "Yes." He said, "Go down to studio A. We'll find a pianist. You're on tonight's news hour." And that's exactly the way it was. I was given a bale of hay as a prop, put in a rustic check shirt, and sang – what else could it be – *The Floral Dance*! That was the beginning of many programmes with Westward and, later on, even more with their successors West Country Television, where I had my own series called Steal Away: out and about in Cornwall, interviewing all kinds of interesting, exceptional people from all walks of life – and tons of music.

I had my wish come true. My career became an international one. Almost everyone in Cornwall knew what I was achieving. Other Cornish singers were following fast on my heels: Alan Opie [Redruth], John Treleaven [Porthleven], Wendy Eathorne [Four Lanes], Margaret Polkinghorn [Pool], Richard Jackson, and some, like me, were also moving on to the international circuit.

Through all of this I still came down to do the occasional concert in Camborne Wesley Chapel or Redruth Centenary Chapel. Even did one later in the dilapidated Truro City Hall!

When home occasionally, someone would come up to me and say, "We're some proud of you, boy," and that meant so much to me. I had become "a prophet in my own land" and I was very proud of that.

So, although I was so involved with the Duchy, mainly from a distance, I actually didn't know much about the overall musical scene there.

Chapter 4

Ben's Masterclasses

CW: But before we go on with the tale of the masterclasses and the seventy-two singers who sang their hearts out over the course of a week, it's important to say that Cornwall at this time was definitely not a cultural desert due to the lack of a venue. We should remember and applaud all those who made and continue to make fantastic work, often under trying circumstances, and especially those companies and individuals who made superb site-specific – and indeed Cornwall-specific – work in iconic Cornish settings. I'm thinking of events like *Selling the Wind* in Boscastle, where the witches danced magically on the surface of the water mid harbour, of Kneehigh – who sadly I failed to catch when they played Beijing – on beaches which left us all with retinally-etched visual images – like the actress who emerged from the sea with a fish in her mouth – which I can recall forty years later. So many and so excellent. Not forgetting Wild Works, which I saw at Colchester and Felbrigg. We should also play tribute to the wonderful music performed by both international and Cornish musicians at the Three Spires Festival, St Endellion, in so many other draughty churches, and of course at Prussia Cove.

Beggar's Opera at Cotehele – why we needed a new hall…

In 1985 I had the privilege of directing two shows simultaneously, one in each type of venue. *The Beggar's Opera* with Duchy Opera opened in Truro City Hall and then went on to give several outdoor performances at National Trust houses, and *Murder in the Cathedral* was performed in Truro Cathedral as part of the Three Spires Festival.

We had great fun with the make-up in *Beggar's Opera*, using copydex to raise scabs and ghastly running sores. The costumes were pretty impressive too, though I nearly came to blows with the wardrobe mistress. She made perfect 18th-century costumes - which I then distressed till they became filthy rags. I don't know why she got so upset…The drawing by Wendy Shier, below, shows the costume for Diana Trapes, who is one of the main women in Peachum's gang, a sort of madam, and a companion to Macheath.

Edmund Dehn played both Macheath in *Beggar's* and Becket in *Murder in the Cathedral*, and many other actors and singers were in both shows. Rehearsals overlapped and there was such a vibrant creative mix of imported professional luvvies with the best of Cornwall's hugely experienced amateurs that I truly believed that this was the beginning of a Cornish repertory company which would eventually have its own fit-for-purpose venue. The Beast was stirring again. But you don't make a garden by sitting under a tree …

Wendy Shier's design for Mrs Trapes in Duchy Opera's Beggar's Opera

BL: Out of the blue I was invited by Chris Warner to come and sing the Toreador in a production of *Carmen* that he was directing for Duchy Opera in Falmouth. I knew nothing of Chris or Duchy Opera. The Toreador was not a role for me, and anyway I didn't have enough time free to join the rehearsals and performances.

However, when I was down for a quick visit, I was able to take my mother to see a performance. Well, I didn't like the way Chris had set the production, somewhere in Latin America infested with guerrilla soldiers, but was impressed by the quality of much of the singing. I also knew Leon Lovett, the conductor, well. He had bought a second home in Cornwall, loved it, and had gotten involved in the musical scene, namely Duchy Opera, through Chris, of course.

Chris was determined to pursue me and asked me next to be Chairman or President of the company, I can't remember which. I said yes, I was interested, but someone would have to do all the donkey work: I wouldn't be around that much.

Chris had succeeded – he had my interest and involvement – but on condition that Duchy lived up to its name: that its singers came from all round the Duchy and that Duchy Opera should serve the whole county and not be focused in just Truro or Falmouth. Big thinking, right up Chris's street!

CW: Gotcha! Ben agreed to join Leon, I and Duchy Opera on the condition that we found out more about the singers in Cornwall, their standard and their whereabouts. So we hatched a plan whereby Ben would offer six public masterclasses in six towns, each attended by twelve singers. These would eventually lead to a revitalised Duchy Opera developing into an impressive, largely amateur, opera company with regular chorus, orchestra and soloists drawn from the county, a revitalised Arts Centre Trust, the Hall for Cornwall Campaign and eventually the Hall itself.

BL: We decided I would come down for a week and do six days of masterclasses, working with twelve singers a day, and see for ourselves what and where the talent was. We started at Bude, then Lanhydrock [Bodmin], St. Austell, Truro, Camborne and Penzance.

And the singers came – from age sixteen to sixty-six! Such a mix of talent. And what fun we had, no one was scared, and how totally heart-warming. We performed two concerts, one at Truro School chapel on evening three, and finally in Camborne Wesley on evening six. Everyone who had taken part in the masterclasses had a chance to sing and hopefully show what they had learned.

It was a triumph! Such excitement and spirit. By the end I was exhilarated but absolutely exhausted, Chris was in tears because it had all been so real, moving and inspiring, AND we had discovered a good number of very fine singers!

CW: That week saw the beginning of the most amazing creative partnership and a wonderful friendship. I couldn't sing a note – I'd been chucked out of the choir at school – but I could bring my theatre skills to bear and I could help Ben from a non-singing point of view. For example, in one of the masterclass sessions, Ben suddenly challenged me in public: "What's the matter with this singer?" I replied that she was so tense that the only time her body relaxed was when she turned the page. We "unlocked" her and she sang like an angel.

We were so astonished by the quality and quantity of the singers who turned up that we resolved to double cast *The Magic Flute* with Ben singing Papageno and take it on tour back to the masterclass towns. Leon was to conduct and I would co-direct with Ben. Duchy Opera would be the company.

BL: We had chosen an opera where we could cast all of our talent, myself included, and take it out into the Duchy accompanied by a good orchestra of mainly professional musicians.

Mozart's *Magic Flute* is full of beautiful music, comedy, mysteriousness and magic, and with approximately twenty singing roles divided pretty evenly between male and female voices. Also, a nice mix of major and minor roles, so that we could give stage opportunity to some of our less experienced singers – PERFECT. Oh, and a small chorus!

And all our best singers from the masterclasses joined the company!

CW: We were determined to take the show to the best venues we could find across the county, starting in Bude Leisure Centre, down to Liskeard Town Hall, then St. Austell Town Hall, Truro City Hall, Carn Brea Leisure Centre and St. John's Hall, Penzance. With orchestra, singers, stage staff, sets and costumes, there were the best part of 100 people on the road. The two leisure centres were totally unsuitable for theatre of any kind, the town halls largely abysmal.

The Duchy board was very concerned by the significant cost of taking the production on tour but how could they possibly turn us down? *The Magic Flute* has lots of parts for female singers, and by double casting we were able to make use of many of the singers from the masterclasses, with the added advantage that by going on tour individual singers were able to perform in their home towns. This was good for both publicity and the box office.

What none of us anticipated was the challenge for an amateur company touring to six venues all of which needed converting into performance spaces in order to make them even vaguely suitable to host a large production. All the sports halls needed temporary seating, a blackout, a lighting rig, dressing rooms with mirrors, a bar, to say nothing of a "pit" for our thirty-piece orchestra, cast, chorus and staff – around 120 people! We squeezed into other venues but the sports halls were particularly demanding. We kept blowing the fuses at Bude, and Ben and his son Jonathan risked their necks trying to get a blackout using rolls of black polythene held down by breeze blocks on the roof of Carn Brea in a gale. We must have been nuts! I was glad I didn't have to sing that night.

BL: But we did it: performances were great in spite of the conditions, and the whole company took it in their stride. Adapting the show to some very challenging venues was really tough for everyone involved and we often had to improvise but somehow we managed to pull it off. I don't remember how many people actually saw the show but it must have been around 5,000.

One specific memory I have of this tour was the performance at Carn Brea Leisure Centre. We arrived to find the roof of the sports hall built with multiple rows of glass skylights. It was summer, and they had to be blacked out or we couldn't light the show.

It was my son Jonathan, who was staying with me in Cornwall at the time, and I who had the task of blacking out the skylights with rolls of black plastic attached to the lips of glass roofing with bulldog clips. There was no one else available for the job. The stagehands and Chris had all they could do to erect a stage and set, and set-up our lighting system and seating for an audience. Jon and I were on the roof all afternoon, but it worked – the muse was with us: the wind didn't rise and lift off our plastic and the show was lit. Incidentally, from the roof of that leisure centre we had wonderful views out to the coast and behind us Carn Brea, with its small castle and monument. It wasn't all hardship!

The lesson that we learned from this tour, without setting out to, was that Cornwall did not possess one venue suitable for medium-size, let alone for large-scale, theatrical enterprise. It was a sobering reality to face after our huge effort and the artistic success of *Flute*.

CW: Over the course of the tour, we achieved some significant publicity. Ben was a magnet for both press and audiences and on the last night at Carn Brea we had an audience of 2,000. Although it was a cracking show many people were predictably disappointed by what is known in the trade as "the quality of the night out". Despite all our Herculean efforts, the acoustics were grim, the sightlines were grim, and grim doesn't begin to describe the experience of trying to get to a loo or securing a drink in the interval.

I think it must have been the next day when Ben, Leon and I sat down to have a mop-up meeting. We were joined by four friends of Ben's – Claire Bowden-Dan, Jane Lofthouse and Robin and Delia Spence. Robin was the son of the distinguished architect Basil Spence and was an architect himself – another bit of serendipity there, as it turned out.

Everyone was chuffed. We'd done it, and what the National Lottery is pleased to call "early indications" confirmed that, in spite of production costs of around £30,000, we had not bankrupted Duchy Opera. But soon everyone around that table was moaning. We realised that not only did we have a quality product which deserved to be seen in a proper venue, but, more importantly than that, everyone in Cornwall was denied access to a whole range of shows because there was no suitable venue. We chewed over how much the Cornish rugby team meant to Cornwall and wished that Cornwall could be equally proud of a Cornish venue.

I remember saying, "It's no good just sitting here moaning. We need to do something about it." "Well," said Ben, "You live here, you'd better do something about it." I reflected (foolishly) that taking on "doing something about it" wasn't going to cause any collateral damage because I was single at the time. "I'll need some money to get started," I said, secretly hoping that this request would dampen their enthusiasm. Not a bit of it – in a twink, four cheques, each for £100, lay upon the table.

And with that they all stuffed off back to London …

It was a bit of a facer!

Luckily Sarah Smith, would soon enter stage right. In a Wayfarer.

Chapter 5

Everyone else has got one!

CW: People in Cornwall were passionate about their music, and communities in many, many towns and villages throughout the county had their own choirs and brass bands. They performed in churches, village and school halls and leisure centres, as well as within their own communities on special occasions and to celebrate festivities. In addition to the talent within these choirs and bands, folk music was popular and there were small clubs scattered around the county where musicians shared their music.

I remember trekking out across the fields to the Folk Cottage to see fabulous singers such as Brenda Wootton, John the Fish and Ralph McTell. The Cornwall Coliseum in Carlyon Bay was by far the largest concert venue and it was a draw for national and international pop and rock musicians. Legendary bands – such as Genesis – would often start a UK or world tour at this venue, which had a capacity of 3,300 during the eighties.

The new Hall wasn't just about presenting theatre and opera – we were determined that it would embrace the eclectic mix of performances throughout the county. There was no doubt that Cornwall was home to many talented artists, but their inability to showcase their talent was something the Campaign was determined to rectify.

Having set the scene, I would like to go back a few steps and tease out other forces which came together like cord in a rope and which also contributed to the success of the Hall for Cornwall Campaign.

Quite soon after our production of *Carmen* in the Falmouth Cinema, we heard to our horror that Carrick had plans to demolish it and replace it with a car park. All entreaties from us and many others fell on deaf ears. It was really quite a useful town-centre middle-scale venue, which, with a modest bit of investment, could have been smashing. And there it was, gone!

Leon and I became aware of a campaign by the Cornwall Dance and Theatre Trust to provide an arts centre in Truro. St Austell, Falmouth and Penzance had one, so why not Truro? The venue they proposed was, however, no use to Duchy or indeed to any of the middle-scale touring shows which never got further west than Plymouth. So Ben, Leon and I – and later Stef Brammar (SB) – hijacked this modest initiative and set up the Arts Centre Trust (ACT), which quickly achieved charitable status. Our aim was simply to show people what they were missing by promoting a hit-and-run programme of well-known performers and companies into inadequate venues in the Truro area. Stef Brammar who had joined us as a trustee became the first Director. She was dynamic and well connected!

Jenny Arquati, Chris, Ben and Stef Brammar at one of the many events organised by Stef

SB: When I first came to live in Truro, the City Hall was mainly used for live cattle markets and flea markets, although TOADS (Truro Operatic and Drama Society) did perform their shows there. I discovered and joined the Arts Centre Trust - a group campaigning for a permanent performance space.

But it was meeting Chris Warner that propelled me into a partnership which eventually included Ben Luxon. Together we rose to the challenge - later taken up by the Hall for Cornwall Trust - of transforming a municipal building that was by then a very tired, sad shadow of its former self, into a Hall for Cornwall. I could write reams about our negotiations with Carrick District and the County Council, and many hot debates with other Cornish towns about whether Truro was the right location.

Somehow I discovered I had a talent for spotting opportunities to raise grants and to book drama, music, and dance tours. Chris's professional theatre experience was invaluable - he taught me how to budget for shows and events, and he was a genius at managing the lighting and logistics for the range of companies we booked.

CW: Stef's triumphs included securing the Royal Shakespeare Company (RSC), which performed *The Merchant of Venice* in the City Hall, and then several more RSC productions in Truro School Sports Hall. For every RSC visit, she had to find a team of strong volunteers to do the get-ins and strikes of an entire portable raked auditorium. And for each RSC visit she had to find substantial sponsorship – a new concept for Truro businesses, who rose to the challenge. She also went for big-name jazz performers like Ronnie Scott, Courtney Pine, and Slim Gaillard, who had been a driver for the Mob in the Al Capone days. Larry Adler was a bit of a gamble but he sold out, with people travelling from all over the county. We provided Truronians with somewhere to go on successive New Year's Eves with a series of Bustopher Jones Jazz Band Balls.

SB: I have so many memories - Chris and I fly posting around the city, persuading the local fire brigade to hang banners across Lemon Street during their training sessions. Probably the best one was "The Cossacks are Coming!" (and they did). Handing out leaflets at the station to trainspotters who then turned up at Bristol Old Vic's touring show *God's Wonderful Railway*. Cornish bands and Cornish choirs, Duchy Opera. And of course, the Royal Shakespeare Company for whom we had to raise major sponsorship and provide a team of 20 to get their entire touring theatre, set and costumes into the City Hall and then take it all out again at the end of the week's run. Worth every aching muscle when we saw the matinees packed with Cornish schoolchildren. I've had a lucky and interesting career since but watching the RSC lorries roll into Boscawen Street was a very special moment.

CW: The pop-up entertainment was of course most enjoyable in its own right, but we always took care to point out how lovely it would be to have a proper venue which would have first-rate facilities – including enough loos and a long bar. And we started a proper box office, which sold tickets for our own and other events, thereby generating both a county-wide profile and a new income stream for ACT. Stef made sure that every show had its own media attention, which helped us to get our message out to a very wide range of people.

SB: In 1985 ACT commissioned Wendy Shier to build a model to illustrate a proposal to replace the old City Hall with a flexible new one which would cost £2m. The West Briton ran a feature, but nothing really came of it. I still have the chunk of Cornish granite given to me by Bert Biscoe when I left the Duchy. It's a reminder of some very special people, a historic building, Truro, and Cornwall.

CW: Bert Biscoe (BB), a Cornish politician, historian and bard of the Cornish Gorsedh, represents Cornwall Council's Truro Boscawen District as an independent Cornwall councillor and Truro City councillor. Bert, Mayor of Truro in 2020/21, remembers those early days:

BB: The Truro Beat Group Contest was compered by Peter Boggia. It featured about ten finalists, nine of which played "Walk Away Renee" (The Four Tops). The tenth band, The Fantastics, blew my head off. Roger Taylor was the drummer and Mike Dudley the guitarist, with Rick Penrose on bass. A French girl called Joelle danced as this trio played "Morning Dew" and "Land of 1,000 Dances". I discovered rock music one night in the sixties at Truro City Hall. It blew my head off and changed my life.

Twenty years later, having toured the UK with my own bands, I found myself playing in a pub in Kensington one night and thought: "I've had enough of this. I'm going home!" I pitched up in Truro and, with a couple of mates, tried to hire Truro City Hall to put on a gig – it was only available for a full twenty-four hours – we wanted it for three! Outrageous! I went to a Town Meeting to tell the Council it was off its rocker! My first taste of Truro politics!

Within months I found myself working with a group of people campaigning to stop Carrick councillors from selling off Truro City Hall. By now I was working for the Arts Centre Trust and putting on events regularly – we promoted Andy Sheppard, Bill Giles (the weatherman – the Newlyn fishing fleet stayed in port to hear him!), David Icke (who came on stage with the Ukelele Orchestra of Great Britain playing I can't get no satisfaction), Courtney Pine, Kneehigh, and many others. On New Year's Eve I spent my time walking narrow planks above the barrel ceiling hanging up baskets of balloons, and all night putting away heavy old cinema seats to make way for the flea market at 7 a.m. In all this I was instructed by the late John Ashby, manager of Truro City Hall.

John Ashby was the person who held the place together during his twenty-five years as Manager. This lengthy service was to prove immensely valuable in itself, as the cost of his possible redundancy played figuratively on Carrick Council's corporate calculating – John

Ashby used to chuckle and say, "Ah! I'm that expensive, they can't afford to be without me!"

He had an office along the aromatic corridor of cloakrooms, dressing rooms, cupboards and spaces on the other side of locked doors that I, for one, never got through. His was the last vestige of the days when the City Hall complex was the headquarters of Truro Borough Council. His desk, his chair, his filing cabinet and stapler were all vintage. It was a warm, comfortable place in which many pipes were smoked, many jokes discreetly and lengthily chuckled over, and many bollockings handed out to hirers and firers.

John was a Yorkshireman who found his natural place in Truro. Despite his gruff persona, he was a quietly sentimental chap who, as the threat to his place of work grew, became more and more emotionally entangled with it. He worked like a beaver, but with a measured pace that meant that everything got done according to Ashby Time. No problem. I worked with him on many occasions, and we stacked and unstacked those old cinema chairs hundreds of times, setting out for shows, putting away for markets. I began to feel the wood and sweat; the long maroon velvets and clacking lights began to grab at my heart strings, too. We got along fine.

SB: ACT began to use different seating layouts - we added theatre in the round and thrust stage to the traditional proscenium arch productions. We also set up a theatre bar and a properly functioning box office. We found a school hand bell to ring for the end of intervals.

Very soon we had a committed team of volunteers including Bert Biscoe. We had a stage manager, stagehands and front of house staff, bar and box office staff. I will always be eternally grateful to them, and to Mr Ashby: I guess we caused him many headaches, but he bore it well with infinite patience.

BB: John knew local government inside out and, despite hostility at the offices up the road, he filed, forgot, remembered, buried and quietly, guilefully and with impeccable honesty and abruptness, preserved City Hall so our campaign could succeed. His role in the great public meeting which saw the developers off and presented the community with the challenge that eventually became Hall for Cornwall was heroic in an understated sort of way. He risked his job and pension, and did so silently, with a gruff inward chuckle as we heaved the chairs under the stage and ran the tables into neat lines for the next day's flea market. We should not forget either that sweeping the remnants of rhetoric and the split ends of realpolitik off the floor was the eminent Truronian and quiet soldier Mark Wotton – a long-enduring and quietly amused Trurra boy.

John Ashby was an obdurate grumpy old hero who kept the place going, held his employer at arm's length and proved so expensive to lay off that Carrick DC couldn't do it! But he loved the place and refused to let it die when all about him were for scuttling and running – I don't think any of us will ever really know how much Truro owes to him for his obduracy, skill and will.

CW: My day job continued on Loe Beach teaching sailing with my team of instructors whilst pondering my vision for a purpose-built venue. It was during one of my lessons in a Wayfarer that I met Sarah Smith (SS), who wanted to learn something new to keep up with her young children.

SS: Loe Beach in Feock near Truro was an idyllic place to go after school and during the holidays. A few boats were moored there, the pebbly/sandy beach and water were relatively sheltered and safe for children, there was a café, and most importantly there was a sailing school. It was a busy beach with lots of activities, boats being pulled in and out of the water, lots of sailing, and it was a meeting place for young families.

The main attraction was undoubtedly the sailing school, with its rather eccentric owner, who taught so many children to sail and gain confidence in boats. Chris Warner was like a Pied Piper! It was not only about the sailing, but it was about enjoying messing

Wayfarer with spinnaker up.
Photo by Hartley Boats

about on and in the water, learning to respect the sea and understanding its unpredictability, but above all just having fun. Chris had a way of getting the best out of his pupils, and after lessons they seemed to stay around sailing Toppers, Mirrors and Lasers.

Watching all this activity on the beach with my children, it was not long before they wanted to join in, too. Many of their friends were learning to sail or could already sail, and so in the summer of 1989 when I first met Chris, he agreed to teach my daughter Georgina and son Adam to sail. They were taught with friends to sail small dinghies by Chris's team, and it wasn't long before they got the hang of the basics and were off on the water. Two in each dinghy, sailing with a number of other children from Loe Beach, whilst Chris and helpers supervised in a motorboat. The children loved it and after all these years, still remember those summers hanging about Loe Beach enjoying Chris's humour and sometimes even offering to help him. It was a happy place to be!

Having seen Georgina and Adam becoming quite competent in a Topper and then a Mirror dinghy, a friend and I decided to ask Chris to teach us to sail … but not in a small dinghy! Chris agreed to take up the challenge and we started our lessons in a 16ft Wayfarer. Lyn and I learnt a lot about the sea, the boat, and what we had to do to get the boat to move. We took it quite seriously, and as we became more competent, we started to use the trapeze, a harness attached by a wire to a high point on the mast. It was on one of the early occasions when, harnessed to the trapeze, standing on the side of the boat which was moving along the water quite well, that I ended up flying off the boat at some speed into the Carrick Roads. The wire had snapped, causing a great deal of hilarity as Lyn and Chris fished me out of the water.

During one of our lessons, Chris started to talk about his dream of finding or creating a performance space in Cornwall to showcase the wealth of talent in the county and to attract and accommodate performances that did not cross the Tamar because there was no suitable venue. He felt it was time to stop making do with school halls or sports halls and that Cornwall should have a dedicated space with comfortable seating. He told me that he had been working with Duchy Opera as its Artistic Director and had been disappointed with the venues where his productions had to be staged. There was just nowhere suitable in Cornwall. I agreed with him, as most of my children's theatre experiences had either been in Bristol or Plymouth. Cornwall had the Minack Theatre in the summer months, an open-air theatre, magical when the weather was fine but not great when it was too hot, cold or raining! There were several theatre companies based in Cornwall, and out-of-county theatre companies like the RSC did tour to Cornwall but usually had to perform in sports halls. Music and dance also struggled with performance spaces, and choirs and brass bands, which Cornwall could boast about, ended up performing in unusual places with poor acoustics. For a county that loved its music and song there was little opportunity to showcase it.

We talked a lot about his dream during those sailing lessons. Chris often talked about Duchy Opera, which included professional and amateur singers and actors who performed throughout Cornwall. He talked about how successful the operas had become due in part to Ben who had joined the company. He said that there was no doubt that the appetite for performances was there but there was definitely a need for a performance space with at least 500 seats and an orchestra pit. That was his dream … to get hold of a greenfield site for his project, and we would talk about the best location for such a venue. I remember feeling quite frustrated with him because he had so many ideas, had talked to a number of people about it, such as Ben Luxon and Leon Lovett as well as a number of locals, but that seemed to be as far as he had got. I remember saying something like, "Dreams don't often just come true… do something about it!"

Chris had a clear vision and was so enthusiastic and determined but couldn't see how to move forward. He already had the ideas, the right connections through the work with Duchy Opera and through the sailing school, but it was the next step that was needed to launch Chris's ideas. His enthusiasm was contagious, and I thought it was a brilliant idea. He now needed to see if he could sell his idea to the people of Cornwall. It sounded so easy – but what were the next steps?

Chapter 6

Dramas at Truro City Hall

SS: At that time, I was co-owner of an employment agency in Ferris Town. Smith and Reed was a successful business providing temporary and permanent people, mainly in admin, accountancy, secretarial and clerical work, to organisations throughout Cornwall. Smith and Reed owned its premises and Jennie Reed and I decided that there was enough room to offer Chris an office to use as a base for his campaign. So, in October 1989 Chris moved into our office and started to organise the campaign for the new Hall.

CW: This was an absolutely brilliant arrangement because I could be out and about but there was always someone to answer my phone, to take messages, which were always passed on efficiently, and, in those pre-computer days, Ann Jennings typed professional-looking letters. It was also a professional address, a couth place to see people, and, for an "organisation" that didn't really exist, it provided much needed credibility.

SS: Now aptly called the Hall for Cornwall Campaign Chris and Ben spent a lot of time and energy talking to and sounding out people in Cornwall about their ideas. For the next few months, Smith and Reed saw a steady stream of visitors coming to the offices to see Chris, and Ben when he was in Truro. They made quite a nuisance of themselves pestering all sorts of people for support both in Cornwall and beyond. Chris explained that sometimes they were well received and sometimes they were greeted with indifference or even downright hostility. It just seemed so blindingly obvious to them that Cornwall needed and deserved a decent performance space that they were oblivious to the old adage that one man's passion is another man's boredom.

At this stage, Chris was still looking for a suitable site for a hall. It wasn't easy, as the idea was to find somewhere that was accessible and that would attract anyone and everyone in Cornwall and beyond. Really, he was looking for a location in the middle of Cornwall. It felt like a slow burn to those involved but Chris and his supporters were making progress, the idea not only taking root but beginning to grow as a result of timely circumstances. This would be the turning point for the Campaign.

By the end of that year, I had sold my share of the employment agency to my business partner, Jennie, in order to pursue other opportunities. I spent the new decade busily setting up my own consultancy and began working with different organisations in the Truro area. Chris stayed at Smith and Reed and I had little contact with him over the next few months, although I did try to keep up to date with the progress he was making. He was busy juggling his passion, skills and keeping the wolf from the door during those times, trying to find a way forward for the Campaign, continuing to direct productions with Duchy Opera, and teaching people to sail.

During the summer of 1990 I met Chris by chance in Truro and he told me that he had, with help from Annette Penhaligon, started to talk to Carrick District Council about the possibility of leasing City Hall in Truro. His ideas of a greenfield site had come to nothing but coincidentally, following a particularly tricky time for Carrick, they were now looking at other options. Bert Biscoe remembers the fight to keep City Hall:

BB: Truro people were incensed that the Council wanted to flog their City Hall for a shopping development. Passions became inflamed. I found myself, week after week for months, making leaflets with stencils and photocopiers, which we would hand out in the foyer on Saturdays when the Flea Market was in its heyday. Some councillors would come and harangue us (a leading Liberal Democrat once shrieked: "You are an Anarchist!" at me), but the people were with us. A property developer – Shearwater – made an offer to the Council. A public meeting was called.

I was now editing the Truro News, a free newspaper owned by two friends. We were one of the first to use e-mail, and we printed the paper on a press in the garden shed. When the late Bill Cheshire was elected Chairman of Carrick, I printed the Council's celebratory press release alongside his official photograph. The motto of the Citizens of Truro, "Let Time be the Judge!" was the headline. At his first meeting Bill, who later became a friend and a mentor, grew quite heated at the attitude of the Truro press!

The Mayor was Lorrie Eathorne. I offered to make a special edition of Truro News and the front page carried a message from the Mayor asking all those who loved Truro City Hall to come to the meeting to "Save Truro City Hall". All week the developers skulked around town rehearsing their hi-tec picture-show – "an audio-visual presentation", they declared, proudly.

On the night, a crowd turned out which filled the Hall. Truro's dander was well and truly up! Most Truro City councillors met outside and, as the Chairman took his seat on the stage, we marched in. The Mayor was preceded by the late and wonderful Reg Little conducting Truro City Band playing "When The Saints Go Marching In". The audience stood and clapped along. Bill Cheshire, a retired football referee, blew a whistle, and, eventually, a hush fell. The Mayor had been given permission to open the meeting. This she did, stating that this was "our" hall. She sat down to applause.

The developers rose to start their presentation. Somebody called: "Lights!" Nothing happened. "Lights!" The only man who could work the lights was the Hall Manager, the late John Ashby. He was not in his office, and not backstage. The Developer was forced to proceed. Their presentation was ruined. John could not be found. As they finished, the Planning Officer, Steven Watson, stood up to outline the planning issues with a stick and a flipchart. As he opened his mouth, all the lights went out. John Ashby had finished his break ("A quiet pint") and returned from the Market Inn. Steven proceeded in the dark.

As the lights reappeared a burst of noisy applause broke out. John Cockle whispered in his wonderfully penetrative way, "That's done it!" The Shearwater people were to be seen trudging disconsolately off stage and out through the back door, never to be seen again. Now what? Many plans and ideas were put forward. The situation was becoming fractious and it looked as though no solution would be found. Certain Carrick councillors were beginning to say "I told you so!" and to sharpen their quills ready to sign another contract to sell.

Not long after this debacle Chris Warner asked to speak to Truro City Council. He was his usual buoyant and optimistic self and persuaded the Council that everybody should come together around a project which he would lead with Ben Luxon.

SS: So enter Chris down stage with his ideas for a hall for everyone somewhere in Cornwall but which would be best placed in Truro… After all, Carrick District Council officers would have to go on paying the annual running costs of £60,000 and Chris's proposal might be a way of getting rid of this white elephant for a while… until even he couldn't make it work. Then, having built up a case, Carrick would be in a much better position to sell City Hall to developers.

CW: Thus City Hall became a realistic candidate for us. It was an interesting proposition for Carrick, particularly as they could not see how we could pull off running City Hall, launch the Hall for Cornwall Campaign, achieve charitable status and get listed building consent to demolish part of a Grade II* building. Leave alone jumping over all the regulatory hurdles of planning permission and building regs. Oh! and not to mention the little matter of raising several million pounds to fund the construction of the new Hall for Cornwall.

Not one of our three local authorities were enthusiastic. Shoulders were not to the wheel. Mugs were generally at least half empty, if not worse. When I went to see him, the County Librarian, responsible for the Arts, was sitting in his plush office, newly furnished to Chief Officer standards, but didn't have any beer at all in his mug. He made me feel like a beggar and I got really cross, telling him that the provision of a decent hall for Cornwall was the County Council's responsibility not mine, and I enquired – possibly a little too forcefully – why it had not been provided years ago. He wittered about lack of money while I made a silent guess at the cost of his new carpet. If only Sarah had been there to kick me under the table …

The City Hall-ers had done nothing about its scandalous neglect by their elected representatives. This neglect was in part caused by Carrick allowing the profit from the flea-market operation to be retained by one private individual who made a tenfold return on the rent paid. This faction had no clear view of how its refurbishment and future running costs could be met. United by their love for it – and often to preserve it for their own benefit – the Luddite "Save our City Hall-ers" were faced with three main threats.

These were:

- The unaffordable cost of repairs to the hall, which were the result of Carrick District Council's dismal track record of failure to maintain their Grade II* building.

- Cash-rich predatory developers, who had plans to demolish and replace city-centre City Hall with a profitable (to them) shopping mall.

- The Hall for Cornwall Campaign, which had a clear vision for a combined community and performance space and a business plan to go with that vision. The plan required the demolition of the central section and promised the refurbishment of the Back Quay end of the building. But as yet the Campaign did not have any money in its bank account.

An unpopular Council, stereotypical developers and a bunch of idealists with no money were lining up to slug it out while poor old City Hall limped along. While there might have been strength in an alliance between Carrick officers and the developers, the fact remained that most people sympathised with Mercutio's famous line from Romeo and Juliet: "A plague on both your houses." Everyone loves to hate a developer, and most are not overly keen on councils.

We had two things going for us. We wanted to keep City Hall as a centre for community activity of all kinds, which meant that for the Save our City Hall-ers we were the least worst option. Additionally, because we wanted to right an injustice – namely, that it was manifestly unfair that middle-scale performances of subsidised dance, theatre and music were not available in Cornwall despite the residents of Cornwall paying their taxes. This meant that there was a large body of articulate people who cared about the arts and entertainment, who would get behind our campaign.

People who wanted to discredit our proposals nicknamed Hall For Cornwall, the "Hall for Warner", and as part of their campaign to hang on to "their" City Hall, they alleged that Ben and I wanted to build it so we could have a lovely new toy for our operas. There was a small truth in that allegation, but the greater truth was that loads of people really wanted it, even though there were also many who felt so deeply about "their" dilapidated, underused, inadequate City Hall that they could not bear to part with it.

Stalemate!

Ironically, Carrick's demolition of the cinema in Falmouth led eventually to Carrick granting us our 125-year lease on City Hall and giving us their £500,000. One might be forgiven for wondering why on earth they hadn't spent at least some of that money on the upkeep of City Hall.

Chapter 7

Spaghetti Lift Off!

CW: In Truro City Council, there was some support but also a lot of opposition. Councillors were however very sensitive to the Save Our City Hall faction, most of whom were Truro residents who had a vote. Many councillors were also deeply suspicious that we wanted to get our hands on their part of the building; plus, there was constant tension between the City and Carrick councils. Carrick was the City Council's landlord and the not-so-proud owner of the City Hall.

Mr. Winskill, the generally rather unloved Chief Executive of Carrick District Council who Ben and I had nicknamed The Weasel, clearly had his own ambitions, which were to develop City Hall as a prime retail city-centre site. I don't know if he had a nickname for us, but I bet it wasn't complimentary! Ben and I were trouble – and might, just might, derail his plans, which had already experienced serious community opposition, as expressed in no uncertain terms at the very rowdy presentation by the developers. I think The Weasel decided to buy some time by asking us to do some research into multi-purpose arts venues and then to make some recommendations as to how City Hall might be developed and run. He probably thought he would find it easy to kick our can into the local government long grass. How wrong he was! With equal hubris, thinking we were about to become some sort of artistic Trojan Horse, we set off on a tour to look at the design, build costs and revenue implications of various halls in England and Wales. He couldn't/wouldn't pay us for this work, but we could claim reasonable expenses.

For someone who worked his life around a five-year diary, earning significant fees singing in opera houses all over Europe, including La Scala, this was an impressive commitment from Ben. It was easier for me because I was self-employed – meaning I had lots of time, although little money. We set off like two truant schoolboys on an exciting road trip. Ben drove his plush Renault Espace and I navigated. He drove exceptionally fast, talking nineteen to the dozen all the time. It was occasionally quite alarming – like when I was trying to clear the condensation off the windscreen and he casually remarked, "I wouldn't bother if I were you – you'll be dead before you see it anyway." The trip also had its lighter moments. In those un-PC years, we ran a daily competition of how many ladies we could get to smile when we caught their eyes. This light-hearted game came back to bite us when one day in Newport I cried out in triumph, "I got one, I got one!" and Ben turned to look – and bumped a stationary car at some traffic lights.

I can't remember all the venues we went to. The Corn Exchange in King's Lynn and the allegedly multi-purpose hall in Bracknell stand out. The Corn Exchange was very smart but suffered, as did the old City Hall, from what we called "shoebox syndrome", i.e. the building was a finite rectangle with no wing space and with seating in straight rows reminiscent of a village hall. Bracknell was much more interesting – very inviting, ironwork painted in primary colours, and lots of loos and a decent bar. We learnt a valuable lesson there because, although truly multi-purpose, it took so long and cost so much in labour to effect the changes that in reality it was not used to its full potential. It was ironic that Tim Brinkman, the Director at the Corn Exchange Bracknell, would become my successor at HfC.

Around this time, an arts consultant called Crispin Raymond came to Cornwall to see us. He talked to us about his Arts Council-commissioned publication Clear Sightlines, which was a manual for people who managed receiving houses (theatres that bought in touring productions). In it he considered what he called the five successes – financial, artistic, community, the building itself, and service – needed for a venue to thrive. What he had to say chimed with what we were trying to do and I quoted it many times when people asked why we needed or planned such and such. A very brief précis: it's no good having a brilliant performance in a crap venue, no good having a brilliant performance which doesn't sell, no good having a brilliant venue if you programme rubbish. It's not good enough just to sell loads of tickets – you need to know who is sitting in your seats and you should listen to what they have to say. And everyone who works in the building must be aware that they are working in a service industry and that they must make every effort to make sure that all interactions with the ticket-buying customers are positive experiences.

Above all, he talked about "the quality of the night out". This concept really resonated with us because so much fabulous work in Cornwall was in venues which were inaccessible, which were cold or too hot, had uncomfortable seating, had poor sightlines, poor acoustics, lacked a bar and had poor toilet provision. In other words, to state the obvious, you might think twice about attending a venue where last time the tickets were expensive and difficult to get hold of, where after the interval you were still busting to go to the loo, where you were freezing, couldn't see, couldn't hear, and worst of all, perhaps, you had turned up to an outdoor performance only to find it had been cancelled due to bad weather. Like a restaurant, for a venue to be a success, the quality of the night out is the most important factor, although of course it also needs to be an artistic and a financial success. And often forgotten, and just as important as all the others, the venue must be attractive to visiting companies – a level get-in for stage kit, good lighting and sound systems, decent dressing rooms properly kitted out, a good piano if needed, and with the ability to generate good audiences. And in order to attract touring companies, other similar venues must be within a reasonable travel distance in order for their tour to be financially successful. All travel and no play keeps a company away …

For our road trip we decided to focus on Wales because it seemed to have much in common with Cornwall – a strong choral tradition, Methodism, small towns and scattered rural settlements, not many large venues. The biggest venue we saw was St David's Hall. It was really impressive, with acoustics to die for achieved by complex architectural devices such as stepped balconies. One dressing room still had the full-sized bath which had been installed for Sir Thomas Beacham because he needed to cool down in the interval before having a complete change of clothes for the second half. Quality all round, but definitely not multi-purpose. We began to think we needed five different halls – for concerts, cattle shows, markets, theatre and dance. How could we resolve the competing demands for acoustics: resonant for singing, crisp for theatre and dead for rock and pop? How could we shut a venue down from a stage wide enough to seat the sixty players of the Bournemouth Symphony Orchestra to a space intimate enough for a piano recital?

Venues in Wales were generally not much help, but we were mightily impressed by the energy and creativity of the Mid Wales Development Board. As well as supporting several small-scale venues, they had supported the creation of artists' workshops and shops in a number of locations where travellers might pause for some reason – e.g. to buy petrol or to look at the view. These were beehive units where you could watch craftspeople and artists at work and then buy their produce. The arts-and-craft tenants were clearly valued by the Board for their contribution to the quality of life in Mid Wales. How we wished we had such a board in Cornwall!

Ben and Chris on their travels

Perhaps most importantly, as we hurtled through the Welsh mist in the Espace, we had time to talk, to think and to test ideas. We came to the conclusion that at least three different halls, ideally in one large complex, were needed if the job was to be done properly, and that they should all be in a town centre. We favoured Truro but we were aware of the likely familiar outcry, "Why should Truro always get everything?" The 1974 local government reform which led to the creation of district councils had, in Cornwall, brought fierce town rivalries under one political roof – this was especially true in Truro, where Carrick and the County Council had their offices. And let's not mention the law courts or the police HQ. Or the Royal Cornwall Hospital. And, of course, the cathedral.

BL: Apart from the fun we had on our tour of halls and arts centres, we became increasingly aware of the business of staffing these establishments and the salaries involved.

There was also lots of advice about the buildings themselves, such as making sure there was enough office space, ladies' toilets (an all-time favourite), dressing rooms – the list went on and on.

Although both Chris and I had spent our working lives in halls and theatres, our knowledge and experience came from the performance aspect not the administrative. Our tour was very informative and we returned home with a pretty good idea of how many people would be employed by our hall and the kind of money needed to run it, as well as all kinds of necessary facilities.

Nobody had done this before as far as we knew, or town councils and various governing bodies would have realized that it is impossible to have a place like Truro City Hall run by "one man and his dog", as in the case of John Ashby, assisted by occasional volunteers like the young Bert Biscoe.

CW: After a week or so away, I got home flat broke but inspired to set pen to paper for our report, which we called "Towards a new City Hall". A lady typist kept a horse on my small farm and I engaged her to type it up for us. In it we set out our thinking on how a truly multi-purpose venue could be created and operated on the City Hall site while retaining the impressive frontages to Boscawen Street and Back Quay. We delivered it in triumph, thinking that now Carrick District Council had a blueprint and would hopefully get on with the job while we could get on with our lives. Wrong! We also delivered our expenses for fuel, food and hotels for our week away. Wrong again! The Weasel had "no recollection" of agreeing to pay expenses. He took the report, and I have "no recollection" of what then happened to it. I was so broke after the trip that I had to pay the typist in hay.

BL: We had just about had enough; nobody was taking much interest, so we decided to go public at a press conference at the swish Alverton Manor Hotel in Truro.

We had facts and figures all sectionalised for anyone to see: the level and type of staff needed, numbers of volunteers, salary costs, type of activities to take place – it was all there. And just as important, we had Robin Spence's full-scale architectural plans approved and chosen as the winner of a subsequently aborted competition promoted by none other than Carrick Council themselves. At the Alverton, we used the white model of the proposed new Hall, which we had used for presentations to Carrick.

CW: To explain this in more detail: in the early days, I had been working with London architect Robin Spence, who was one of the group which had sat around the table moaning about the scandalous lack of a decent venue after the Carn Brea *Magic Flute*. He and his wife had come to support their friend Ben Luxon, who had drawn an audience of 2,000 who had been determined to hear their boy from Camborne sing Papageno on the last night of our Cornish tour. Even if it meant crossing their legs for the second half due to the woeful lack of loos, or not being able to get a drink in the interval. To be fair, it was a sports hall.

Eat your heart out, John de la Cour!

The Spence name should have rung bells of the alarm variety. Robin's father was the distinguished architect Sir Basil Spence, who, among other achievements, including Coventry Cathedral, had designed the theatre at Southampton University. The theatre was well known for its copper-clad roof and in moments of irreverence I had always imagined an army of cleaning ladies in Marigolds, wearing harness and crampons, using copious amounts of Duraglit to burnish the copper and keep it from turning green in the sea air.

The grim reality was that when we pitched up for the get-in of my Northcott Theatre production of *Look Back in Anger* with a lorry load of eighteen-foot-high flats, we soon found there was no easy dock access to the stage. Normally, the scenery lorry would back up to a loading platform which would afford level straight-line access from the lorry bed to the scenery dock at the back of the stage. At the copper-sheathed wonder, you had to get the flats down a domestic corridor, through domestic doors and, at one point, round a right-angle bend.

Bearing in mind that at the "moaning table" we had no plans to build the Hall ourselves, we were grateful for Robin's offer to make use of the drawings with which he had won Carrick's aborted competition to design a replacement for City Hall in the mid-eighties. He had demonstrated how a new multi-purpose hall might be all things to all people – comfortable, with good "quality of the night out" facilities, capable of being transformed quickly and economically from a flat floor market or a rock concert into a seated concert hall or theatre, with technical facilities which would attract the very best national and international touring product into Cornwall and inspire and nurture indigenous Cornish talent. Not much of an ask, really.

Robin's design looked impressive. Using the very latest technology, he proposed simple and dramatic solutions to the problems inherent in operating multi-purpose halls. Retractable seating, although representing a big step forward from the tedious business (suffered by caretakers and others in halls up and down the land) of unfolding individual seats and locking them together, hopefully in an order which might correspond to a seating plan, tended to be uncomfortable, worked loose and squeaked. And audiences were likely to be reluctant to pay top whack for an uncomfortable, squeaky seat, even if they were watching the National Theatre.

At a stroke, Robin had dealt with all these problems and prejudices by proposing four large movable blocks of permanent non-folding seating. These blocks were to be stored in a large underground "garage" and would be moved into position on the sort of compressed air hovercraft-type trolleys which had been developed to manoeuvre vast jet engines on a factory floor. The individual blocks of fixed seating would be moved by the trolleys onto hydraulic lifts and thence into position to form an apparently permanent auditorium. It was the principle of the orchestra pit lift bringing up the grand piano from its basement storage, now applied to an entire 1,000-seat theatre. Most appealing.

I knew that if we could build a working model, people would be able to see what a neat solution we were offering. The model would be a real game changer, far more persuasive than drawings. The breakthrough came with a grant of £5,000 from The Moorgate Trust, which allowed us to build a schematic model based loosely on the City Hall site.

Now back to our decision to go public at the Alverton…

BL: With my reputation riding high and my fairly regular working relationship with West Country TV, they agreed to come down to the Alverton and film the press conference. With the model working overtime, we got some great exposure on local television, on Radio Cornwall and in the papers.

CW: Ben and I were very pleased with both the quantity and the quality of the media attention that Ben generated at the Alverton Manor Hotel. It's worth pointing out that our aim was simply to break the logjam by publicly underlining the deplorable fact that Cornwall did not have a middle-scale performing arts venue that was fit for purpose. That was a fact – no one could argue against it. We wanted to provoke a debate that would lead to a real solution. We hoped that the press conference would be the catalyst for "someone doing something about it". We never intended to build or to run a new venue.

But, just like the silence after we presented our report to The Weasel, in spite of all the media and press hubbub at the Alverton, there was just another resounding silence.

We waited for something to happen ... Then my phone rang and someone offered us a site next to the large roundabout at Carn Brea. It was quite an exciting thought – the location was as Cornish as you could hope for. But I knew that, although it would be eminently visible to lots of passing traffic, it would be Northcott all over again because there would be no daytime or casual footfall. No means of earning a diverse regular income to support an arts programme. So we said thank you but no thank you.

It was a good start – it showed that someone was listening and was prepared to help. But then the silence descended again like a fog on a moor. I began to doubt our wisdom – were we just a hopelessly romantic couple of middle-aged fools?

A few days later, I had the phone call that was going to change everything – including our lives for the next few years. It was Dame Annette Penhaligon, who, you may remember, took sailing lessons with her family at Loe Beach. I assumed that was what she wanted to talk about. But she explained that she had her Carrick District Councillor hat on and that she wanted to talk about Truro City Hall. She told me that she had secured cross-party agreement from several councillors and that she wanted to make us an offer and could I come to lunch the following day at her house?

She was a sort of grand dame of liberal politics at Carrick and possibly in Cornwall. Hers was often the voice of common sense amid the internecine warfare of local politics. She told me that after the press conference she had called together a cross-party group of Carrick Members and that she might have found a way forward. Slightly mystified, I accepted her invitation to lunch the next day.

So off I went to meet what became known as the Spaghetti Group – because that was what Annette had cooked for lunch. As soon as I entered her house, I sensed a palpable air of almost smug excitement. I can't remember how many councillors were assembled –

half a dozen, perhaps, maybe more. Most of the faces were familiar and several had been carefully supportive of our cri de coeur over the need for a decent Cornish venue. It reminded me of Christmas when the kids have a very special gift for someone and they want to see the reaction of the recipient when the wrapping paper comes off. With knowing looks and a sense of supressed anticipation around the dining table, we had to consume an enormous bowl of spaghetti Bolognese before I was allowed to unwrap my present.

I was a bit startled by the deal they proposed, which went like this: what would I feel about a 125-year lease on City Hall with a rent of £1 a year, plus £500,000 from Carrick towards the capital costs of a new hall?

They – the group round the table – reckoned they could get together enough votes to get this offer through full council.

I don't know what got into me, but I remember replying that we'd be happy to take it off their hands for £750,000. Annette told me rather firmly not to be silly. Thinking on my feet – even though I was sitting down – I could immediately see that it would be a huge benefit to our cause if we could have a campaign and fundraising base at City Hall and where we would be able to run a demonstration programme like Stef had done at ACT. They thought this was a distinct possibility. I decided to push them one step further and said that we would need a clean break with the old management regime. We would run City Hall. They said the Council would have to consider this request.

The Hall for Cornwall would probably not have become a reality without Annette and the people she had gathered around her table. That they stuck their political necks out when others around them bickered should be celebrated. I'm ashamed to say that I don't think we ever thanked them properly.

Walking back to my Land Rover, the euphoria began to wear off. It rapidly dawned on me that I had just been well and truly lumbered. We were about to become the "someone" who was going to do "something" about it …

BL: It took us totally by surprise! We knew we couldn't do it, as did Carrick Council, but we also knew that there was nobody else even remotely as informed as we were, or as resolute. Our thinking was that if we didn't accept this challenge – and that was what it was – the idea of a Hall for Cornwall would die, possibly for years to come.

So we had to pick up the glove which the Spaghetti Group had thrown down.

CW: Following this exciting and daring offer by a group of councillors who had put their political difference to one side, less cordial negotiations with the officers at Carrick began. They set out the list of conditions they required us to meet in order to turn the outline offer from the Spaghetti Group into a legal reality acceptable to the Council.

BL: Apart from various things like becoming a charity, the deal which emerged was an uncomfortably blunt instrument – "you fund it, you get all the consents, you build it, you run it".

CW: Eventually we found ourselves at a full Council meeting which had to vote on the deal we had thrashed out with the officers. The Weasel, whose aim had always been retail development and was therefore not the ideal advocate for our plan, told Members that, as there were currently no other plans for City Hall in the pipeline, they might as well let us have it because we would probably fail after a couple of years – and then the Council could do something more commercially viable with it.

The deal was approved by the Council. I think everyone there was quite amazed that we had got to this point and the atmosphere was ever so slightly festive. Although there were still multiple hurdles to jump and mountains to climb, we would soon walk down Lemon Street the proud possessors of the large bunch of keys to City Hall.

A few years later, when contractors were appointed and we needed to draw down the £500,000, we were amused to find that Carrick had not set the money aside – probably because they had tacitly assumed that we would fail. But for now, it was full steam ahead – with conditions.

All we had to do now was become a charity, obtain planning permission, listed building consent to demolish a large part of a Grade II* listed building, and meet both local and Home Office fire regulations for places of entertainment. Oh, and raise £6m to build the new Hall. In the meantime, as soon as we had charitable status, we could take over the loss-making City Hall, put down a deposit and pay Carrick a monthly rent. What could possibly go wrong?

"We" had become "Them".

We had our outline deal with Carrick but the council had made it clear that there could be no progress until we became a charity. We had to create an ordinary company, register this at Companies House and then make an application to the Charity Commission for charitable status for our new company.

The key to success with making a charity application is to write both your Memorandum and Articles of Association – which have to be signed by the first members who then elect the first trustees – and your Charitable Objects which set out what the charity is going to do. You need to frame these very carefully in the broadest possible terms taking care not to mention anything that has a whiff of trading about it. To save time, we adapted Duchy Opera's "Mem and Arts" which concentrated on emotive aims such as education, development and opportunities for young people rather than on people dressing up, singing and having fun on stage. It was not difficult, but it was certainly a bit laborious, and it seemed to take for ever. I just couldn't wait to get on with the exciting bits.

Here we are posing with our brand new charity number and smiling the broadest of smiles because we knew that City Hall would soon become the very visible base for the Hall for Cornwall Campaign.

Ann and Chris proudly holding up Hall for Cornwall Trust's charity number!

Chapter 8

We get the Keys to City Hall!

City Hall's auditorium – photograph by Martin Howse

CW: Unlocking the back door and walking into our new home was an amazing but daunting experience. Like Emperor Jones, I sensed what O'Neill called "little formless fears" scuttling about in the shadows…

SS: Chris took over City Hall in April 1991 after a licence between Carrick District Council and the Hall for Cornwall Trust was signed, to be reissued on an annual basis.

We think this is a photograph of Chris and Ben signing the agreement with Cllr LeWarne, Chair of Carrick District Council; Carrick's legal officer; Peter Dexter, solicitor for Hall for Cornwall; and John Christie, who was the very supportive Mayor of Truro!

Carrick lent Chris £5,000 so that he and a small team could decorate parts of the Hall, the annexe, make trestle tables for flea markets and sort out an office. He worked hard on putting together a schedule of activities including mini-markets, flea markets, amateur dramatics and other events, with flea markets as the main money earner. Chris brought in Ann Jennings from Smith and Reed to run and manage the flea markets, which were extremely popular during the nineties, attracting regular stallholders and weekly customers to City Hall.

The Campaign now focused on developing the design of a multi-purpose hall on the City Hall site. The architectural design was by Robin Spence and the estimated cost of the build was over £6million without a technical fit-out. There was support for the Campaign and Chris received small donations from coffee mornings and individuals, but not enough to keep City Hall and the Campaign going. Soon Chris had no alternative but to ask for a loan from Midland Bank.

CW: The only way I could secure that loan for £5,000 was by offering my beloved farmhouse as surety. It felt like things were getting a bit hairy. Make or break time!

My main focus needed to be on how we were going to transform City Hall into the Hall for Cornwall. We had continued to discuss the plans for City Hall with Carrick officers and many other interested parties, using the plans and the white model which had been such a significant step forward.

People who struggled with two-dimensional plans for a multi-purpose hall could now see how it might actually work – and better still, they could move the model seating blocks around for themselves. It proved a most persuasive toy which everyone enjoyed playing with and we soon made a short demonstration film which was first shown on Look East. It was extraordinary how quickly this stylised white model acquired a momentum of its own; people even began to ask about – and argue over – the colour of the seats.

There was suddenly a sense that the project might actually have legs, that we weren't just a bunch of idealists with a hare-brained idea. But the model had other unintended consequences, not least for poor Robin.

It provoked a raft of sometimes rather awkward questions. Such as "How are you going to stop the enormous basement flooding at high tide?" Or "Given the huge hydraulic pressure caused by the rising water table at high tide, how are you going to prevent the tanked basement floating like a boat?" "How are you going to able to ensure smoke integrity with so many moving parts?" "How are you going to contain a fire in the huge storage basement which will be underneath the auditorium?" Or "With such large blocks of seating, how are you going to be able to meet the Home Office guidelines on the minimum distances of travel to places of safety?"

Er … We didn't know. We hadn't got that far. We were simply trying to show how this thing might work. And Robin didn't know either.

In spite of all the politicking and negativity, we had somehow rolled our boulder up to the top of the hill. And suddenly it was setting off on its own down the other side and we needed to look sharp and chase after it.

Our boulder might have been on the move but no one "in authority", as Ben put it – least of all Carrick – seemed to have much of an appetite to roll with it. Unfortunately, the current design was perceived as both too expensive and unlikely to achieve approvals for building and licensing regulations. We had to think again … fast.

SS: I met up with Chris that summer and he asked me to help him raise the profile of the Hall for Cornwall campaign in its new home, particularly with the businesses in Cornwall. Arthur Pickering, an artist based in East Cornwall, had offered to help by designing a caricature map of Cornwall which would include all the landmarks and businesses in the county. To be included, a business or organisation had to buy its space on the map. The idea was clever!

The business or organisation would be named and depicted on the map, and these maps would then be sold as a poster printed on tea towels, mugs and T-shirts. The plan was to meet as many businesses as possible throughout Cornwall and talk about the plans for the Hall for Cornwall, and, if they supported the idea, persuade them to sponsor a space on the map, which would be promoted as a marketing tool for the Hall for Cornwall.

Cornwall is a long county, and so, willing as I was to gauge the interest in the Hall for Cornwall, I needed help. We asked Tina Evans, a councillor in Padstow and well known as a member of the Tourist Board in North Cornwall. She knew that area well and had many, many connections throughout Cornwall. Tina and I set forth on our mission to sell the Hall for Cornwall idea to businesses. We talked about the vision of a middle-scale venue based in City Hall and the response was very positive. Most businesses agreed that Cornwall needed a decent venue, but at a realistic cost. We visited every type of business: breweries, creameries, hotels, tourist attractions, quarries, iconic landmarks in every part of Cornwall – and filled up the map with logos and Arthur's interpretation of Cornwall's busy life at that time! It took several months. There was indeed support for a new hall, but not for the elaborate scheme that had been proposed. We had the feedback we needed, and we succeeded in raising the profile of the Hall for Cornwall whilst managing to generate £28,000 from businesses towards the Campaign.

Just as well I did! One of the businesses I visited was Midland Bank (now HSBC) where the meeting with the manager was very enlightening about the Hall for Cornwall's financial situation. The bank had given Chris a personal loan of £5,000, but the manager was very concerned about how the Campaign could move forward in City Hall. It was not good, and the bank manager politely suggested that I had a frank conversation with Chris about the Campaign because Hall for Cornwall had no money. He still sponsored the map, though, and was relieved to see that we had managed to sort out the finances for the moment thanks to Arthur's map.

Nevertheless, Chris and I did have a conversation about how we would manage going forward. He asked me to take away the chequebook, manage the finances and say no to him when necessary. Chris, after all, was an ideas man, a visionary, and these skills don't usually meld with finance and admin.

Arthur Pickering's caricature map of Cornwall 1991

I said I would think about it because this was no ordinary business and it would be such a huge challenge. Did I have the energy, experience and passion for this campaign? The original agreement with Carrick District Council was that the Hall for Cornwall Trust would run City Hall as well as raising the funding (£6m at the time) to refurbish City Hall. I definitely believed in the Campaign: Cornwall did need a hall and I believed that City Hall was the perfect location for it. However, I didn't have much time to pontificate. Carrick was already losing confidence in the Hall for Cornwall team and suggested that the following had to be addressed:

- Find new local trustees
- Set up and operate the City Hall in a commercial way and prove that the operation could be financially viable
- Look for a fundraising consultant
- Develop revised plans for the new Hall.

A stark warning, and quite a challenge!

But we were determined to sort this! It was clear that Robin's scheme was just not going to be accepted. After all, what did someone from London know about City Hall and what Cornwall wanted? Chris started having conversations with Paul Newton, a local architect who had originally taken part in the Carrick competition to find an architect to transform City Hall. Unfortunately, he had been beaten by Robin Spence, but remained very interested in the project and was aware that things were not going well. More about him later, but Paul did join us in a meeting with John Wilson (one of our trustees) and the Carrick officers to discuss the situation.

Alongside this, there were other changes afoot. Some trustees resigned for a variety of reasons relating to the design not being acceptable and other commitments meaning that some could not give enough time to the project.

I agreed to join Chris as General Manager of the Hall for Cornwall and became Director of HfC Ltd (the trading arm of the HfC Trust). First things first, I took away the chequebook from Chris and we started to become more commercial in our approach to running City Hall.

We had a lot of work to do to prove that Hall for Cornwall was serious. Our priorities were: plan the fundraising campaign, develop an alternative design and turn the loss-making City Hall into a profitable business.

The hub of the Hall for Cornwall Campaign was located on the ground floor of the grand granite building called Back Quay at the rear of the City Hall. The main entrance to the office was here and people could come to a window and buy tickets for events or talk to any of us at any time during the day. It was a busy place and most days saw a constant stream of people coming to find out what was happening or passing the time of day.

CW: One day I had a visit from a very senior Lib Dem Carrick councillor, who stressed the importance of their annual fundraising event in the Hall. He also, quietly but firmly, suggested that it would be in our best interest to continue to offer the Hall at discounted rents for the Lib Dem Fair and other community events. A conundrum! On the one hand, we needed to prove that HfC could be a viable business, but on the other we were obliged to offer the Hall at uncommercial rates – the very thing which had previously contributed to Carrick's annual deficit of around £60,000 on the running of City Hall. This conundrum was never solved, and it became an increasing source of tension when local groups started booking the new Hall. I suggested a whacky subsidy scheme to Terry

Beckett, Carrick's Head of Tourism, Leisure and Economic Development Services, whereby Carrick would offer discount vouchers to every Carrick resident. If the subsidised vouchers were used to buy tickets, the Hall would claim the discount from Carrick. I thought it was rather a jolly win–win marketing ploy; but Carrick declined to engage.

SS: During the day we booked in flea markets, commercial markets, events, the Christmas Farmers' Show, exhibitions and parties. Our flea markets were already fairly well established by Ann Jennings, who was an excellent manager and organised and controlled these regular markets well, building a long list of regular stallholders as well as a waiting list. She was popular, and loved by the stallholders, and always had a tale to tell after each market. One constant, though, was the stories that different stallholders shared about sightings of a gentleman dressed in Victorian clothes who used to walk up and down the dressing-room corridor. This corridor stretched along the Lemon Street side of the Hall, with doors into about five or six dressing rooms, was dimly lit and always felt a bit chilly. Even Ann saw this character once, as large as life! He was called Mr Brown who was once the manager of the City Hall and was clearly continuing to keep an eye on the place.

Flea markets at City Hall – photograph by Martin Howse

The flea markets were a great success and really helped us with a steady, albeit small, regular income during those difficult early years.

CW: I used to pray for a wet August so that sodden tourists would throng the stalls. We used to programme four markets a week for around six weeks, and if it did rain everyone was very happy. If it was a dry summer then the only happy people were the tourists!

SS: Every day, business was carefully monitored and the programme of activities within the City Hall slowly increased.

We were always looking at ways of generating more income and decided to start up a proper café serving coffees, lunches and teas during the day. Chris persuaded an experienced catering manager, Mandy Rolleston (MR), to come and help us set up the café. She had some great ideas, and with a small team, including Caroline Enfissi and Jackie Pound, she opened the café with some success. It was very hard, though, given the surroundings and with such limited facilities. Terry Beckett found some funding to update the catering facilities so that we would meet hygiene standards. Together with a coat of paint and some basic café furniture, the cafe did become a bit of a meeting place and we did attract regulars who supported us over the years whilst we were trying to run the old hall and plan for the new one. Mandy Rolleston, Catering Manager and licensee of the Hall for Cornwall looks back:

MR: I had known Chris Warner and Ben Luxon for many years; I had been involved with Duchy Opera and Chris's own theatre company, Warner's Corner. Chris approached me and asked if I would like to join the Hall for Cornwall fundraising team as the Catering Manager; my answer was of course "yes". This came at exactly the right time: my children were old enough now for me to do a job which had less sociable hours, so that was the start of my time as Catering Manager and licensee of the Hall for Cornwall.

What fun we had: hard work, long hours – a real team. Our surroundings were definitely a challenge: a run-down hall, mice running along the beams, pigeons flying in through the broken windows. A haunted spiral staircase going down the back of the old stage. A beer cellar with no cooling; limited cooking and storage facilities. Did it matter? No. My wonderful team was made up of Caroline, Jacqui, Liz, Ruth and Jeanette. In all my years of management, this team has to be the best team ever and nothing fazed us. Then a body of friends volunteered to help out on big bar nights by manning the beer heads (New Year's Eve, gigs, dances, theatre productions, brass band contests, flea markets, beer festivals, Cornish fayres and much more). The hours didn't seem to matter, late finishes straight into early starts. We all just loved the buzz of the place and the feeling that what we were doing was shaping the future of the Hall. Chris's dreams and ideas were endless, Sarah keeping Chris on track, Ann running the flea markets, Debbie being the PA to all this activity, Ian doing all the odd jobs around the Hall. A string of other individuals also brought their expertise to the team.

For me personally, the highlights must have been firstly getting my personal license to sell alcohol after I completed my licensee course up at St Austell Brewery. Catering for bands like The Levellers and Radiohead, with great big pans of bean stew and jam sponge and custard to follow! New Year's Eve events, where the Hall buzzed and a good time was had by all, including us behind the bar. And on a day-to-day basis, the baking of cakes and quiches. Making soups and bacon sandwiches from ingredients sourced from the local businesses at the Pannier Market. Locals coming in for refreshments and lunches. Even our own tramp, who would come in from busking under the underpass for soup and a beer at lunchtime. The amazing stories he could tell … it's a shame he is no longer with us. The excitement of the plans for the new Hall falling into place, choosing the furniture for the new restaurants and bars. Exploring the unused derelict corridors of the City Hall. Viv Prideaux making the beautiful silk hanging banners for the new foyer. Nameplates on the back of the new theatre seats in row "M" as a thank you to all of us for our hard work. Shame the current Hall management managed to destroy/lose them before the rebuild of phase two. We did ask for them to be returned to us …

When I think back, the most powerful tool we had was the individuals involved in the project. Chris Warner has an incredible talent for engaging and taking people with him, and I can only thank him for giving me the opportunity to be part of this fantastic team, it was one hell of an experience!

Chapter 9

Growing our Business at City Hall

SS: We gradually started to introduce an arts programme in the evenings. We presented some small theatre productions and managed to beg, borrow and keep some pretty good lighting, which we moved around on scaffolding both on stage and in the Hall, depending what we were putting on.

We even tried to bring back wrestling, which proved a step too far. The audience was more aggressive than the wrestlers, and one night we ended up with not just the usual shouting and screaming at the referee and the "baddie", but with the audience hurling chairs into the ring. It was not a good night and after that we decided that we would avoid programming wrestling again.

Lighting rigged at City Hall for an event - possibly Wrestling! – photograph by Martin Howse

CW: Of course, I absolutely loved this raw audience involvement – pure theatre! But sadly, Sarah was right and it was not the image we needed to project while we were trying to raise £6m. Of the wrestling events that we put on, the highlight for me was Giant Haystacks. And by Jove he was a giant – so heavy that his feet were blue, bruised and swollen. When the wrestlers were setting up, there was a constant procession of people who sneaked in just to look at him. But we had real trouble finding a B&B that would take the risk of him sleeping in one of their beds.

SS: We widely advertised the space for hire and contacted a number of impresarios in the hope that they would bring their acts to Truro without charging much. We did work successfully with a couple of promoters who brought in bands such as Chumbawumba, Radiohead and Hawkwind, all of which were very popular and more or less sold out. The trouble was that our backstage facilities were so outdated and shabby. The lighting board was positioned so that the operator could only see the stage from the side, and the switchboard was on the right of the lighting board, so the operator had to work with their back to the stage. It was quite embarrassing!

City Hall lighting board and prompt corner – photograph by Martin Howse

We knew we had an audience for popular and rock music, which would prove to be really important to us during the fundraising campaign a couple of years later. But in the meantime, we were experimenting and looking at opportunities to showcase different arts genres in the hope of discovering audiences who would like theatre, dance, music and art.

CW: I often hung out with Roy Walker, an abstract expressionist, who occupied what had once been Ben Nicholson's studio above Porthmeor beach in St Ives. I loved visiting Roy there, and if the weather was fine, we would climb down a ladder onto the sand. One of his specialities was etching images onto large untreated steel sheets, and one day he told me how frustrating it was that he was unable to show these larger works in Cornwall. Just as Steph had set out with ACT to show people what theatrical treats they were missing due to the lack of a venue, I determined to do the same for the visual arts when we got our mitts on the City Hall. So we converted part of the Hall into an art gallery and Roy used this space, or the Gallery, as we called it, to exhibit his seriously large metal works on the long side walls.

Over a single weekend the staff worked with a huge floor sander, a big tin of Ronseal and a few gallons of brilliant white to transform the tatty old annexe into a fabulous gallery. The floor was sanded, the sliding wall was covered in MDF, painted a pristine white, and exhibition lighting was installed. The invitations from Dame Hilda Bracket had already gone out for a Private View of Roy's exhibition and the guests literally gasped as they entered the space we had created. A half-size Coco-Chanel-lipstick-red helicopter, complete with pilot, was attached to the new wall, and down the centre of the room there was a forty-foot long, six feet high, double-sided etched steel wall. "Smaller" works adorned the long outer masonry wall. Job done. I think Roy actually sold his steel wall. Say no more, nudge, nudge, wink, wink!

Roy's exhibition lent a touch of class to our jaded home and brought new people into City Hall. I loved watching newcomers being astonished by the new space, which of course wasn't really new at all. It showed everyone what a bit of imagination, elbow grease and white paint could achieve. It wasn't a perfect art gallery, although we worked wonders with the lighting.

SS: We programmed the annual Young Farmers' Club Christmas Party, Beer Festival and New Year's Eve parties, all of which were really successful and very, very busy.

Caroline Enfissi (CE) recalls her time at City Hall:

CE: I first got involved with the Hall for Cornwall campaign when they needed someone to work in the kitchen.

Once Mandy Rolleston had taken over the catering, there were six of us working there regularly: Mandy, me, Jacqui, Lizzie, Ruth and Jeanette. Anne Jennings's niece Beverley worked with us for a while, but her vegetarianism didn't really fit with our bacon-sandwich-and-pasty regime. My daughter Genny used to work at weekends and in the school holidays.

We had very basic facilities in the kitchen, although life became easier when we got a dishwasher. Washing up by hand after events like the Mayor's Banquet had been a real marathon! The menu was limited to what was practical with the equipment we had. Our mainstays were homemade soups, quiches, cakes and scones. And, of course, wall-to-wall bacon sandwiches on flea-market days! The best thing about working at the Hall was the variety; flea markets and antique fairs meant an early start and a day-long queue for food; weekdays were quieter and we might be finished by 3 p.m.

The first year was very much learning on the job. On our first New Year's Eve, we ran out of beer and had to get more in from the pub next door. We also ran out of change, which was more difficult. The queue was about six deep at the bar and in the end people were just handing us £10 notes to get any sort of drink! We were better organised the next year. The Young Farmers' Club Christmas Party was another memorable affair. The boys were mainly inexperienced drinkers, and when the beer started running low they turned to other options. "What's that green stuff?" "Crème de menthe." "Is it alcohol? Give me a half." (We didn't!)

The annual Beer Festival was always really busy. The amusing thing was the number of men who would come over to our bar clutching their commemorative glass and whisper, "Could you just give me a lager in it?" or even better, "Could I have a Coke or a lemonade?" After a couple of years we took over the cheese stall at the festival, managing to find some really nice cheeses in the Pannier Market next door.

We had quite a few well-known performers over the years. I remember cooking breakfast for The Levellers and Chumbawumba, an after-show party for Dame Hilda Bracket, and knocking up a quick birthday cake for Kenny Ball! On one occasion Chris

Jackie Pound and Caroline Enfissi suporting the Art Auction in 1995 – photograph by HfC

asked me to make "one of those up-market canapés you're so good at". I had a vague idea that a canapé was something on a bit of toast, but what constituted an up-market one? I imagine I just made some things on toast!

It wasn't unknown for us to finish a day in the café and then stay on and help with setting up the Hall for an evening event, where we would be running the bar. The hardest one was probably the International Dance Festival. We would start with breakfast at 7.30 a.m. (the Russians used to bring in their own tins of caviar for breakfast) and work through till midnight (with a short break somewhere in the day). Then it was hopefully home by 1 a.m. and back again for 7.30 a.m. I still remember being taught a Breton dance by a Belgian dancer at around midnight. Way beyond tired at that point.

In the end of course, the best bit was the customers.

"I'll have a bit of that flat round thing." (Quiche.)

"Give me some of they crud-eyets." (We'd branched out into serving crudités with a dip.)

We were accused of serving French onion soup with too many onions in, and omelettes that were too eggy.

The customers had great faith in our abilities, though. When the roof leaked and the kitchen was a foot deep in water and we were trying to clear up in near total darkness because the electricity was off and we only had thc light from the gas stove, we still had a few hopeful souls coming to the kitchen door wondering if we could make them a bacon sandwich or egg and chips.

CW: Life at City Hall could be so unpredictable, and the Great Knicker Heist was a lovely example of this! I was called out one night by the police, who had found the back door smashed. And wide open. Inside, I found a ghostly flea market set up in the gloom and it soon emerged that the only thing missing was a quantity of excessively large knickers from the underwear stall. The police had given chase, and the thief, encumbered by the knickers and unable to escape because the ground-floor doors were all locked, had, in true B-movie style, made good his – or her – escape onto the roof. Next day it rained and then it pelted. Water started pouring in, soaking several stalls, much to the chagrin of the stallholders, some of whom, if they ever had an entry in Who's Who, would probably have listed complaining as one of their hobbies. Up on to the wet and slippery roof I went, only to find that the deluge had been caused by armfuls of discarded knickers which had blocked the gulley in the valley between the two roofs. Like the dead pigeon in the Back Quay downpipe, the voluminous knickers had caused the water to back up over the lead flashing.

A while later, very early one morning, I was called in to another mystery. There was no sign of a break-in but a few of the lights were on and I could hear someone moving about inside. I had taken my large Lab with me and I picked up a handy bit of 4x4 timber as I crept in through the stage door. Suddenly I was almost flattened by a running figure. We collided with a mutual "Ooof!" The figure collapsed. I stood over it gripping my bit of 4x4 in both hands. The Lab, who clearly had not understood his role in the proceedings, started to lick the prostrate intruder. "How the f**ck do yer git outta here?" he demanded belligerently in a strong Irish accent. It turned out that he had dossed down while the show was running and had got himself locked in.

SS: Improvements were made to City Hall although there were continuous problems with the roof and plumbing. Carrick were not always swift in their response or actions to repair the Hall. The leaking roof was the worst, as whenever we had rain, which in Cornwall is often, we had to place buckets strategically to avoid hazardous puddles. Thankfully, most people attending flea markets and events were very relaxed about the conditions and would side-step the buckets. It all added to our compelling argument that what was needed was a refurbished Hall.

CW: I remember one show when the assistant stage manager had to use an umbrella to protect actors from a deluge in the wings. And the same night someone in the audience complained about the noise backstage – it was the rain beating on the wooden floorboards of the stage!

Jacqui Pound (JP) shares her memories of those days:

JP: I worked in the City Hall when Chris and Sarah ran it. I worked in the catering department; such a great place to work (early mornings on flea-market days, which ran through from Thursday until Saturday most weeks). I can remember the frenzy of Saturday early evenings: all the tables being put away, and straight on to getting the Hall ready for a night of entertainment, which was so eclectic, from opera one night to the Levellers another time. Desmond Dekker was a great night!!! My kids had a great time coming to watch a lot of shows – so much so that my youngest daughter, who spent most of her formative years coming to work with me (there was usually a space available for her to watch the shows while I was working) was given a real taste of the theatre world. She has gone on to be a West End performer ... definitely my favourite job of all time.

SS: We continued to work hard to stabilise the commercial side of the business, streamlining the staff and growing the programme of events. Two key members of staff were Mary Sheppard (MS), as our part time Accounts Officer and Debbie McCrory (DMc), who helped with box office and administration. Both Mary and Debbie made our lives so much easier. We were no longer juggling everything but becoming more orderly in the way we operated. We were becoming more professional, and it was also becoming a lot of fun. Mary was excellent at keeping our income and expenditure in order – she challenged us and chased us for information, too. Her attention to detail was amazing, and perfect for what we needed. Debbie, who had been training to become an actress, returned to Cornwall when the grants were withdrawn. Lucky for us, as she joined the team and was a breath of fresh air: energetic, funny and hard-working, plus she was absolutely wedded to the idea of a hall for the people of Cornwall. Both Mary and Debbie stayed throughout and left a few years after the new Hall had opened.

MS: My involvement was with the day-to-day running of the old City Hall, just book-keeping really. The flea markets were so important for us. I remember how Yvonne Allis, our cashier, would walk through the streets of Truro to the bank with hundreds of pounds from the flea market stall fees in a shopping bag. In retrospect it was very dangerous – perhaps we were a bit naïve.

As the business developed, I had to produce accounts and a cash flow for the trustees, which frightened me to death, and the accounts became even more complicated as we moved into fundraising and then the refurbishment of City Hall. At times I used to find Chris's grand ideas quite scary, but Sarah was always able to rein him in, or, more often than not, she would find the necessary funding.

I always thought Sarah was the brains behind the whole thing; she worked so hard, with great success, to get it off the ground. I recognise it was Chris's idea, but without Sarah it would not have happened.

SS: Financial constraints and hard work paid off and by the end of the financial year in March 1993 improvements were showing on the balance sheet. Thankfully, Tony Hill of KPMG had worked closely with me, controlling the finances and organising the Trust and commercial company. Carrick began talks with us about a full licence, which would make the Hall for Cornwall Trust responsible for the City Hall and pay a rent of £12,000 per annum.

HfC mug and Ben Luxon's Proper Job!

We decided to use our caricature map printed on posters and mugs as well as tea towels just to generate money towards the campaign. Thankfully, these did sell steadily – as did a recording of Ben Luxon's "Proper Job"! Mary Sheppard tells me that the song has stood the test of time and is still aired on Cornwall radio stations!

BL: As you can see, we were moving into an incredibly exciting period with a determination to show the public what was possible, even with the tatty old City Hall as our venue.

So many new people joined us, among them Goff Richards, like me a musician, but who had come into the profession from the Cornish brass band tradition. Now he had a huge reputation as an arranger and composer for brass bands world-wide. Although based in the north of England, Goff was very much a Cornishman and offered to write a couple of songs for me to record in order to promote our cause and hopefully add some funds. He set to music two poems by David Dearlove from Penzance – "Proper Job", which was a really lively up-tempo number all about "meeting you at the hall", and a beautiful nostalgic song called "West Of The Tamar". They were fun to sing and record.

Goff eventually became a trustee and for our opening concert in 1997 he composed the musical centrepiece, a medley of Cornish folk songs for choirs, brass band, orchestra and soloists – perfect for the occasion!

SS: Alongside all these activities and ideas, Chris and I felt that we had to prove that the Hall for Cornwall was needed. Yes, we had got a terrific response from businesses, we were generating support and interest from those living in the Truro area, and the message was certainly getting out and filtering around Cornwall; but how could we test it?

We decided that we should undertake a survey and focus it on young people in the county. After all, they would be our audiences of the future. We had no money to pay for a survey but knew that we had to make sure it was robust and substantial enough for us to refer to. We approached Cornwall College, who were willing to take this survey on as part of their course. The survey was undertaken by full-time students in their final year of a two-year BTEC National Diploma Course in Business and Finance within the Trevithick Business Centre. It involved the Sales and Marketing group together with the Statistics group. The survey was designed by the different groups with Chris and I working with them to ensure that we covered all the questions that we needed to ask.

They took on the task during the winter and spring terms of 1992/93 within the BTEC format, and this was coordinated by Tricia Noble and Keith Vingoe. The survey covered all the main towns in Cornwall, with up to three students assigned to each town armed with twenty questionnaires. The results were analysed, and the conclusions were quite a relief! The majority of people who took part agreed that there was a definite need for a new hall – here is an extract from the survey in which we share the findings:

The Hall in the community Market Research Survey

A SPACE FOR YOU

Findings

A total of 851 questionnaires were completed, which compares favourably with the 1,200 of a Mori 'national' poll.

From the 851 people interviewed 162 were in the under 20 category, closely followed by the 46-55 age group with 133 people. The 20-25 category had 114 with the 56-65 group having 96 people. The remaining five groups were close with the 41-45 group having 86, the 36-40 group with 75, the over 65's with 65, the 26-30 with 56 people and the 31-35 age group with 55 people.

When people were asked whether Cornwall needs a new hall 673 said Yes and 175 No, with 429 people saying that they had heard of the Hall for Cornwall Campaign and 412 saying they had not.

When asked how they had heard of the Campaign 253 said word of mouth, 142 said newspapers, 113 radio and 49 television. There were however 62 people who did not respond to this question.

When the public were asked what events they had attended at the City Hall 434 replied fleamarkets, 43 said opera, 315 craftmarkets, 188 pop concerts, 139 people said that they have attended art exhibitions and 115 people said the theatre. Other responses included dances, film shows, jumble sales, dog shows and beer festivals.

The majority of people had heard of the above events by word of mouth, some 394 people. 221 said newspapers, 209 had seen posters, and 78 had responded to fliers.

On average most people travelled over 20 miles for an event with 186 in this group. This was followed by 184 people travelling between 11 and 15 miles. There were 140 in the 6-10 miles and 122 in the 16-20 miles category. There were 84 people who travelled under 5 miles.

The majority of people wished to see a restaurant in the new Hall, some 501 responses. With a bar 426, coffee shop 423, box office 286 and a souvenir shop commanding 224 responses.

The restaurant would be used mainly after performances, 235 responses. Although 291 people would use it during the day. Very few people would use it in the morning, 47 responses.

The types of food which should be served in the restaurant was 287 responses to snacks, 187 to a set menu, 184 to vegetarian meals. Light hot and cold meals was the most popular result with 374 responses.

People mainly wished to see craft fairs at the new Hall, 414 responses; closely followed by pop concerts 396, fleamarkets 363, community events 357, and antique fairs 308. It was interesting to note that all responses were in the hundreds, the least popular being wrestling. With 148 responses.

People were willing to pay between £5 and £10 at the Hall for Cornwall, some 346 persons, this did not include the ticket price.

Most people would seek concessionary prices if they fell into the category of an OAP, student, group, etc.

It was interesting to note that the majority of people interviewed do not leave the county for art/cultural events.

Chapter 10

Tea with the Minister and Designing the Hall for Cornwall

SS: With Hall for Cornwall now firmly on the map locally, we needed to find funding to develop plans to convert City Hall into a multi-purpose hall. Chris had worked hard with Ben's help to get the attention of the government and managed to get a meeting set up in Whitehall. In February 1992 Chris, Tina and I met up with Ben in a pub in London to have lunch and to plan our meeting with the Culture Minister, Tim Renton. It was a very jolly discussion, particularly as Ben, with his booming baritone voice, managed to draw everyone in the pub to listen to our conversation. It is fair to say that they might well have recognised him, as he was at the height of his fame as an opera singer who performed all over the world. But I doubt whether they understood why he was part of a discussion about Cornwall and why we should want to attract some attention and possibly funding from a government minister based in London.

CW: We actually managed to get to speak to two Culture Ministers – Richard Luce, who I met informally at a reception in Cornwall, and his replacement, Tim Renton, who, in February 1992, invited the four of us to tea in his rather plush ministerial office in London. Tim Renton was interested and talked about possible sources of funding including Foundation for Sports and the Arts, the Arts Council and European Funding through the urban renewable scheme. He gave our campaign his backing and we got some good publicity – "Tea with the Minister" was the banner headline in the West Briton. We hoped that Ministerial interest might unlock Arts Council support. Wrong. Nick Capaldi, the chief executive of South West Arts (SWA), the regional arm of the Arts Council England (ACE), was sympathetic but, like so many others, tended to be sceptical. SWA was worried about the side-effects of building the Hall. What impact would it have on Plymouth Theatre Royal's Arts Council tours? We explained patiently that Plymouth was a bit of a schlepp from Penzance and that we were concerned to offer product to new audiences who lacked wheels, didn't leave Cornwall, or who couldn't afford the time or money to get to Plymouth. What about all the small venues in

Cornwall, most of which lived on or near the breadline? What about the thirteen small theatre companies in the Duchy who also struggled to survive on less than subsistence funding? What would the impact of the new Hall be on them?

The Eden Project some years later experienced similar antipathy from the established Cornish gardens, which were seriously concerned that Eden would put them out of business. The answer was that Eden would draw in a new – and large – audience which, having "done" Eden, would want to visit other gardens. We were sure the new Hall would generate increased audiences for the arts centres. In this we were proved right, particularly in relation to modern dance and emerging dance companies, who needed small venues before they were ready to tour middle-scale venues.

Finding ourselves in London one day marching down Piccadilly, Ben suddenly turned to me and said, "Let's go and see Luke Rittner!" (who was the Chief Exec at Arts Council England, which in those days was based at 105 Piccadilly). Ben had never met this man, but undeterred by such a trifle we strode into 105 as bold as brass and asked the reception desk if we could see the head honcho. We faced the usual prevarications, such as, "Who are you? Does he know you? Do you have an appointment?" On the back wall of reception there was a set of named pigeonholes. Ben, who was getting grumpy by this stage, spied a name he recognised. "I know Jack Phipps" (who was ACE Head of Touring), he boomed. "He married so-and-so's sister, he'll see us. So, we asked to see Jack. Just as reception went into a prevarication encore, who should come down the magnificent balustraded stairs but Jack. Like long-lost relations we were whisked upstairs, where we were given tea, Arts Council biscuits – and some really useful advice.

SS: At this point in our story, we ought to explain the complexities of the challenge before us. City Hall was built in 1845 and was a Grade II* listed building. Originally designed with handsome granite façades to the front and back of the building, it was situated in the centre of Truro. The front entrance faced onto Boscawen Street, which was the main street, and the back entrance faced onto Back Quay. The hall was sandwiched between these two grand ends which were monuments to Truro's prosperity and importance in the 19th century. Originally an open-air market which later came to be roofed over, the middle section had been a civic centre, market hall and entertainment venue. It had been sadly neglected over the years and the rooms in the Back Quay end of the building had been unoccupied for several years and were semi-derelict.

The original cavernous main entrance from Boscawen Street was large, dark, with a high ceiling held up by a number of granite columns. It was wasted space and was leased by Truro City Council, whose offices, along with the Magistrates Court, were on the floor above. The Council was very resistant to any use of the main entrance by Hall for Cornwall, so when Chris took over the lease of City Hall, he decided that Hall for Cornwall would operate from Back Quay, which was traditionally regarded as the back entrance. Our campaign office and a new box office were based there on the ground floor and were thus easily accessible from the street.

The Hall itself was accessible from both the front and back entrances, with the stage located towards the Back Quay end of the building. The hall was licensed to accommodate a maximum of 650 people standing and 450 seated.

CW: In those days the fire regs for buildings with a seated audience of under 500 were relatively simple. It soon became clear that Robin's design was going to struggle to comply with the far more stringent Home Office guidelines for seated audiences over 500. These regs are very detailed on a range of matters such as fire and smoke integrity – how fire and smoke can be contained in one area in order to ensure safe escape from the rest of the building. They prescribe the maximum distances to be travelled from auditorium seats to places of safety, such as escape corridors, the width and integrity of fire doors, as well as things like sprinklers, smoke detectors and the fire alarm system. Robin's building as designed would not meet the regulations. A particular concern from the fire regs point of view was that the audience would be sitting over a very large cellar which was structurally part of the auditorium. The relationship with Robin became increasingly strained as we struggled to get answers from him. After he commented in anguish that the necessary changes would "compromise the purity" of his design, Ben and I knew that we had to say a sad goodbye to him.

There was also another not-so-small problem – the whole site from street to street was listed, which meant that we had to get consent to demolish a large chunk of a Grade II* listed building. Not an easy thing to do at the best of times. And the Save Our City Hall camp, which had proved such a useful alliance in thwarting the developers, was, understandably, not particularly enamoured of our proposal to knock down half of what they loved and cherished and wished to save.

We knew that to develop a successful building we had to find an architect who understood the parameters within which we needed to work and who could provide us with some new ideas which would stand up to scrutiny.

Apparently, it's quite common for the first architect to get sacked. This principle allegedly holds true when the successful second architect becomes the first architect on a subsequent project. Robin's departure, sad as it was in many ways, led to the appointment of architects Hocking & Newton, who were an architectural practice based in Perranarworthal near Truro. Ex Redruth Grammar School pupils Roger Hocking and Paul Newton understood the local politics and had originally submitted a design as part of the design competition which Robin Spence had won.

Their appointment was to prove a significant breakthrough on the public relations front. People felt that the choice of a firm, based Cornwall, was infinitely preferable to one from up country. I loved Paul and Roger because they listened. Some of the happiest and most fulfilling days of my life were soon to be spent in their design studio.

SS: Our brief for Hall for Cornwall was to provide a sympathetic restoration of the Victorian elements of the listed building combined with an innovative and modern approach to the provision of a new multi-purpose hall.

Roger Hocking of Hocking & Newton Architects Ltd explains:

RH: My involvement with the Hall for Cornwall started when I was an Associate Architect with MWT Architects, a.k.a. Company of Designers. Paul Newton was the Director in charge.

I received my Diploma in Architecture from the School of Architecture, part of the Plymouth Polytechnic (now University of Plymouth). My first job on leaving college in 1972 was with Marshman Warren Taylor (later known as MWT Architects Ltd and Company of Designers PLC) and not long after I started work, Paul Newton joined the practice. Although Paul and I had both attended Redruth Grammar School and the Plymouth School of Architecture, Paul was six years older than I and we had consequently previously never met.

Although the opportunity to design a theatre is not a common occurrence for an Architect, I was able to draw on the knowledge that I had obtained from preparing my RIBA Part 2 qualifying design thesis, which was a cultural centre for Truro incorporating a theatre. Being aware that Cornwall was short of adequate facilities for the performing arts "which were essential to the quality of life ... to the region's capacity to attract and retain people of lively minds ..." to quote from South West Economic Council's A *Region with a Future* at that time, I was keen that my thesis would be related to the needs of the area where I was born and brought up. Before preparing a design for my thesis, I carried out desktop studies of certain theatres in the country, viz.: The Playhouse, Leeds; The Repertory, Birmingham; The Playhouse, Weston-Super-Mare; Bristol Old Vic, The Northcott, Exeter (including a visit) and (the one that particularly caught my attention) The Crucible, Sheffield. The site I chose was what was then known as the Pydar Street redevelopment area, using the building known as Cathedral Chambers as the entrance; otherwise, the design was for a new building rather than a refurbishment of an existing building. I became familiar with terms like proscenium and fly tower and learned about auditoria layouts, sightlines, reverberation periods, etc., so not only was I able to put what I had learned to good use in preparing a proposal for the design competition but being involved in what was to eventually become the Hall for Cornwall was the realisation of something that I believed in strongly.

We submitted a competition design for the redevelopment of the City Hall to form a multi-use theatre and community hall. This was before the days of computer-aided design, and whilst preparing the competition entry I spent a considerable amount of time projecting and drawing by hand a perspective illustration of the Boscawen Street foyer restored to its original glory, it at that time being divided up into individual small retail units. In the event, the competition was won by the architect Robin Spence. However, that proposal eventually floundered.

Paul Newton advised me on my thirty-fifth birthday that the Truro office of MWT/CoD was to close and that we would all be made redundant. With my redundancy money I bought my first computer (a Viglen with a 100MB hard drive and 4MB of ram!) and set up my own company, Roger Hocking (Architect) Ltd. Paul Newton similarly started practising on his own.

In those days, the City Hall was the venue for the annual CAMRA Beer Festival in Truro, of which I was an avid supporter. That same year I attended and met fellow supporters Bob Moore and John Stenglehofen, employees of MWT's rival practice John Crowther Associates (JCA). They told me that two of those Associates, Mike Lilly (d/d) and David Lewarne (d/d) were leaving JCA to set up their own practice, to be known as Lilly Lewarne Partnership. On my return home I phoned Paul Newton to advise him of this development and we agreed to combine our practices and formed Hocking & Newton Architects Ltd.

Paul told me that, following the dropping of Robin Spence's design for the redevelopment of the City Hall, he had been approached by Chris Warner, then running the City Hall on a licence from Carrick Ditrict Council, to progress the design for the redevelopment of the City Hall submitted by MWT/CoD, on which I had worked, but on the basis of minimum construction cost, as it was envisaged that obtaining funding would be a major issue.

I then set to work putting the design on to my newly acquired computer. The principle of the design was to retain the Boscawen Street and Back Quay buildings, to demolish the central hall and to construct a new multi-use hall/auditorium with retractable seating and a variable height orchestra pit, enabling concert, theatre and flat-floor uses. It was deemed important to achieve a seating capacity of 1,000 in concert mode. The Back Quay building in particular was severely dilapidated, with part of the roof having collapsed, leading to rain penetration into a panelled room (now called the Arbon Room after Dennis Arbon, a significant financial contributor), resulting in dry rot developing. I also particularly remember a toilet at the back of the Boscawen Street building, where pigeons were able gain access to roost, with a toilet covered in a pyramid of guano.

As part of the licenced operation at that time, Chris and Sarah Smith were running a café which they called the Back Stage Café. I volunteered to paint a sign for them, which I did on Saturdays. On one occasion I stayed on to complete a section of the sign unnoticed by the café staff, who left, locking me in. In those days the locking mechanisms were not Building Regulations compliant, i.e. not free to escape. I managed to contact Sarah by phone, and she came and let me out. Whilst waiting I sang the opening lines of "Oh For The Wings Of A Dove" on the stage to an empty auditorium. At least I can honestly say that I have performed in the City Hall!

Chapter 11

Hocking & Newton's Design

SS: Chris, Roger and Paul had several sessions looking at the City Hall site in order to see how it could be transformed into a multi-purpose hall with a stage large enough to accommodate choirs, bands, ballet, dance, musicals and theatre with enough seats to make the Hall financially viable. Not only was this critical to the vision for the Hall but also, if we were going to present theatre in all its guises, we would need a fly tower which would inevitably rise above the old City Hall roofline and which would therefore be very visible from some parts of the city.

CW: The biggest challenge was fitting everything into the finite space between the two grand granite structures at either end. To get into the old City Hall, people parked in the Lemon Quay car park and then trudged round to the Boscawen Street entrance, sometimes in the rain. That seemed daft so we determined to make the new entrance on Back Quay, which was also more suitable – or perhaps less unsuitable – for accommodating the huge scenery lorries and rock bands' tour buses which would need to park outside for several hours.

The old City Hall stage backed onto the rear of the Back Quay building. We decided to rotate the position of the new stage to the Lemon Street side and I had a wild plan to buy and knock down the rather seedy Market Inn on Back Quay in order to create an off-street loading bay which would give us the techies' dream of a direct level load-in onto the side of the new stage.

SS: We finally had some plans to share with Carrick District Council and so arranged a presentation to the Councillors. It went fairly well until we talked about the fly tower, which was vehemently challenged by Mrs Carlyon and others. We were told that it would ruin the view of Truro Cathedral from the top of Lemon Street, that it would have to be a compromise and would need to be redesigned. The arguments and aggressive meetings continued for months as we tried to share slight changes in design, including a model showing mirrors on the fly tower. Inevitably, we compromised, but not without a fight by Chris, who seemed to get the rough end of everyone's tongue. Chris was so passionate about the project and meetings would start with him describing the plans with help from the architects, explaining the need for a fly tower and the benefits of having one, which would enable us to attract well-known touring companies to Cornwall and so on – but to no avail. The meetings would disintegrate into a battlefield, with Chris losing his temper. After a couple of these sessions, Chris asked me to go with him to the meetings and if he started getting heated, I was to kick him under the table … It sort of worked, but I began to think that people were actively trying to provoke and bait Chris to get a reaction.

CW: Barbara Spring, the Cornwall County Council member for Saltash was a real ally. Her son was a professional musician who knew Ben. Barbara was a couth lady, a generally good egg, a supporter of Duchy and the Hall. Ben and I often visited her in her beautiful house in Saltash which enjoyed views of the Tamar, in order to discuss the progress – or not – of the Hall for Cornwall Campaign.

Barbara Spring was chairman of the Library, Arts and Records Committee of Cornwall County Council and when things became a bit sticky with the Carrick planners on account of their aversion to the fly tower, she agreed to call a conference in the Long Gallery at County Hall at which Ben and I could set out and explain our plans for the new Hall.

The conference to be held on Tuesday 7 April 1992, was an opportunity for Ben and I to bang home the message that if there were to be incoming tours then the building had to be fit for purpose. We invited two "witnesses" to help us make the case for the fly tower and the other technical facilities which we knew were needed. One was Charles Vance who was big in the touring business, bringing shows out of the West End. He was a charismatic, charming person and he said he very much wanted to bring his national tours down to Truro. He then explained that he would only be able to do so if the Hall was a properly equipped receiving house.

SS: The other was Stephen Hybs, Director of Tomorrow's World Exhibition & Conferences. Having known Stephen for most of my life, I was aware that he had set up and developed a very successful company in exhibitions and conferences. He more than most had the experience of confirming whether a venue was suitable for a conference or exhibition and was in a perfect position to put forward a convincing argument. We definitely wanted Hall for Cornwall to be part of the exhibition and conference circuit as these would provide us with an important income stream. We had already planned to provide the appropriate technical equipment with the the ability to support those sorts of events. We also wanted Stephen to demonstrate that conferences and exhibitions would have a positive economic impact for Truro and Cornwall.

From memory we didn't have a huge gathering but those who attended were key for us. Officers and councillors from Carrick and Cornwall County Council were there and I think the conference did help to persuade them of the benefits of a new hall in Truro.

CW: There is a very simple formula for calculating the height of a flytower. The height of the grid above the stage must be at least one and a half times the height of the proscenium opening. The tower would have to be at the right height in order to fly out the scenery brought in by the national companies we hoped to attract. If the tower wasn't tall enough, the bottom of the flown scenery would remain visible to the audience. If the tower wasn't fit for purpose, big shows simply wouldn't come. It was so important to the project that Paul proposed mirror cladding for the whole tower in order to make it "disappear". When that didn't cut the planning mustard, I threatened we'd take the project somewhere else. The planners still refused to budge. I felt they were being – in Army parlance – wilfully obtuse. And it drove me absolutely crazy!

Mulling this over with Paul and Roger, I suggested – partly for a joke – that we could move the stage to the opposite (Morlaix Avenue) side of the space and dig out the whole site down to the Back Quay level. There was snigger, then a pause as it gradually sank in to all of us that this could be a solution. It would position the fly tower so it was less intrusive in relation to the cathedral, and it would reduce its apparent height by three feet without compromising our ability to provide more or less full-height flying. And it would give us a reasonable level load-in for scenery and, for audiences, street-to-seat access to the auditorium, which would particularly benefit people in wheelchairs.

Roger Hocking recalls the somewhat organic way the design of the new Hall developed:

RH: The space between the Boscawen Street and Back Quay buildings, which was to become the main auditorium/hall, stage and wings, was an irregular rhombus shape. For simplicity of construction, a regular rectangular-shaped steel frame was proposed, with the left-over spaces between that and the existing adjacent buildings becoming toilets and dressing rooms. I remember the first time we electronically passed, with bated breath, copies of our drawings to Ian Hick of structural engineers Warren Greig and Partners.

For this first version of our design, the biggest hurdle, however, was obtaining listed building consent, particularly for the fly tower, which would literally tower over the existing roofs of the City Hall and which, at that time, was proposed to back on to the Market Inn and was visibly prominent when seen from higher up Lemon Street. For some reason I shall never understand, this was not acceptable to the Conservation Officer (who was known in my profession as Dr No). To minimise this impact, I think Chris suggested turning the auditorium through 180 degrees so that the fly tower backed on to the Pannier Market, which is where it was eventually built.

A major decision was that the Back Quay building would become the entrance foyer, with the first floor becoming a restaurant and the second-floor accommodation used for meeting rooms.

CW: The first row of seats would now be on the same level at the Back Quay pavement, allowing less mobile people to buy a ticket, get a coffee and go on through to their seats without facing steps.

In another life I attended a disability awareness course which had proved to be an eye-opener. The tutor used a wheelchair, and I shall never forget her opening remark – "I'm not disabled! It's the ****** steps which disable me."

Roger, Paul and I were absolutely determined to do everything we could to make sure that access for people facing mobility issues would be easy and unobtrusive. I decided we needed to get some advice, and who best to advise but actual wheelchair users. Twelve people in wheelchairs came to visit us in the old City Hall and each person faced different problems and most had special chairs. We talked about turning circles if you had your legs sticking out horizontally, how hard it was to get through doors, how frustrating and disheartening it was for them not to be able to reach door handles, light switches, mirrors and taps. And the buttons which opened power-operated doors needed to be positioned so that the doors didn't whack the wheelchair. And not least how important it was that the new building should have sufficient special toilets which would be designed to cater for the various needs of wheelchair users. We really tried to get this right.

Twenty years later, it was really sad to hear a distinguished lady Paralympian describe on television her anguish at being forced to wet herself because the train she was travelling on did not offer an accessible toilet.

RH: The floor of the auditorium was lowered to the Back Quay ground floor level, about a metre lower than the Boscawen Street foyer. This necessitated excavation of the Hall floor down to its historically original floor level, which revealed the slate floor from when the Hall was used as a cattle market. Some of the slate slabs were reclaimed and reused in the refurbished Boscawen Street foyer, which had the dividing screens removed, allowing the foyer to be opened up as in my earlier hand-drawn perspective sketch – a dream come true. I only wish I still had that drawing.

The design of the balustrade to the mezzanine-floor restaurant was the subject of a competition. The panel of judges on which I sat, headed by Professor Alan Livingston, selected the design submitted by James Horrobin of Doverhay Studios, Porlock.

To comply with fire-escape regulations, a wider stair was required than then existed in the Back Quay foyer. On removal of that existing timber stair, an earlier, previously unknown, granite stair was discovered beneath. Despite opposition from the Conservation Officer, this also had to be removed, but the granite treads were reused in the Boscawen Street foyer leading down to the lowered auditorium floor. Unfortunately, the replacement curved steps in matching granite had to be imported from China.

To construct the roof of the auditorium, which spanned the space between the Boscawen Street and Back Quay foyers, scaffolding had to be erected for the width, height and depth of the auditorium.

I especially remember the day I visited the site following removal of the scaffolding, walking into the auditorium, lit by the contractor's temporary lighting, and seeing the uninterrupted space for the first time. I felt my heart jump and I can honestly say that is the only time in my life where I found myself saying "wow"!

SS: The breakthrough came when Paul walked into Chris's office bearing a new set of plans. These revealed the fresh design approach of moving the stage from the Lemon Street side of the building to the left of the site when walking in from Boscawen Street. This not only enabled us to increase seating significantly to 1,000 seats, but also gave us a large stage and enabled the fly tower to be placed more discreetly, which would hopefully cause less upset to local residents. There were dressing rooms, and areas allocated for toilets, a restaurant, front of house, an exceptionally long bar, box office and office.

These plans were so exciting, and we suddenly felt that these ideas just might be acceptable to planners and locals alike. We asked Paul to work up the plans a little and share them with Peter Greig of Warren Greig and Partners, structural engineers, to see whether structurally the plan was feasible. We then took them to quantity surveyors and cost consultants J. Derek Reid & Associates, with a brief to keep the costs under £4m. I knew that keeping costs down was essential, and so, with much debate and discussion, agreed that we would only be able to build a basic hall without the technology or gizmos that we would like. It would be a robust, quality building but basically a shell with seats, which we would complete through fundraising over time. The cost was just over £3.5m, which we –well, perhaps not Chris and Ben – felt would be a more acceptable cost of a Hall for Cornwall.

These plans felt right, and at the right price, too. We now had to make sure we got them accepted by Carrick.

Roger Hocking has kindly given us permission for us to share the plans for Hall for Cornwall:

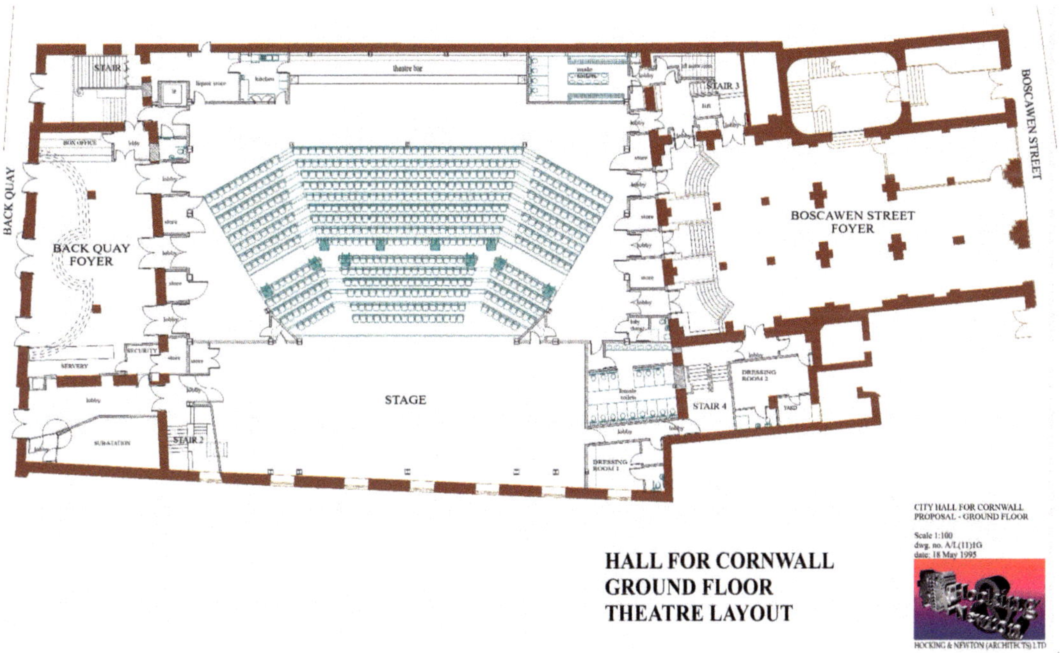

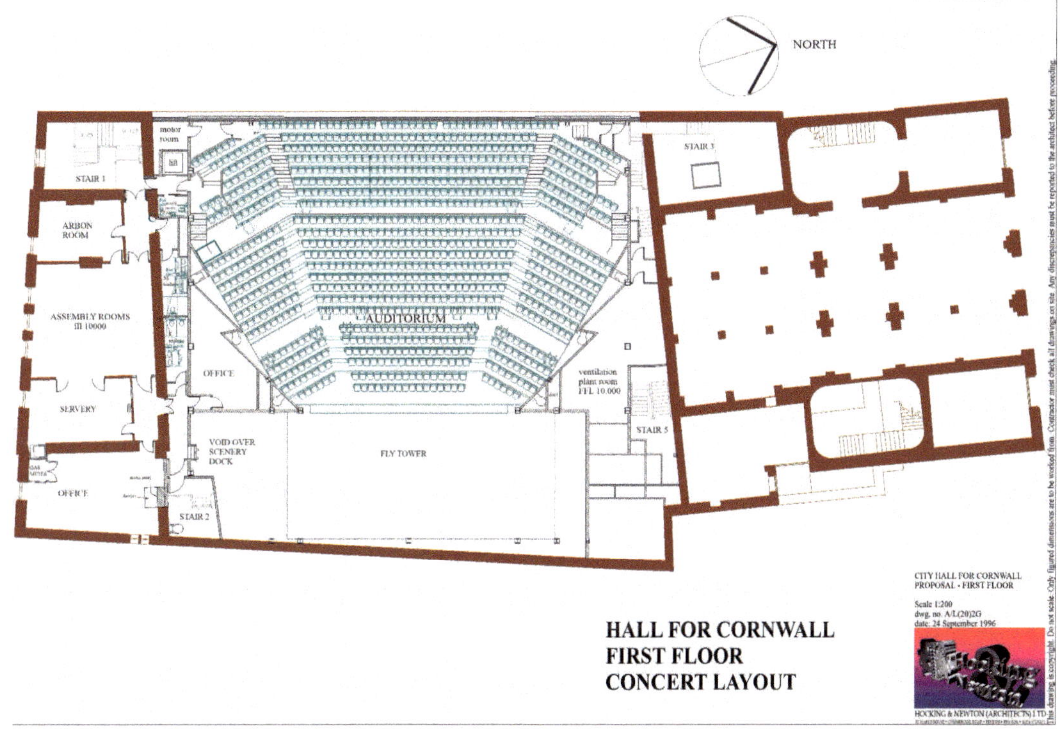

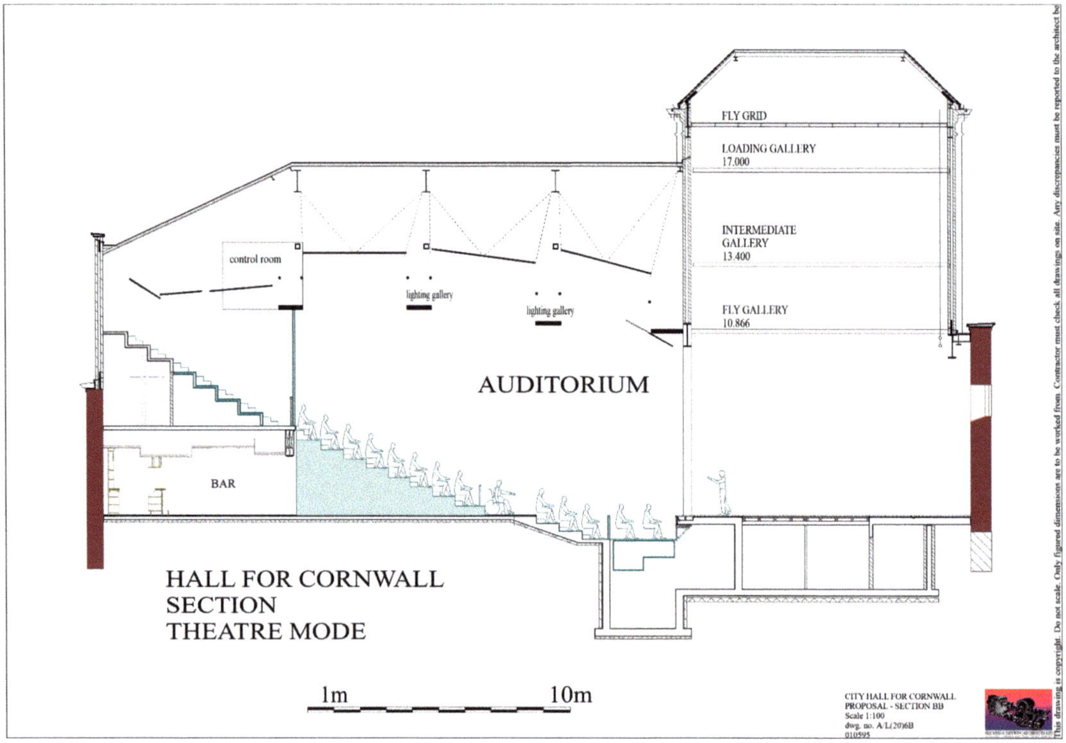

CW: Ben and I were really annoyed – we felt that behind the cost reduction there was an implicit belief that Cornwall somehow did not deserve the best.

SS: I understood why Chris and Ben were disappointed but felt that one of the criticisms of the past scheme was the price tag. Rightly or wrongly, people were really freaked out by the costs and refused to entertain the idea that Cornwall could raise that amount of money. And sadly, they would revert to the question: Well, does Cornwall honestly need a hall? We had to prove that Cornwall did need a hall and that £3.5m was a palatable amount, so I felt we had to grasp this nettle and just run with it. But in the end all was not lost for, as we know now, fate had a habit of playing its hand in this project …

CW: After all the effort to satisfy the planners regarding the impact of the fly tower, it's amusing to note that the new M&S building did a grand job of obscuring the view of the Cathedral from Morlaix Avenue and that the Lemon Quay car park is long gone! And the tower regrettably remains forever about three feet too short.

SS: We should highlight that from early in 1992 work on the plans for the new Hall continued with Paul Newton, Roger Hocking, Peter Greig and Derek Reid. The design team were not paid for their time at this stage, and Hall for Cornwall relied heavily on their goodwill during those months. We could not find any funding to finance the fees to develop the project and gradually we came to a bit of a halt. However, we had applied for a grant from the Foundation for Sports and the Arts, and remarkably, with a bit of lobbying from Ben, who knew one of the Foundation trustees, in May the Hall for Cornwall was awarded £300,000. So off we went now able to appoint and pay our existing design team for their work and appoint a range of specialists consultants to advise on technical details.

Chapter 12

Trustees with Gravitas

CW: One of Carrick District Council's conditions of their support had been that Hall for Cornwall must become a charity. This was understandable and was a prerequisite in those days before a project could receive public money or grants from charitable foundations. First you create a limited company, then you apply for charitable status. I think Hall For Cornwall was probably the seventh charity I had helped to set up, so I knew the ropes. But this time, for me there was a serious catch because if you create a charity you have to appoint trustees. Even if you personally have created the organisation, you can't draw a salary and be a trustee and therefore you no longer have sole control.

When you first have an idea, you get together with a group of like-minded people. They all have fire in their bellies, share a common vision and give their time. As the project develops, it starts to need things: phones, stationery, postage, possibly an office, a bank account. Expenses become overheads. Just as when starry-eyed young lovers get a mortgage, buy a house, start a family, buy a Volvo, your project needs a bit of organisation, a respectable board, so you have to become a charity. Some of the people who sat around the table moaning after *The Magic Flute* became trustees. The original HfC board included Ben Luxon, Claire Bowden-Dan and Jane Lofthouse. Because we were all friends, shared a common vision, things remained fairly informal. And I made sure that they were the original Members of the company and signatories to the Articles of Association. Members elect trustees. I had learnt from experience that some of the original group could fall by the wayside and that others would get recruited to replace them. And that can be the start of a process of fragmentation and dilution. By making sure that the Members were from the original post-Magic Flute group, I hoped to retain at least a measure of control over the development of the board. If you want to make the gods laugh, make a plan …

Other people who genuinely believed in and who had something to offer the embryonic HfC became trustees, particularly when we got our hands on City Hall. For example, one guy, Roger Lockett, donated and installed a whole phone system when we moved into the leaky old venue that was so hopelessly inadequate yet so loved by so many people. Another chap who joined the board was an ex-bank manager. Unfortunately, he got the heebie-jeebies and left when I could tell him the gross take for the catering operation but couldn't tell him what the profit margin was. It would have been more helpful if he'd tutored me. Another chap, John Wilson, who had experience in marketing large corporations, joined us and was incredibly helpful. The most useful thing I learnt from him was how to avoid selling the negative and how to make a short, memorable, no-waffle pitch, either on paper or to camera.

It was, however, rapidly becoming clear that I was more suited to leading the campaign and was not qualified to run a complex business, which by now included a multi-faceted performing arts programme in the old hall, an emerging box office serving events across Cornwall, a commercial programme with regular flea markets and business lettings and a catering operation, an art gallery, and of course the campaign – which was the real reason we were doing all the other stuff! If I couldn't make a success of running the City Hall it would be a PR disaster, The Weasel would be thrilled and the campaign for a new Hall would be severely damaged. There's no doubt in my mind that Sarah Smith saved my bacon by agreeing to become the General Manager. We made a great team. Looking back, I am sure the project would have foundered without her steadying hand, her diplomacy, her amazing contacts and her business acumen.

As the Hall for Cornwall Campaign gathered momentum, it became clear that our dreams for a new Hall were likely to become a reality. Sarah agreed with Carrick that we needed some new trustees who had the expertise and the credibility to manage a £3.4m building project. I knew she was right and so I had to bite the bullet and reluctantly go along with it.

The thing is, the trustees of a charity are the company directors which means they are the people who have ultimate responsibility for governing a charity and directing how it is managed and run. But that can also be a problem because the trustees may well have their own agendas or ideas. For example, they will unduly worry about costs, whereas the creative person driving the project is likely to be more interested in excellence. This dichotomy at Hall for Cornwall was to surface later with a vengeance. And there's another really serious catch – the trustees also become your employers. Which effectively means not only do you give them control of your project but you can be sacked by them.

Scary stuff. Moral: choose your parents, your partner and your trustees with the utmost care. Because appointing a board is a bit like getting married. Disagreements are inevitable and it may well all go pear-shaped later on because boards tend to go through a predictable life cycle which sometimes leads to divorce.

But there was now no doubt that we needed to recruit some new trustees who had the influence, connections and gravitas to help us to build our Hall. As a charity, we already had a few board members – Ben Luxon, Claire Bowden-Dan and Jane Lofthouse had all been stalwarts – but none of them lived in Cornwall.

SS: Because our financial position had become more stable and the plans for the new Hall began to look more achievable, we felt we were in position to recruit the new local trustees required by Carrick. And I had some ideas…

CW: Sarah approached John Worlledge, a qualified accountant, who had formed Lark Developments and Lark Construction Ltd, which operated almost entirely in Cornwall and had an impressive annual turnover. He was very well known in the Duchy, having lived here since 1968, and even better he had recently retired. It took a bit of persuading but eventually John agreed to join the board, promising that he would help recruit a few more locals.

Sarah then approached Jim Beeching, OBE, JP, a surveyor who had worked in Cornwall for over forty years and who was highly respected and well known. Importantly, he was at the time President of Truro Amateur Operatic and Dramatic Society and had a great interest in the arts. A friend of John's and someone Sarah had known for many years, Jim agreed to join the board. John then, thinking about who might be available to chair the board, suggested Brian Mansell OBE. Brian had moved to Cornwall in 1969 having worked for a number of county councils designing and constructing roads. He was Deputy Surveyor and then in 1972 became County Surveyor until 1993. He had recently retired but was involved with a number of professional activities and appointments both locally and nationally. He was also awarded an honorary degree of Doctor of Technology by Plymouth University in 1994. Brian was very well known and, with his connections to Cornwall County Council, we knew that if he agreed, we would be in a strong position to move the project forward. Brian agreed and also accepted the position of Chair of the Board. So we were becoming a force to be reckoned with!

I knew Jim through Truro Operatic and Dramatic Society (TOADS) and warmed to his appointment. When I was introduced to the other two, I was horrified. They were so alien, from a very different culture, even spoke a different language, and had no experience of or sympathy for the arts. Or indeed artists. Brian particularly appeared to take rather a dim view of creative people in general – he felt they should stop asking for handouts and get a proper job. He was later to ask me what I did all day. If Prufrock measured out his life in coffee spoons, Brian measured his in yards of tarmac. Outsiders were also shocked, but most were impressed. There was a feeling that these three brought a new credibility to the project.

SS: It is true to say that these three new trustees who focused on their specific roles were our strength. They joined the Hall for Cornwall Trust board in the summer of 1992 and immediately got stuck in.

Whilst John spent a lot of time keeping his eye on our finances and supporting Mary, our Accounts Officer, Jim and Brian were busy talking about the plans for City Hall and would spend time presenting to colleagues, not only in Cornwall but London, too.

Jim focused on a particular contact who might help to secure some funding form one of the Trusts set up by the Sainsbury family. It wasn't easy as Hall for Cornwall was not a natural fit for any of their Trusts. Jim persisted and worked very hard on our behalf and thankfully after meetings and visits managed to secure an award from the Headley Trust for £30,000.

Mavis, Brian's wife, remembered him being so proud of Hall for Cornwall. She said that he sat on various panels most of which were based in London. On one of his trips to London for a meeting, unable to stay at the RAC Club because it was full, he stayed at the Army and Navy Club. In the morning he went down to the restaurant and discovered Lord and Lady Falmouth having breakfast. He approached them and started talking about the Hall for Cornwall. After a little hesitation they became enthusiastic, and Lord Falmouth offered his help by agreeing to mention the project to HRH The Duke of Cornwall. Brian's chance meeting must have helped us in our quest to secure The Duke of Cornwall as our Patron.

Bert Biscoe (BB) adds his memories:

BB: I had found myself running between the Citizens of Truro and the Hall for Cornwall Trust, trying to encourage a positive relationship. It was difficult. Many CoT members wanted a community hall. Chris Warner and his supporters saw a different future and believed that a reconstructed Truro City Hall could act as a catalyst for enlivening our rather dull city centre. Money started to come in and plans advanced.

By now I was a member of Carrick Council, and strongly supporting the 125-year lease, as well as trying to persuade the Council that it would need to put money in to the project. Many "I told you so's" remained sceptical – it was not an easy ride.

One day I realised that everything would be OK. I was coming out of "County" Hall one lunchtime when I spied my old sparring partner, retired County Surveyor Brian Mansell, who had become Chair of the Trust. He said: "Ah! You'll do! Give me a hand!"

We had never exchanged a friendly word before. I then found myself, at 5'6", walking backwards carrying one end of a large model of the Hall for Cornwall at urgent speed and being pushed by the 6'-plus Mr Mansell through the door of the "County" Council Chairman's office into a scrum of the great and the good. "Put it down here!" said Mansell and a startled Chairman in unison. The G and the G saw the little anarchist and the great engineer carrying the model of HfC and put two and two together! You could almost hear the "Aha!"

CW: It was clear from the start that integrating Brian, John and Jim with the original board members was going to be a challenge. Speaking personally, I did not welcome TWO cuckoos in my nest, and I felt very threatened.

SS: That was Chris's view, which I didn't really understand at the time but got to understand over the years whilst working with artistic directors at Bristol Old Vic who often felt threatened by their trustees. This is mainly because trustees bring a different set of skills as well as experience to a board, as their purpose is to govern and have the overall legal responsibility for the charity. Few have artistic or creative skills and so inevitably this can cause friction and tension.

For me, the arrival to Hall for Cornwall of Brian, John and Jim meant we were in a different place from now on. We had highly respected people of influence to back us and it was now up to us to deliver. Yes, we had a lot of persuading, cajoling and reassurance to play out, but I felt that we could do it. All I had to do was to keep Chris calm and focused on the project and help him find a way to articulate it so that everyone would one day understand what we were trying to achieve.

It had dawned on both Chris and I that we didn't really have the expertise to coordinate the detail of the developing plans or eventually the building works, and in any case, we were just too busy. Brian Mansell had the answer. He had worked with a project manager at County Hall over the years, namely Peter Fazakerly, who was also a golf club buddy. Brian suggested that Peter would be the best person to take on the role of Project Coordinator. We were happy that we now had someone with solid experience in this area, but we were determined to keep an eye on things and to make sure that Mr Fazakerly didn't try to make savings which would endanger the ability of the new Hall to deliver on the programme promises we had made.

CW: It's fair to say that Brian was a very forceful person – which of course was just what we needed in our new Chairman – and he was used to getting his own way. This meant that he often found it difficult when Sarah and I disagreed with him. Whenever we thought that the viability of the new Hall was going to be compromised, we simply refused to back down.

SS: One saving grace for which I was personally very grateful was that we also had the support and in-kind advice from a well-known local solicitor and notary, Peter Dexter, who was a partner with Nalders Solicitors. He helped us hugely and from time to time proved to be a great mediator when things got challenging. He always believed in the Campaign and helped us through the years until we opened the Hall in 1997.

The Hall for Cornwall Trust met every two months and when necessary, more frequently, and in those early days our trustees were a small group – Brian Mansell (Chair), John Worlledge, Jim Beeching, Jane Lofthouse and Claire Bowden-Dan. James Williams (JW) joined the Board a year or so later followed by Martin Schute and Goff Richards in 1995. Martin had a background in film production and theatre, had worked with Ray Cooney at the Theatre of Comedy and later became Chairman of the South West Film Commission. Goff was born in Cornwall and was a composer, arranger and conductor. He travelled world-wide conducting and was regularly to be heard on BBC Radio Two.

Ben Luxon, during the mid-nineties, was working all over the world and was unable to commit as a trustee, but in recognition of all his input and help in the early years he became President of Hall for Cornwall and joined our board meetings when he was in Cornwall and when we needed support … well, when Chris needed an ally!

I happened to be friendly with James and Sarah Williams, who divided their time between London and their Cornish home at Tregullow, near Redruth. James worked for Baring Asset Management and spent much of the time travelling all over the world and was frequently away from Cornwall. We had sons of the same age who used to spend most holidays together, so when poor Sarah and James were in Cornwall they heard a lot about our plans to develop City Hall and our campaign. Looking back, I am not sure whether friends considered me a crashing bore, obsessive, or slightly mad, as I talked about the Hall at every conceivable opportunity. On one such occasion I brought over the three-dimensional model and set it up in the dining room at Tregullow under the gaze of James's collection of John Opie portraits. I introduced James and Sarah to Chris, and between us we explained what the plan was.

JW: Sarah was a hugely enthusiastic ambassador for the project. We knew her well, and our sons were good friends. My times in Cornwall were limited by the pressures of work in London and abroad, but I always knew that we would come back to Cornwall and spend far more time here. Both Sarah (my wife, to avoid confusion) and I were lovers of theatre and performance and felt keenly the lack of opportunity to enjoy these in Cornwall. It was early days for the cultural renaissance of Cornwall that followed in years to come, but it just felt wrong that there was a great big vacuum in a part of the country that had spawned so many great artists, performers and musicians. In short, I was easily hooked by Sarah and Chris's enthusiastic sales pitch!

SS: We searched for trusts and foundations that were interested in Cornwall, the South West, the arts, communities in remote and deprived areas, development plans for buildings that were of heritage interest, and updating entertainment venues. We compiled a healthy list of potential trusts which we planned to approach. One such trust was the Baring Foundation. It was during one of those conversations with James Williams over a drink or two when I mentioned that we planned to approach the Baring Foundation and would James advise us and point us in the right direction. James was not terribly optimistic but knew Nicholas Baring and agreed to think about the best approach. The Baring Foundation was the owner of Barings Bank and diverted all the dividends it received to philanthropic causes. James pointed out that their regional focus was based around the poorer parts of London, and around areas of deprivation on Merseyside. True to his word, he came back with how we should proceed, which we did immediately, but he warned us that the trustees of the Baring Foundation only met a few times a year and so we had to be patient.

CW: I seem to remember that we received a rejection letter fairly quickly from the Foundation saying that they were interested in the arts but not in Cornwall. So off went Sarah to chat to James in order to see whether the situation was retrievable.

SS: I think we had been a bit too enthusiastic and should have waited for James to have a conversation with Nicholas Baring. So I confessed to James that we had got a bit carried away and asked for his help. We agreed that Nicholas Baring would not have known about our first application. James, as always, was sympathetic and agreed to talk to Nicholas about Hall for Cornwall the next time he saw him.

We did as James suggested: we were patient, and when James had discussed it with Nicholas, he gave us advice on the best way to steer the application. We submitted it to the Baring Foundation and one afternoon a few weeks later, I was sitting on the beach at

Porthtowan with James and Sarah whilst the boys were surfing. He said that he had some good news and that the Baring Foundation had awarded us with £20,000 towards the capital cost of the Hall for Cornwall. This was fairly early in our fundraising efforts and it was a truly significant moment for us. It was a huge compliment for the appeal to be acknowledged and associated with one of the oldest and most famous banks in the world.

JW: In the early 1970s the Baring family had placed all their interests in the 200-year-old bank into the Baring Foundation. The Barings are a remarkable family and have a deep core of philanthropy, something which belies the image of many City organisations. The bank was professionally run and for all that time extraordinarily successful, and each year the surplus income was paid to the Foundation, which would use its sizeable endowment to fund good causes. The family had, among other things, a particular bent towards the arts, and for that reason I felt that it would be worth approaching them to become a founder supporter of the Hall for Cornwall. Like all charitable foundations, they had criteria, one of which was geography. The East End of London and Merseyside were the limits of where charitable donations would go. Nicholas Baring, I knew well, a cerebral, gentle, and scholarly man with a deep sense of pride in the history and the achievements of the family. I was working on a project with him in South America, and a twelve-hour flight to Sao Paulo sitting next to him enabled me to persuade him that an exception should be made where Cornwall was concerned. At that point he promised to bring this up at the Foundation's next meeting.

SS: Chris and I were ecstatic, and we felt that we would love James to be much more involved with Hall for Cornwall. We asked him whether he would be interested in becoming a trustee. He said he would give it some thought, as he was still away from Cornwall a lot of the time. Thankfully, James agreed to join the Board in May 1994 and we accepted that he would not be able to attend meetings regularly. In early 1995 the world was shocked by the collapse of Barings Bank, brought about by Nick Leeson, who worked for Barings as a derivatives trader. A lot has been written about this rogue trader but suffice to say that his actions led directly to the collapse of the UK's oldest merchant bank. It also had a tragic knock-on effect on the Baring Foundation, which lost its annual dividend from the bank, meaning that funds donated to good causes fell by over 90 per cent.

Thankfully, and selfishly for us, James was able to spend more time in Cornwall. He was a great asset and had a good understanding of the sensitivities that we would all face when once we got on site and the capital works began.

JW: It was with some trepidation that I became involved as a trustee of the Hall for Cornwall. I was born and brought up in the county, and as a Cornishman I knew enough about how things worked in this unique part of the world. However, my time at home was limited and I did not always have a feel for the nuances that the project had to face. It proved to be a steep learning curve for me, and it took time for me to understand clearly what all the moving, and in some cases immoveable, parts were. I learned about the art of being positive when so many people would come up with a reason for not doing something rather than providing a solution. It proved to be the first of many things in Cornwall that I became engaged with, and it provided me with an education second to none as to the priorities that the great Cornish institutions needed to consider. I was involved for many years with, among others, Cornish charities, the Royal Institution of Cornwall, Truro Cathedral, Falmouth University, and the Duchy of Cornwall. All of these will have gained from the, sometimes painful, experiences which I had at Hall for Cornwall in those early days.

A charitable trustee is ultimately responsible and of course liable for the financial probity of the institution. Without necessarily having the expertise in other things that were in front of us, I would consume the accounts, the budgets and the cash flow forecasts. Where funds were expected, what would be the probabilities of them being received? Were the expenses manageable within the funding that we had available? Were budgets set using conservative assumptions? This was exceptionally difficult in what was effectively a grass-roots start-up, and sometimes the inherent disciplines had to be parked when there was no choice but to take a gamble. I would like to think that I helped during those crucial early years, but there were many occasions when I felt out of my depth.

Our meetings used to take place on Sunday mornings with a promise that they would be over in good time. Sometimes four hours later I would be wondering whether I would have time to get home for lunch before driving back to London with the children that afternoon. Another of the lessons that I learned about the Cornish voluntary sector is how much people liked the sound of their own voices!

Chapter 13

Refining the Design

CW: Many people – of a certain age – may remember a seventies TV advert with the slogan "Go to work on an egg!" The guy that made the ad was called Bernard Miles. Although a well-known actor, he is probably better remembered for his egg ad than for running his independent Mermaid Theatre in the City of London. Apart from admiring his grit and determination at the Mermaid, I've always treasured his advice on theatre design. He felt that the most important thing to get right was the relationship between actor and audience. An actor should be able to "command" the auditorium simply by standing still at the front of the stage. The actor should be able to see everyone in the audience without what Bernard called "machine gunning", i.e. without having to move his head. And, just as importantly, everyone in the audience should be able to see the actor's eyes and should feel that the performer was looking at them personally. Ideally, the first few rows of seats should be below stage level. This gives the actor an added sense of power, of commanding the space. It works. It worked in the Mermaid, it worked at the Northcott in Exeter, and it worked for the new Hall for Cornwall. When you walked out onto the new Hall stage you really felt in contact with every single one of the 1,000 people in front of you. Some time after the Hall had opened, I was very chuffed to be buttonholed by a well-known actor who wanted to tell me how much he and his colleagues enjoyed playing HfC.

Carr & Angier were appointed as our Theatre Consultants. They had a tremendous reputation – they had been associated with the design and technical installation of a long list of national and international concert halls and theatres. At our first meeting with Martin Carr, I recounted Bernard's thoughts on auditorium design and my own happy experience of the auditorium at the Northcott Theatre in Exeter. He listened politely to my "Go to work on an egg" tale and nodded. He understood exactly what I meant. Although hugely experienced, Martin was without the arrogance that so many experts bring to the table – and he was a Cornishman, born in Penzance. Straightaway I knew we were going to get on and that, in him, I had a kindred spirit and a valuable ally in the fight to make sure the new Hall would be "a proper job" rather than just another overgrown village hall unable to take the major tours which we so wanted to bring across the Tamar.

After taking him through our plans and ambitions for the new building and its programme, I emphasised something that Ben had said several times after our fact-finding trip at the very beginning of the project. Every place we visited had the same high street retail chains, and all the theatres had much the same programme of events – with different dates, obviously – as every other town. I explained that we were determined that the programme in the new Hall should reflect Cornwall's cultural identity and that we were not interested in building just another high street theatre. Once more I reeled off the long list of companies which we wanted to attract.

"OK," said Martin quietly, "Got that. Tell me, what do you want it to do best?" I didn't immediately get what he meant. "Well, if you want to be able to take the Bournemouth Symphony Orchestra (BSO) – you are going to need an opening of around 16-20 metres and a resonant acoustic. That's a long reverberation time – what we call the RT. Like singing in the bathroom. But for theatre and the spoken word you're going to need a much shorter RT, and the open proscenium (prosc) which suits the BSO will be too wide for most scenery. For ballet and modern dance, the wide prosc will be a dream. Opera will need a resonant acoustic, but the prosc will be too wide for the scenery and you'll need an orchestra pit which runs back under the stage in order to damp down the woodwind and brass sections, which compete with the human singing voice. And rock bands need a totally dead acoustic. And don't forget that the width of the proscenium arch will have major implications for sightlines – an auditorium with a very wide opening will have sight-line problems when you reduce the prosc opening for theatre – seats on the ends of the first few rows will have a restricted view as well as being able to see into the wings on the opposite side of the stage. Not only will you have masking problems, but you will have to discount those tickets, and that will impact on the bottom line."

"Ah!" I said, "Yes, well, but we do need to be able to present the widest possible range of events in order to attract the widest possible range of people from a relatively small population. We need to give the Hall the best possible chance of breaking even financially. If we present just one type of show, we reckon we'll run out of audience! We really need to build two or three different buildings, but we've only got one shot at this. If the new Hall has a solid proscenium arch suitable for theatre, that's all we'll ever put on. We reckon that it's got to have a wide opening which can be masked down when needed, even if it does cause sight-line problems. We would rather try to dampen an acoustic than beef up the reverberation time electronically. So, the answer to your question is music: orchestral and opera, plus ballet and modern dance. We also want to present chamber music and piano recitals by international pianists."

Martin took all this in for a moment or two. He explained how it was possible to modify the acoustics in each auditorium format by introducing fabric or by exposing hard-wall services. For example, we could make use of the full-width metal safety curtain (known as the "iron") in order to create more resonance. He reckoned that in 400-seat mode, with the pit lid level with the main floor and the piano in front of the iron, we would have a delicious little recital venue. Add in a couple of large flower displays and Robert would be our musical uncle. But the other modes were going to be more challenging. For example, if you do a concert and you raise the choir on rostra at the back of the stage, all their sound will tend to get lost in the fly tower. For concerts, ideally you want the audience to be in the same "room" as the musicians – one resonant space, no proscenium. For rock concerts you also want a single space, but you need a completely dead acoustic. You can dampen an acoustic quite easily with fabric or even rubbery egg-box-type material and by breaking up large flat surfaces in the design, but it would be very difficult for us to make a dead space more resonant unless we installed some sort of sound-enhancement system. We were definitely going to need an acoustic engineer on the team …

While we had a rough idea of what our auditorium would look like – and perhaps more importantly, what it would feel like – it was now Martin's job to make all five auditoria function properly from an audience point of view. He was also responsible for the technical specs for all backstage equipment – flying, lighting, sound, communications, get-ins, dressing rooms, etc. And it was also now his job to find a way through the minefields of the Home Office guidelines on escape from places of entertainment, and the more local Fire Regulations – including our old friend smoke integrity, which had caused so much grief with Robin Spence.

SS: Sound Research Laboratories joined Carr & Angier to help us achieve the right acoustics for all the different genres of performances we were planning. We now had a formidable team of expertise within our architects and consultants, who were absolutely determined to design a hall for the people of Cornwall that was indeed multi-purpose. Our professional team throughout the design and delivery phases of our project included:

Architects	**Hocking & Newton**
Theatre Consultants	**Carr & Angier**
Acoustics Consultants	**Sound Research Laboratories**
Mechanical & Engineering Consultants	**Hoare Lea & Partners**
Quantity Surveyors & Cost Consultants	**J. Derek Reid & Associates**
Structural Engineers	**Warren Greig and Partners**

They were a wonderful team who put their hearts and souls into this project, and for this Chris and I will be eternally grateful. Twenty-five years later, we have learned that some of them are no longer with us and so it has been up to Roger Hocking to put pen to paper on their behalf.

RH: In 2000, subsequent to the completion of the Hall for Cornwall, after having worked together for eight years, Paul Newton advised me that he was contemplating retiring sometime after his sixtieth birthday. To cut a long story short, we formed CAD Architects Ltd with a former colleague. This resolved how Paul might gracefully retire and how I might continue until my retirement, after which the practice would continue. Unfortunately, Paul died suddenly before he could take full advantage of his retirement. This came as a great shock to me and our colleagues as well as to his family.

SS: Paul was a really lovely man. Patient, sensitive and very caring.

CW: We could find only one photograph of Paul. Here he is on site with Jim Beeching and Peter Fazakerly in 1997.

SS: In 2014, Martin Carr also sadly died - long before Chris and I even thought of writing up our memories. He was one of the early theatre planning consultants and had so much experience in his field. The Hall at the design stage was almost a blank canvas for Martin and he made an invaluable contribution to the Hall for Cornwall, maybe because he was so proud of his Cornish roots.

Peter Greig, our Structural Engineer, is also no longer with us, but we would like to highlight his significant contribution to our project. He was involved in the early stages and it would have been good to capture some of the tales he could have told about the Hall for Cornwall. Peter was generous with his time, a warm-hearted and clever man who helped develop the designs even when there were no funds to pay professional fees.

RH: Peter was old school. He always got his PA to make and answer phone calls for him. He was a kind and gentle person who let Ian Hick get on with the job, which Ian did, quietly and professionally.

SS: His colleague Ian Hick started at the structural design stage of Hall for Cornwall and worked on site through to practical completion. Although the construction phase definitely had its challenges, these were relatively easy to overcome compared to the wilful intransigence we encountered early in the development phase of the designs.

IH: The overriding recollection with the HfC project was one of pride within Warren Greig and Partners that, as a local engineering company, we had been appointed on a major project of this nature. I can recall that the initial structural input was provided by Peter Greig and that he was able to make use of his vast experience in the design concept of steel-framed buildings to help develop a working solution within the confines of the City Hall buildings.

Once the project was moved to a more formal stage, most of the office became involved with the drawings being produced electronically for the first time by Mark Gendall, who was our principal Technician. I was then privileged to be tasked with coordinating the initial information and undertaking the detailed design of the structural aspects, as well as overseeing the on-site works. As a young engineer, this was a big responsibility, but thankfully almost everything progressed well on site.

CW: That brings us to Derek Reid, our cost consultant, who made a very significant contribution in the early days before we had the funds to pay the professional team. Now in his nineties, this account would not be complete without recording how much he did for the Hall for Cornwall and subsequently for the construction.

As a performer himself, he had great sensitivity for the project, and we know that he had many a "full and frank" discussion with Peter Fazakerly, when he "explained" to Peter why he shouldn't make cuts which would compromise the artistic integrity of the Hall. Derek had a great interest in music and understood what we were trying to achieve.

His guiding hand, his firm's name and his membership of the professional team gave great credibility to a project that could so easily have been pooh-poohed by the pie-in-the-sky brigade.

RH: I spoke with Derek Reid recently, and although unwell I found him his usual cheerful self. Derek brought a pragmatic approach to the cost aspects of the project and at all times performed his duties professionally and in a way that earned everyone's respect.

SS: We could not have found anyone better than Derek in this role and we had a lot of respect for the way he managed the costs as the project unfolded. He was a real ally and we owe him a great debt for helping to protect our dream. Undoubtedly one of the best ever!

Our aim was to develop the plans to RIBA Stage 3 so that we would submit our planning application to Carrick District Council during 1994. We had ironed out all the contentious physical problems with the building and by then had agreed that we would not be able to do much with the Boscawen Street end of the Hall despite many meetings with Truro City Council. We really hoped that we would be able to take over the entrance and the rooms above, as well as the street-facing shops and café that were situated either side of what had always been the main entrance to City Hall. However, when we realised that this was probably a bit ambitious, we focused on developing the plans for the new hall with the entrance foyer in the Back Quay building.

One part of the design that Chris and I did bang on about was our need to provide enough female toilets for a full house when we reckoned 500 females would need to use the loo in a twenty-minute interval! Inadequate provision was a constant criticism of so many venues around the country, and inevitably whenever there are plans being developed to refurbish or rebuild theatres and halls the feedback is always the same: please provide enough female toilets. Every time we met the design team during those early days, we reminded them about the need for a decent number of toilets. It was a particular concern for Ben, too. He often reminded us during Board meetings about the importance of ensuring that we did not have long queues to the toilets during intervals and told us that his mother had told him that it was very important for us to get this right.

We squeezed in as many toilets as we could but suffice to say there are never enough and I am sure that Julien Boast, current Chief Executive and Creative Director of Hall for Cornwall, will have gone through the same discussions as we did with their design team twenty-plus years later!

As our design team continued to develop our plans, Chris and I also talked about the need for a really long bar so that audiences could be served quickly and efficiently, thus avoiding queues during intervals. We had experienced this problem so often during our days running events at City Hall with our makeshift bar, which was not easy to operate efficiently. During big music events Mandy would arrange for as many staff as possible to be on duty, but often Chris or I would be called in as well. It was so difficult to work effectively, as it was such a squash behind the bar. We did sell a lot of barrelled beer during those events and often had to rush to the Market Inn next door and buy extra barrels. The main reason was that we tried to order in advance only what we thought we could sell on the night because beer served in that way doesn't have a long life. We had very limited space to store the barrels, as we didn't have a cellar. However, we did get caught out occasionally, and thankfully the landlord at the Market Inn was patient with us!

We had an example of best practice at the Cornwall Coliseum, which was a very popular music space housing a standing audience of over 3,000, and it boasted the longest bar in Cornwall. Sadly, or thankfully for HfC, it reduced its rock concert programme and finally closed its doors for redevelopment in 2003.

With this requirement for our new bar in mind, Paul and Roger came up with a design that stretched the entire length of the old dressing-room corridor, with several workstations, meaning that numerous people would be comfortably able to work behind the bar. Chris and I thought this was brilliant! It was located under the top tier of stalls seats and was easily accessible on ground-floor level. Once we got planning permission, we approached St. Austell Brewery, one of the few independent breweries left in the UK at that time, and they helped us hugely to develop ideas. They also sponsored the bar and one or two fundraising events and remained great allies of the Hall for Cornwall for many years.

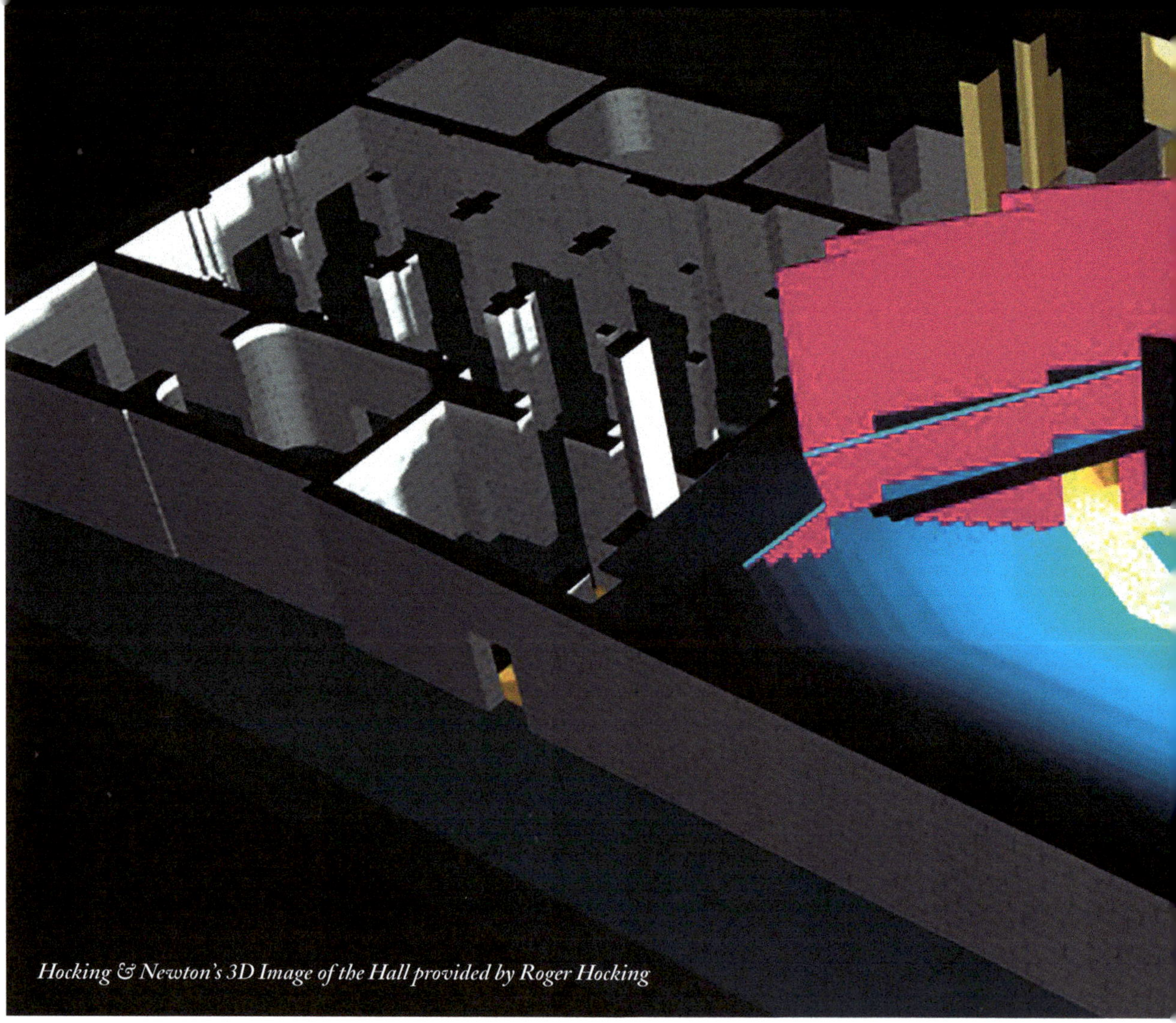

Hocking & Newton's 3D Image of the Hall provided by Roger Hocking

CW: As well as the internal practicalities of the design, there were other significant problems to be solved. While it was our laudable intention to breathe new life into a Grade II* listed building, the fact that we wanted to demolish at least a third of it was always bound to be a sensitive issue. We wanted to scoop out the whole of the old City Hall, replace it with the new auditorium and stage, but retain and refurbish the Boscawen Street and Back Quay buildings at either end.

Normally it is all but impossible to obtain consent to demolish a listed building and getting permission from English Heritage was to prove challenging. It was quite a performance! We argued that by building the new Hall, we would bring back to life the semi-derelict Back Quay section, which we said was of far greater value than the middle. Eventually English Heritage reluctantly agreed.

This argument later came back to bite us when, once work had started, we discovered a concealed cantilevered granite staircase in Back Quay. Unfortunately, it turned the

opposite way to our design, and we therefore needed to remove it or redesign the access to the upper floors of Back Quay. To make matters worse, the stair was cited in the original 1971 listing as being of special architectural and historical interest. We found ourselves applying to English heritage for additional consent to demolish a part of the very building which we had claimed we would bring back to life! We were on very thin ice, but after much consideration and discussion and an expensive pause in the building works English Heritage agreed we could remove the staircase.

SS: With the many requests and requirements ironed out or compromises made and agreed, we did succeed in submitting our plans for the new Hall in 1994. In October that year we received the statutory consents for the Hall for Cornwall. This was a huge milestone and triggered our funding applications to the European Rural Development Fund, Arts Council England and Trusts. In addition, we agreed that it was time to share our news and let everyone in Cornwall know what we were planning.

Chapter 14

A Fundraising Strategy

CW: Fundraising is a bit like climbing a mountain. Looking up from the bottom, the ascent seems pretty daunting. People think you're potty, that you have an unrealistic target, and so they are unlikely to make a donation early on. However, lots of people had been prepared to hazard a tenner for the Campaign, and those tenners were incredibly important because without them we would not have got to Base Camp. But with the mountain £3.5m high, even our most ardent supporters were going to be cautious about making larger donations. We knew we had to get near enough to the summit for people to feel that there was a good chance of success before we launched a public appeal.

At this time there was no Lottery but the Littlewoods Pools people had seen the writing on the wall and had set up their own philanthropic foundation in self-defence. Ben was at a dinner when someone mentioned the new fund and also told him that Dame Janet Baker was a trustee. Very early on we made an application to the new Foundation of Sports and the Arts, and to our astonishment the £300,000 landed in our account. It was to prove a useful lever with Carrick because it was such a significant sum. The grant prompted Carrick to formalise their offer of a lease for 125 years at £1 a year and to pledge their £500,000 toward the capital costs to refurbish and transform City Hall. This meant that we had a notional £800,000 before we even started fundraising.

SS: It's also worth mentioning that when offered a £10 note to cover the rent for the first decade, Carrick declined to accept it. It also transpired later, when we called on Carrick for the £500,000 to complete our funding and so make a start on the building, that they didn't actually have the funds. They had never believed we'd succeed, and it gave Chris great pleasure to wave our contract and force them to pay up.

Back to the matter of needing to raise a further £2.7m, we were at least up on the lower slopes of our mountain. Carrick monitored us carefully, and Terry Beckett used to meet us regularly for an update. He advised us to think about employing fundraising consultants as we had no experience of raising money ourselves apart from generating income from the caricature map of Cornwall, and the Council was unlikely to take us seriously without professional help.

Chris and I set about trying to find fundraising consultants, not even really knowing what they would do, and eventually Terry Beckett came up with four consultants for us to investigate, Craigmyle Fundraising Consultants, Donors International, Roger Pearce & Associates and Collyer Finn. We arranged to meet three. Two out of the three were based in London, and although charming, they didn't really fill us with confidence or enthusiasm about being able to raise funds in Cornwall. The last one we met was Tim Finn of Collyer Finn, based in the south of England. He talked us through how he thought fundraising would work but stressed that it would be up to us to raise the money because we lived in Cornwall and knew the people there, whereas he didn't. He would visit us and advise us and for this would take a percentage of the total amount raised, somewhere in the region of 8-10 per cent. We were shocked by this revelation – we had to do all the work and a fundraising consultant would then receive up to 10 per cent of the money raised! We got on well with Tim and we were grateful for his honesty, but we felt very uncomfortable with the idea of having to give away 10 per cent of our funds to someone who had barely been there.

After we had met up with Tim Finn in Exeter, we discussed what we were going to do all the way back to Truro. Then I had one of those brainwaves which I played out with Chris. What if Tim Finn wrote down how to fundraise and agreed to let us use his name? Chris thought this was worth a try, and so the next day I called Tim and asked him how much it would cost for him to write us a fundraising strategy and to lend us his name for the fundraising literature and headed paper. He thought about it and came back agreeing to both requests for a one-off fee of £5,000, and a few weeks later we received our strategy from Tim.

This was going to be a challenge, and mainly my responsibility. I needed to get my head together and spent time researching recent appeals one of which was the Great Ormond Street Hospital's Wishing Well Appeal. This appeal had been extremely successful and brought a fresh, modern approach to fundraising. A brilliant book, Charity Appeals, by Marion Allford, Director of Great Ormond Street Hospital's Wishing Well Appeal was my main prop throughout the campaign.

Tim's strategy made it clear that first of all we had to get key stakeholders on board – the Arts Council England, Carrick District Council, Cornwall County Council. The appeal would also be helped if we could attract a high-profile individual to become our patron. We would also need to identify those trusts and foundations whose interests and objectives matched a project like the Hall for Cornwall. We then had to work on a list of high net-worth individuals who might invest in our project. Finally, after all that, we

A SPACE FOR YOU

Small scale theatre mode with balcony available for separate function. Capacity 400

Mode with orchestra pit for touring opera, ballet and theatre. Capacity 600

Mode for chamber orchestra, conferences. Capacity 800

Concert mode for orchestral concerts, choirs, bands and conference. Capacity 1,000

Rock concert layout with standing on ground floor and seats on the balcony. Capacity 1,500

Flat floor mode for markets and fairs with flat floor balcony available for separate function. Total ground floor of 9,600 sq ft

The Hall for Cornwall Trust
City Hall, Back Quay,
Truro, Cornwall TR1 2LL

Telephone 01872 76461

All donations will be acknowledged

could start thinking about the Public Appeal. Oh, and we would need to develop a case for support and create fundraising literature in order to explain to people what we were planning.

CW: When Robin Spence was the architect, it was agreed that a model would be the best way to show how the multi-functional Hall for Cornwall would look and work. It is so much easier to share a three-dimensional model of the layout of a building. After Roger Hocking and Paul Newton had developed the second plans of the layout of the refurbished City Hall, we agreed that a second model, which we could display and use to demonstrate the revised layout, would be so much more effective than just the using the new drawings when making presentations.

SS: We allocated a small amount of funding and found a man who was absolutely brilliant at producing model buildings off plan. We were so excited with it when it was delivered to us, and I remember Chris lifting the roof, which also had the fly tower attached, to reveal the layout of the new Hall with its various seat configurations. For example, we knew we could fill 1,000 seats with Jethro, a Cornish Choir or a popular rock band but we would need to reduce the seating accordingly for ballet or theatre, a string quartet or poetry. The model also showed the new restaurant located in the Back Quay section and the front of house foyer with its café and box office, as well as toilets, backstage facilities and dressing rooms. We all agreed that this model would really help us tell the story and would hopefully attract the funding and the support we needed.

One further part of our fundraising planning was to find high-profile people who would endorse our Hall; and above all we would need a patron.

The obvious person for a project like ours was His Royal Highness The Duke of Cornwall. We knew that he was a regular visitor to Cornwall, that he was in contact with the Lord Lieutenant Lady Mary Holborow, and often stayed with friends near Truro. We also knew that approaching him would take time and that we had to get on with finding the large chunks of funding.

CW: Whilst through Duchy Opera's Country House Concerts we had made some useful contacts with many of the Duchy's senior families, sadly most of the people who had so generously hosted those concerts in their grand houses remained somewhat reticent about publicly lending their support to the HfC campaign. I do remember Lady Falmouth, who was a stalwart supporter of Duchy Opera, was very supportive. However no one was keen to be involved in what might be a spectacular failure.

When Sarah, in cahoots with Lady Mary Holborow, first approached The Duke of Cornwall about becoming our Patron, his Equerry had echoed that sentiment. I remember feeling rather annoyed that we would only get his support after we didn't really need it. Sarah was not happy and was most offended by the response, so she decided to contact His Royal Highness's Secretary. She talked him through our project, assuring him that the Hall for Cornwall was a high-profile project and not about "buckets and spades" – hence why she was involved! He agreed to think about it. Lady Mary agreed to persevere and decided that both she and Sarah would talk to Michael Galsworthy of Trewithen, a great friend of The Duke of Cornwall. We hoped that he too would help to persuade His Royal Highness to become our patron.

CW: Alongside this, Sarah spent a lot of time researching and identifying high-profile people either living in or connected to Cornwall with the aim of inviting them to join us as Vice Presidents. I had already asked some local influential people including Christopher Beazley MEP, Peter Bickford-Smith, Lucy Penrose, Peter Prideaux-Brune, Elisabeth Prideaux-Brune, The Hon Evelyn Boscawen, Cllr John Christie, Roy Walker and Kevin Platt to support the campaign and their help was greatly appreciated. It was easier than I thought because those people who performed at City Hall were usually enthusiastic and lent their names to the campaign. These included Dame Hilda Bracket, Justin Hayward, Dr David Bellamy, E V Thompson and others from further afield.

We found that the list grew relatively quickly mainly thanks to supporters like Lucy Penrose who was always very enthusiastic and always came up with possible new Vice Presidents. We added these names to our fundraising literature and our headed paper. You can find the full list of VPs under acknowledgements. An early serendipity was nabbing Peter Sissons, who had presented the BBC's Question Time in the old City Hall long before we took over running it. After the show, Sissons commented on the state of the place and, when I told him about our plans he readily agreed to become a VP. All very Wannamaker!

SS: Lady Mary Holborow continued to help us wherever she could and introduced the project to different people throughout Cornwall and beyond. We could not have asked for a better unofficial ambassador for our campaign. She was very influential and highly respected by everyone – for good reason, as she carried Cornwall at the heart of all her endeavours. During the campaign I would meet Lady Mary regularly and she would listen to the progress we had made, the issues we had, and we would discuss sensible ways to solve these. She was so wise and such a huge support to us. I remember her sheer delight on the evening of the gala when we opened the Hall in 1997. Thank goodness we had her as our ally; we will forever be indebted to her and grateful for her enthusiasm.

Apart from reading up on successful fundraising campaigns, we were well aware of a Cornish fundraising appeal that had been a terrific success a couple of years earlier – The Tate at St Ives, a brilliant initiative which was funded from the local community, the Henry Moore Foundation and the European Rural Development Fund. The Tate at St Ives opened in 1993 and welcomed over 120,000 visitors in the first six months! Sir Richard Carew Pole masterminded the fundraising campaign and kindly agreed to meet Chris and I to share with us his ideas about how to raise funds locally.

One idea that had been really successful was an art auction in aid of the Tate at St Ives, where local artists were asked to donate paintings to be auctioned as part of a fundraising event. It raised thousands for the appeal and generated a great deal of publicity, as so many artists supported the campaign. Our meeting with Sir Richard filled us with enthusiasm and determination. We too could do this, as long as we made sure that the whole of Cornwall understood what we were doing and what we were trying to achieve.

One other meeting arranged in our fundraising planning stage was with Tim Smit, who had done an amazing job restoring the Lost Gardens of Heligan. It was pouring with rain the day of the meeting at Heligan, and I got soaked carrying the heavy model into the café, where I waited looking pretty bedraggled. Tim arrived wearing wellington boots and a jacket and explained that he didn't have much time as he was doing a tour of the gardens for a coach load of people. His reputation went before him as an inspirational, energetic entrepreneur who I knew I could learn from, but I was going to have to be quick. I knew Tim had been in the music business and was a songwriter and producer, so I hoped he would be interested in our plans for the new Hall. He was interested in the size of the Hall and particularly keen that we should get the acoustics right for bands. He felt it was important for us to attract class A bands to the county, particularly as the Cornwall Coliseum in St Austell had been redeveloped for housing. I admit that I was slightly out of my depth when talking to Tim about the programme, but I shared our aspirations for what and who we wanted to visit the new Hall once it was opened.

The one thing I did take away from that meeting was his belief that "Fundraising is easy – there is so much money out there – you have just got to find the right way to unlock it." Hearing this from him was just so exciting and it made me feel absolutely determined to prove him right.

I could have continued chatting to him for hours but was interrupted by about forty women who arrived for their tour with Tim. They all seemed to know him, or perhaps that was just the way Tim was – enthusiastic, playful and at ease. I watched him as he led his tour off into the gardens and hoped that I could do a tiny bit as well as he had.

As well as meeting people who had raised significant funding, we had brainstorming sessions with our small team at the Hall to think about the sorts of events that would appeal. I had read and been told that it wasn't worth doing an event unless it raised at least £5,000 because of the work that went into making every event successful. We started making lists of those who could help us; these included schools, colleges, groups, communities, musicians, artists, friends … We recruited associate fundraisers who agreed to help us in different areas of the community. These included John Walton, Chairman of ACT, Paula Thornton who was involved with the Truro Amateur Operative Drama Society (TOADS) and Geoff Aver, the county's head of the advisory service, known as "Mr Education of Cornwall." They all helped to spread the word and generate funding towards our appeal.

Chapter 15

Designing the Fundraising Literature and Going Public

CW: Ben and I were convinced that the new Hall would only thrive if it offered a wide range of events to the widest possible range of people. In spite of what the sceptics alleged, we didn't want to build just a theatre or just a concert hall. Some people were also reluctant to believe that we really needed the flea markets, fairs and commercial events, but we really did – not only for their valuable revenue streams but because they would attract into the building people who would not normally think of going to cultural events. Once these flat-floor attenders became comfortable in the new Hall, they would hopefully be tempted to attend a seated event.

The design challenge for the architects was that the new multi-purpose Hall had to be fit for purpose both culturally and commercially. Once Hocking and Newton and Martin Carr were on board, I never had any doubts that we could make it work.

A bigger challenge was finding a way to get this multi-purpose message across to the Cornish public, the councillors on City Council, Carrick District and Cornwall County Councils, plus the Arts Council and trusts and foundations. We needed to create a diverse raft of supporters in Cornwall who would help us to make the case that the new Hall was not only needed but would be well attended. And we hoped that when we eventually launched the Public Appeal, these early supporters would be prepared, some of them for a second time, to put their hands in their pockets. The multi-purpose nature of the new Hall was, however, both a strength and a weakness: a strength because of its diversity and a weakness (in marketing terms) because it was difficult to brand that very same diversity.

Fortunately, Sarah knew a man called Timothy Guy (TG), who could probably help. He ran a company called Timothy Guy Design, based in Truro and working on projects in Cornwall, up country and abroad. So we went to see him in his very couth offices. In fact everything about Tim was couth and stylish: the man himself, his work place and his actual work.

Tim's portfolio was seriously impressive, but I have to admit that at the time I had no idea just how distinguished and experienced he was. It's only through writing this memoir that I have learnt that his first job out of college was with the "Fathers of Graphic Design" FHK Henrion, where he worked on KLM (Royal Dutch Airlines), Colt Heating and Ventilation, BEA (British European Airways) and the international cement company Associated Portland Cement Manufacturers, a.k.a. Blue Circle. Here's what he had to say about himself when we asked him to make a contribution to this book:

TG: In 1974 I took the brave step to move from London to the more relaxed and creative environment of Cornwall, where we had found an idyllic wooden clapperboard house with a 150-degree sea view, near St Ives – and our own private access to one of the county's best beaches, Porthkidney. Here, at all stages of the tide, we could relax and create. Coupled with that, to my joy, we developed a semi-tropical garden – all for the princely sum of just £4,000. What more could dreams be made of?

To accommodate the rapid growth of the company and to be able to re-employ some of my London staff, we subsequently opened a studio of sixteen in a house which had been General Eisenhower's HQ during the Normandy Landings. It was called "Tullimar" and was in Perranarworthal, near Truro. We were certainly the largest graphic design studio in Cornwall at the time, again luckily growing our international portfolio with clients in NZ, the USA and a small studio outlet in Mallorca which serviced the growth of UK-owned hotels on the island. In 1994 Chris Warner and Sarah Smith's vision to transform the Truro City Hall into the multi-purpose Hall for Cornwall was so exciting and such a big challenge that when they asked if I could help, I jumped at it.

CW: We needed to get our messages across in a stylish but understated way because as a charity it was important not to look as if we were wasting money by being over the top and flashy. Tim was definitely up for some blue-sky thinking. He agreed to help us and gave us some great ideas for our fundraising literature.

It was always a tremendous pleasure to have an hour or two of creative thinking led by Tim. It was time away from the slings and arrows of the Campaign, losing ourselves in dreaming about what the programme would include when all the hard work came to fruition. And we never doubted it would. After several brainstorming sessions, we decided the solution was to go one better than Lord Northcliffe's dictum that a picture is worth a thousand words. We decided to use pictures of evocative objects to get our message across. For example, a pair of ballet pumps instead of the word "ballet", a violin stood for classical music, a rock guitar for a band, a few antiques for a market, etc. We hoped that people

A SPACE FOR YOU!
Now You Can Help.
HFC
THE HALL FOR CORNWALL APPEAL
HFC
City Hall, Back Quay, Truro, Cornwall, TR1 2LL Telephone 01872 76461
Registered Charity 100 16 11
Timothy Guy Design

would identify with the objects that interested them while at the same time taking in the breadth of programme the Hall would offer. The various objects could be real or presented as photographs or as stylised icons. It was neat, visually arresting, and it effectively delivered our complex message on one sheet of paper.

SS: We had very little money for our fundraising literature, so one of the ways we saved costs was to use a beautifully designed folder into which we could insert sheets of paper with different information and detail about the design of the Hall, what we would do, how we would do it, show who was involved, and make the case for support. We would be able to add to these sheets and refresh them during the appeal, which gave us flexibility. We could change the order of the sheets depending on our target recipient. For example, the MD of a business would receive a pack with the exhibition and conference facilities given priority. We also had a leaflet which would eventually be mailed to every single household in Cornwall.

TG: We needed a logo for the new Hall, one that would resonate with the people of Cornwall, so I felt it had to feature the City Hall elevation. I shortened the initials to HfC and of course, being in the heart of the Duchy it had to include the bezant shield. We needed to get all the potential multi-audience sponsors to feel it was their own – hence the list of activities Chris and Sarah envisaged and the "cut-out" square in the sponsorship brochure inviting "YOU" to fill the space.

The endorsement by a range of celebrities, including Dr David Bellamy, Rodney Bewes, David Brierly, RSC, Christopher Nourse, Sadler's Wells Royal Ballet, Peter Jonas, English National Opera, Sir Charles Mackerras, and Sebastian Coe, MP, clearly showed that the programme in the new Hall would include theatre, both classical and modern music as well as modern dance companies like Ballet Rambert.

HfC aimed to attract the best of the best.

CW: After all the fun and creativity with Tim Guy, Sarah told us that we did not have enough money to produce and distribute his lovely appeal leaflets. It had been a long old slog up the lower slopes and now here we were – stuck just below the summit because, despite numerous applications, no charity or foundation seemed to want to fund the Appeal. A real anti-climax.

Fundraising is a funny business. It's a bit like trying to get cash from an ATM. It's frustrating because you know that there is stacks of cash in the machine but you can hit it all you like with a lump hammer and it will refuse to pay out. Punch in the right numbers and you can fill a shopping bag. It is a slog, but actually relatively easy to raise the big money for the bricks and mortar, because that's what most donors – big and small – feel comfortable with. It's safe. Any arts organisation will tell you how hard it is to raise finance for "core costs" like salaries, rent, phone, light, telephone, etc. Financing core costs is not attractive to a funder or a donor because core costs are just not sexy – funders want to fund the front-line work, to make a difference. But without core costs met from somewhere, any organisation will struggle to move forward. We had solved this problem in the early days by differentiating between raising money for the Campaign to make something happen and the Appeal to pay for the actual refurbishment of the building. The profits from running the City Hall and the money given to the Campaign counted as "unallocated funds" and we could spend that money as we wished as long as it was to further the Campaign. On the other hand, funds given for the building had to be spent on the building – and nothing else. To this day, I remain hugely grateful to the hundreds of people who made the project possible in the very early days by chucking a tenner in a bucket at one of our fundraising events, or who put their loose change in one of our yellow fundraising receptacles.

After we finished working with Tim, I was sitting rather morosely in my little room behind the City Hall box office when I heard raised voices. There was quite a serious argument raging and I went through to investigate. I found some of the staff having a row with a stout, very brown and be-ringed lady, complete with sprig of heather, who wanted to tell their fortunes. The feisty fortune teller was vociferously refusing to leave. I don't know why but I asked her to come through into my office – perhaps it was in an effort to defuse what was becoming a rather unpleasant public scene, or perhaps curiosity, or perhaps because, depressed at having no funds in hand to progress the Public Appeal, I had nothing better to do. Anyway, she followed me through, and I sat her down on the visitors' couch and offered her a cup of tea. Her complexion was nut brown and she looked at me with very piercing eyes. I can still see those gimlet eyes and their crows' feet wrinkles twenty-five years later. Her anger subsided, although she still viewed me with a certain amount of suspicion. In Loe Beach language, the wind had clearly been knocked out of her sails.

She took a sip of her tea and asked me if she could tell my fortune and was further unsettled when I agreed without protest. A hint of resentment flickered in those piercing eyes when I said that I didn't have much money on me. To prove it, I emptied my pockets onto the table; there was a fiver and some change. She took my hand and started rambling on in the usual fortune-teller patter; I really can't remember what she said at this stage.

Suddenly she looked up from my hand and said in a completely normal voice that I was very worried about money. I told her that I was. And then she said, "Don't be! Will come soon." With that, she scooped up my loose change and pressed some small bracelet charms into my hand. She gently folded my fingers over the charms, looked me in the eye for the last time and said quite gruffly, "Two, three day. You see."

Three days later, in an unobtrusive brown envelope, we received a cheque for £50,000.

It was from the Esmée Fairbairn Foundation, which is one of the very few funders prepared to support core costs. The application for help with the printing and distribution costs of the appeal literature had been made so long ago that I had given up hope of getting an answer, let alone a cheque.

And so started our dash to the summit! Sarah went into overdrive printing Tim Guy's leaflets and folders and getting them out to every home and business across the whole of Cornwall. At this time there were lots of shuttered shops, and I tried really hard to get permission to set up a display in one. But landlords were wary of the possible impact on their insurance, rate relief and security if they let us into their empty premises. After many frustrating rejections, thanks to the generosity of the Nationwide Building Society, we got the use of an empty window in Lower Lemon Street. In this prime city-centre location, we set up an arresting display of our icon objects, together with big posters and the model of the new Hall. Every now and then we changed the display and it gave me no end of pleasure to see pedestrians stop by the window and absorb the incredible variety which would one day be on offer just around the corner. It made it all seem so possible.

As if he hadn't already done enough by designing our wonderful graphics and a truly brilliant leaflet, Tim went several steps further.

TG: I decided to waive all our studio fees and gave a donation of £10,000, spread over ten years. I also bought a seat and, without her knowledge, had the name of our daughter inscribed on it.

CW: What a guy!

The contents of the Hall for Cornwall leaflet

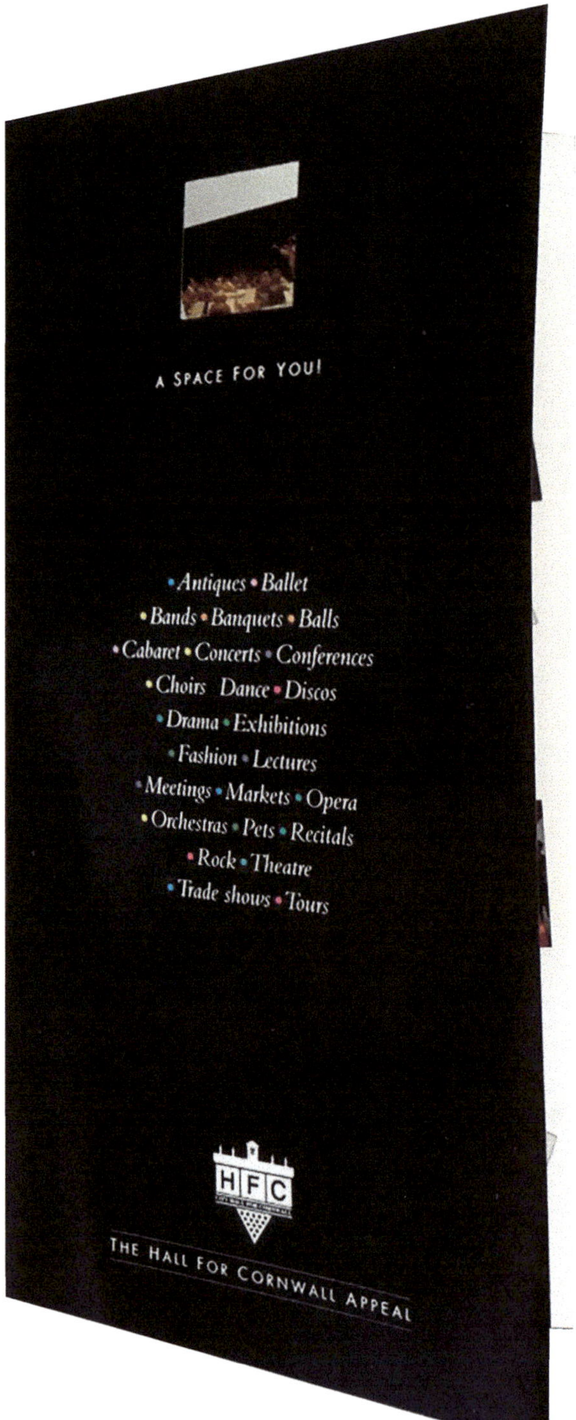
A SPACE FOR YOU!
• Antiques • Ballet
• Bands • Banquets • Balls
• Cabaret • Concerts • Conferences
• Choirs Dance • Discos
• Drama • Exhibitions
• Fashion • Lectures
• Meetings • Markets • Opera
• Orchestras • Pets • Recitals
• Rock • Theatre
• Trade shows • Tours
HFC
THE HALL FOR CORNWALL APPEAL

Our Leaflet

Chapter 16

Going for the Big Money!

SS: At the end of June 1994, we received planning permission and listed building consent from our landlords, Carrick District Council, plus a written agreement in principle to grant a 125-year lease at £1 per annum, and a formal promise of £500,000 if we achieved our financial target. We were, however, still well short of our project cost of £3.5m; we had identified a number of trusts to approach, but first we needed to seek support from key stakeholders. We went to South West Arts and shared our plans for the new Hall, but Nick Capaldi was reluctant to support us at first. I think he thought we were a bit mad and really did not believe that we would raise the money. However, he did reveal more details about a new initiative called the National Lottery, which would provide funds for sports, the arts and health, and would be launched later in the year. Grants would be funded from Lottery tickets which anyone could buy weekly, generating the prize money, and a percentage of the ticket sales would go towards supporting the different "good causes". It sounded too good to be true and Nick agreed to keep us informed. We were determined to be one of the first applicants, as this would give us an opportunity of raising perhaps £1m.

CW: Lottery money for arts projects would be distributed via the Arts Council of England (ACE). Our application would therefore make the case that the new Hall would give access to the people of Cornwall to publicly funded theatre, dance and music, which currently did not get past Plymouth. There would be benefits for ACE and the visiting companies through increased scope and reach, and the Cornish companies who would get a decent venue which would give them a sub-regional platform.

Around this time, Cornwall County Council successfully made the case that the Duchy should qualify for development funds from the European Union. We researched the European Regional Development Fund (ERDF), which supported rural areas such as Cyprus – and now Cornwall - with a particularly low Gross Domestic Product (GDP). To our horror we discovered that Truro was ineligible on the grounds that it was too prosperous. The argument to the ERDF would have to be a purely an economic one because the Eurocrats were not interested in the arts – but they were keen on funding infrastructure. They felt comfortable about building things – like roads – which could secure long-term economic benefit. We were going to need to demonstrate that the new Hall in Truro would be of economic benefit to the whole of Cornwall. I was very grateful when Sarah agreed to lead on this!

SS: My enquiries at first were met with a negative response. However, Brian Mansell introduced me to the Development Department at County Hall where I spent hours exploring how we could make a case to get around the Truro prosperity problem. Thankfully I eventually found the right officer who in turn found the right people to talk to in Europe. Ingrid Heseltine in the Cornwall Economic Development Office understood what we were trying to achieve with our plans for Hall for Cornwall. Ingrid would at later date advise on our ERDF application.

The big challenge was going to be reassuring ACE, that if they were to fund the capital cost of the venue, we would not need to come back to them for annual revenue support. Before we got too excited, we needed to focus and think about how the Hall would work once open. That meant we needed (among a long list of other things) a new business plan which would demonstrate how the Hall could be run on a breakeven basis.

Our early attempt had been pretty feeble. It contained little hard information or informed prediction, and the introductory platitudes were simply repeated several times in a slightly different format. To liberate public money, it was clear we needed a plan which would add clarity, rigour and credibility to a project which, although passionately supported on the one hand, was still regarded by many as – in Cllr Cockle's haunting words – "pie in the sky, boy, pie in the sky".

We did some research and talked to Arts Council England, as we had no idea who could help us with our business plan. Suggestions were made and eventually we both agreed that Peter Boyden would be the best person to appoint as our consultant. He had a very broad range of experience of business planning for major arts projects, was respected by ACE, and had a reputation for rigour. He was also an absolute whizz with nested spreadsheets, which I'd never met before. His daily rate may have been eye watering but I'm sure the business plan he wrote was a very important element in HfC's successful applications both to ERDF and to ACE.

SS: Chris led on the business plan. After the long-overdue removal of a dead pigeon which had blocked a downpipe behind the Back Quay parapet had allowed us to make part of the upper floor fairly habitable, he and Peter set themselves up in one of the old offices. Two floors above the beating heart of the Campaign and the day-to-day demands of programming and running City Hall, it was a pleasant and peaceful place to work.

Talking about pigeons, trustee Claire Bowden-Dan (CBD) describes the first time Chris showed her round the Back Quay building:

CB-D: In Back Quay, there was a narrow staircase at the back of the ground-floor room which Chris first occupied. It wound up to the first floor, where there was the body of a mummified pigeon in the ancient fireplace. No one seemed to want to move it and it stayed there for years, I think until the building work began. My fellow Trustee Jane Lofthouse and I suggested that it could be preserved in a glass case in the entrance of the rebuilt Hall, but that didn't seem to happen.

Mummified remains of a pigeon which resided in the old fireplace in City Hall until Chris rescued it

CW: I rescued it before the builders threw it out and kept it as a memorial to both our time in City Hall and to the disgraceful neglect of Back Quay, which had once been a truly magnificent building. It was eventually beautifully refurbished by HfC as the main entrance, with the box office and café on the ground floor, a full-on restaurant for theatre goers on the second floor, and above that a suite of rooms for hire. One rather plush room was large enough to house the Yamaha practice piano and was suitable for a variety of small performances and meetings. It became known as the Arbon Room – named after Dennis Arbon, who had been such a generous donor in the early days.

The pigeon has survived four house moves. It didn't get a glass case but it now "lives" on my desk in my Suffolk home. Its presence is a nod to the Renaissance habit of keeping skulls in one's study as a reminder one's own mortality.

SS: Back to the business plan.

CW: Peter asked me if we had a notional programme for years one, two and three.

Er, no. I explained the five different formats of the new auditorium – 400, 600, 900, 1,000-plus, flat-floor for flea markets, fairs, commercial events, conferences and standing rock concerts and that we planned to run a very long theatre bar, a café and a restaurant. There would also be smaller rooms for hire. I talked about our ambitions to host a very broad range of seated shows – theatre, opera, dance, ballet, orchestral concerts, chamber music, choirs, pantomime, amateur companies, Cornish companies, entertainment such as tribute bands, jazz bands and stand-up comedy. Oh, and film. Within each genre there would be a range of product which would find a suitable home in one of the auditorium formats. Not much of a challenge then. Peter went a bit quiet.

I had assumed we would have to construct a notional programme based on a calendar. But then for the next four days he just constructed his seriously complicated nested spreadsheet, which allowed us to enter an event by type, auditorium format, price band and ticket price. We could project ticket sales, the deal with the company, marketing costs, casual stage staff required, the spend at the bar and restaurant, and show the overall financial outcome for that event. If you altered the number of tickets sold, or the ticket price, or the bar takings, or anything else, the whole sheet altered itself to give us a new overall outcome both for that event and for the year. As a simple creative, I'd never seen anything like it.

Once the spreadsheet was up and running to his satisfaction, the grilling began. Peter started firing questions. How many markets, how many stalls, what was the rental per stall, how many cups of tea, how many casual staff would be needed to set up a market and take it down, how long would it take to set up and dismantle the various auditorium formats? How many staff for each operation? How many middle-scale (900-seat) theatre performances, how many small (600), how many tickets sold for each, at what price? On and on, always drilling down into the detail. How many stagehands for the pantomime? How many weeks would it run; how many matinees? Decisions, decisions! Creative crystal-ball gazing. Yet all the while, informing our decisions was Peter's vast experience of the business of presenting shows. He knew in his head – or if he didn't, he knew someone who did – the likely cost of this or that show, the deal it would require, the usual ticket prices, and how many tickets had been sold recently in a range of other similar venues.

The business plan grew by day. Each genre a section, each section separated but connected; all feeding down into the summary until the whole plan was distilled onto the last sheet of A4. And at the bottom of the last sheet, plain as day, the bottom line.

I began to get very excited. It was suddenly obvious to me what a tool this was going to be. Not only would the business plan be a route map for planning the programme, it would also inform the economic impact study. For example, if we now knew that there would be three orchestral concerts per year, we would be able to work out the direct spend – accommodation, food, drinks, taxis, etc. – generated by fifty musicians, possibly plus partners staying overnight. We could then quantify the trickle effect of that secondary spend on local suppliers, hotel and bar staff, even delivery people, their transport and their fuel.

In a couple of days, we had a rough draft of the programme. We then set about quantifying other costs such as staffing and salaries, stage staff, casuals, managers, chefs, bar and waiting staff, washer-uppers, etc., energy, rates, comms, insurance and maintenance. Incidentally, the projected maintenance costs came as a big shock to me. We were talking about all the essential kit like fire alarms, smoke alarms, sprinklers, lifts, the safety curtain, heating, ventilation, etc., all of which would have to inspected and signed off at least once a year.

It became clear that maintenance bills in the new Hall would probably come to £50,000 a year or around £1,000 a week. That's an additional cost of roughly £150 a day, every day.

And then the tinkering started. What if we did more markets, raised prices here, changed the price bands for this or that show, sold more ice cream, did more meals, did less ballet? The spreadsheet would chunter out the answers and that final sheet and the bottom line would be amended. Gradually the whole thing looked more and more plausible.

Although we had learnt a great deal about Cornish audiences through programming for ACT and then in the old City Hall, some of our spreadsheet input necessarily remained informed guesswork. There was a whole range of middle-scale stuff – e.g. English Touring Opera, English Touring Ballet, the Royal Ballet, the Bournemouth Symphony Orchestra – that needed 900 seats and which we had been unable to try out in the leaky old 500-seat shoebox that was City Hall. Which was of course precisely why we were building the new Hall. Later, when we came to book events for the first season, this lack of a track record was to prove a bit of a stumbling block, as would the fact that we were trying to persuade these companies to come to what, at that time, was still a hole in the ground.

Ben came to have a look at the final draft of our shiny new plan. He sat reading it for an age. Then he fixed those piercing blue eyes on us and said, "Well, I don't believe a word of it! Any hall this size is going to need around £250,000 a year in grants in order to get by." Someone, and I couldn't possibly comment on who it was, said they truly believed that the Hall was going to be too successful to be allowed to fail. And anyway, we could always do a Mexico …

SS: Both the Lottery and the ERDF required us to submit an Economic Impact Study which had to quantify the social benefits for Cornwall and the number of jobs that the new Hall would generate. We therefore needed to find people with the right expertise to lead on this study.

CW: We eventually commissioned a respected company called Atlantic to do the work; the study would flow neatly on from the notional programme section of the business plan. For example, as I said earlier, when our fifty orchestral players stayed overnight, they would need accommodation and breakfast, lunch, tea and dinner on the day of the performance and a drink after the show. Their coach would need to refuel, etc., etc. Economists use a complicated formula for what they call the ripple effect from a purchase. For example, if you buy a pizza, someone gets paid to make it, they buy the flour and the topping, which makes a profit for a wholesaler, someone has to deliver the ingredients, and the delivery person gets paid to deliver and also needs to buy fuel for their van. Etc., etc.

The bottom line of the economic impact study came as a bit of a surprise. And it also had quite an impact – no pun intended – on anyone who read the study. HfC was going to generate £20,000,000 into the Cornish economy over its first five years.

It was pretty serendipitous that two brand new sources of funding for capital projects should have come on stream just when we needed them. Not only that, but we had a business plan to prove that we could operate a brand new Hall without revenue support, as well as an economic impact study that demonstrated Hall for Cornwall would provide both Truro and more importantly Cornwall with a huge economic benefit.

SS: Things were looking really positive for us. In the meantime, I focused on generating the matched funding to enable us to apply to ACE and ERDF for grants. It was one of the conditions of both funding bodies that we had to generate a reasonable percentage of their funding, and our plan was to raise £1million from Carrick District Council, grant-making trusts and individual donations. Now, with our stylish fundraising literature from Tim Guy, including a beautiful, simple leaflet which described our plans and discreetly asked for donations, we were confident we could achieve this. Our leaflet would be sent to every home in the county and a press release would be issued at the same time to tell everyone in Cornwall about our plans. Timing was of the essence. We knew that the National Lottery was to be launched towards the end of 1994, and so we organised a press conference at Tim Guy's design studio to launch our appeal on 10th October and that day, having negotiated a great deal with the Royal Mail, we sent out our message to every household in Cornwall. All we could do then was to wait. It was not long before we started to receive numerous envelopes containing expressions of support and donations, from £2 to £1,000. We raised over £40,000 in about three weeks. A huge response, and just such a relief that people were going to help us deliver a Hall for Cornwall.

CW: With our business plan and the economic impact study both completed and providing us with the information that was needed by ACE and ERDF, as well as being on course to reach £1million sooner than we had dared dream, we agreed to test the ground with both funding bodies.

SS: We were a very small team, so we had to plan carefully as we were all still doing our day jobs running the 600-seat City Hall and of course still working with the architects and the professional team. We did attract a few volunteers who were helpful with selling raffle tickets and helping at events, but on the whole fundraising was down to us. We put out a press release to schools, groups and communities to help us raise money. We had a great response, with schools, the Scouts and other groups sending in donations from their fundraising activities. We always acknowledged each donation and where appropriate individuals or groups were sent or given certificates to thank them for their efforts.

We put our fundraising tins anywhere we could – they were in private homes, shops, pubs, restaurants, schools and colleges. Every time we took them with us to outside events – for example, when we invited members of the public to try out one of the seats for the new Hall outside Truro Cathedral – we would have to apply for a licence to allow us to have our tins outside in the street.

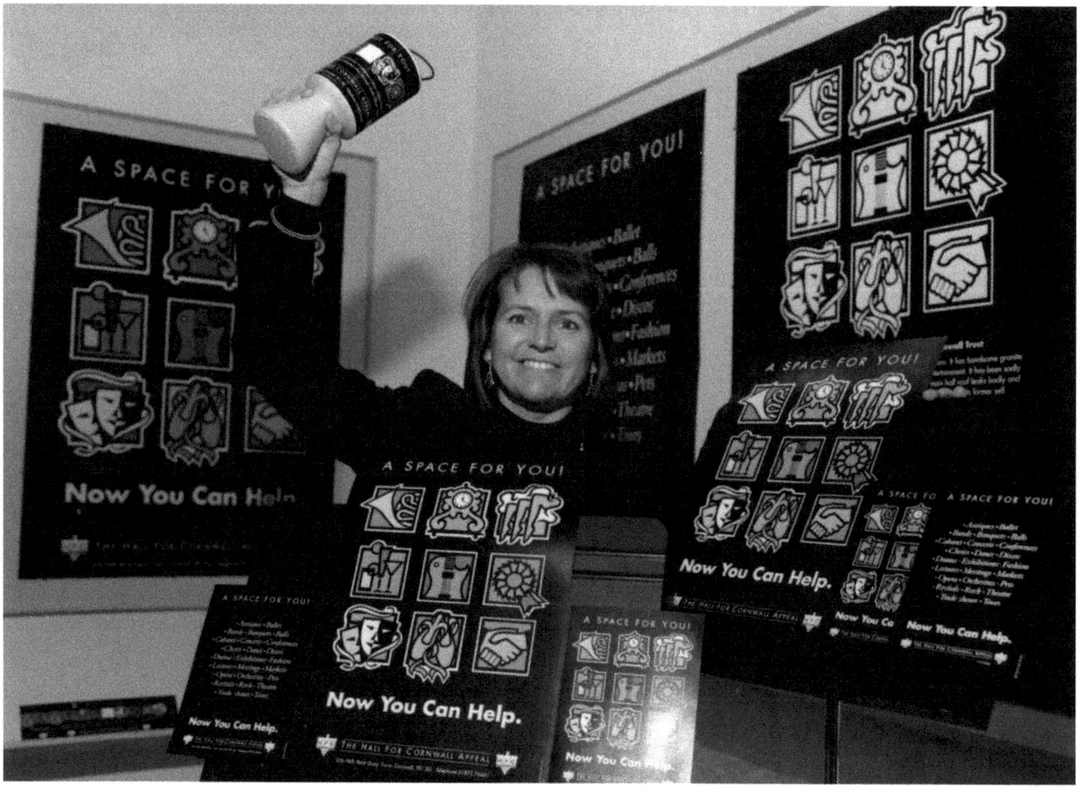

Sarah with our fundraising toolkit – photograph by Cameracraft

CW: Ideas like an art auction, concerts, asking local brass bands and choirs to come to City Hall as fundraising events, contacting rock bands and asking them to come and play without fees, raffling a car, arranging sporting events for businesses, murder mystery evenings, a quiz, New Year's Eve parties, evenings with well-known comedians and actors, were all grist to our fundraising mill.

SS: The momentum continued apace and then we reached a significant milestone – £1 million. The West Briton ran a piece that week with a photo of Caroline Enfissi, our resident artist, painting in the million pound mark on our appeal board "thermometer" in Back Quay.

● *Hall for Cornwall member Caroline Enfissi paints the thermometer appeal board at the rear of City Hall to mark the passing of the £1m.*

Magic million for Hall for Cornwall

SUPPORTERS of the Hall for Cornwall were jubliant this week after an important barrier was broken when the appeal fund passed the £1m mark.

The figure represents more than a psychological victory because by raising such an amount it could open the key to the treasure of grants available from the European Community and National Lottery.

Chris Warner, Hall for Cornwall director, said: "The £1million is not the end, it's a beginning."

He praised the efforts of appeal director Sarah Smith and said: "If both applications to Europe and the National Lottery are successful we could be ready to start in early spring 1996 and open in May, 1997. If the hall does open then it would coincide with the 150th anniversary of the original opening in 1847."

Local amateur societies who have booked the hall for early next year have already been advised to prepare to seek alternative venues for their shows.

Fund-raisers are looking for £3.5 million and Europe could provide up to 45 per cent of that figure and the National Lottery up to 75 per cent on condition individual projects pass 25 per cent of their target.

Mr. Warner is also delighted with the number of town councils who have promised to pay for having their names put on seats. Towns as far away as Saltash, Looe and Bude have promised to contribute.

The appeal continues with fund-raising events such as "Likely Lad", Rodney Bewes performing a one-man show of "Three Men in a Boat" at the Falmouth Arts Centre on May 12, and a jazz night featuring the 100 Club All Stars, with Campbell Burnap and Ritchie Bryant, on June 24 at the Princess Pavilion, Falmouth.

To celebrate the passing of the £1 million mark Caroline Enfissi painted in another band on the appeal thermometer.

CW: This was the match funding we so badly needed to go for the big money! Finally, we were invited to submit the funding applications and so began a very busy period of writing our two major bids – Sarah took responsibility for the ERDF application and I took responsibility for the application to the Arts Council England for an award from the new National Lottery.

SS: As we got into the detail of the applications, an unexpected thing happened with both the Arts Council and ERDF. We were asked about the fit-out of the Hall. We explained that the technology would have to come later and that we would fundraise for it. The ERDF were unhappy about this and basically said that they only supported state-of-the-art capital projects and suggested that I should go back to the design team and draw up a shopping list of equipment and items that would complete the Hall to a high standard.

CW: I received the same advice. When an ACE officer came down from London to meet us and see the old hall, he started asking all sorts of questions: why weren't we planning for air conditioning, showers in the dressing rooms, enough loos, counterweights in the fly tower, etc.? When I explained that the trustees were being very cautious about the cost, he drew himself up and announced: "Money is not a problem, you know – and we are definitely not interested in funding a deficient building."

SS: I think we were the only clients who had ever gone to their design team and told them to design up a more expensive project … which they did, to the total of £5.8m!

The cost of the project had risen significantly because of the need to satisfy the conditions of our key stakeholders. This had been a conscious decision by us, because both ACE and ERDF would not consider our applications unless we were proposing a state-of-the-art building. Thanks to these conditions, we were indeed going to deliver just that, with the most up-to-date technical equipment, the right seating, air conditioning, decent dressing rooms and soft furnishings.

We decided to keep quiet about the revised spec and to continue with the same message – the original cost of £3.5m; after all, what was the point in frightening people by announcing that the cost of the project was £5.8m at this stage? It would be difficult to explain, and in any case we did not know whether we would be awarded these grants. We also had a feeling that costs might creep up once we started the complicated construction work on an old building which was Grade II* listed. It was of significant historical importance, with layers of history and many different uses over the centuries. And it did indeed have a few secrets up its architectural sleeve …

Chapter 17

Fundraising Fun!

SS: It is true to say that we had a lot of support from people all over Cornwall by now but there were still some sceptics who felt that our plans were both ambitious and unnecessary. We were often asked 'What are you bothering to do that for?' Lady Mary Holborow as our ambassador and supporter was very aware of this and felt that we should arrange a conference but that it should be led by Cornwall County Council. We were enthusiastic as always and were very happy when Lady Mary confirmed that she had persuaded Peter Cocks CBE the County Council Chairman to host a reception and presentation for the Hall for Cornwall at County Hall. We carefully planned the evening programme, selected a list of supporters, sceptics and don't knows, sent out invitations and waited.

The Chairman of Cornwall County Council,
Mr. Peter Cocks, CBE,
has pleasure in inviting you to a
Reception and Presentation for the Hall for Cornwall,
in the presence of the Lord Lieutenant, Lady Mary Holborow,
in the Long Gallery, County Hall on
Tuesday 28 March 1995, 6 - 8 p.m.

r.s.v.p *Mrs. M. J. Siddall*
County Hall
TRURO
TR1 3AY, by 24 March, please.

CW: The evening went well and helped us because the reception was led by Peter Cocks in the presence of Lady Mary. Our presentation went down well and dispelled some misgivings and negativity. Quite a relief but back to the day job of writing applications.

SS: Chris completed the Arts Council Lottery Fund application, asking for a total of £2,584,521. It was submitted in the late spring of 1995 not long after the National Lottery was launched and was one of the first sixty applications received. Likewise, I worked up the ERDF application with input from the Development Department at Cornwall County Council. It too was completed and submitted around the same time, requesting the sum of £2,206,557.

CW: With our two big applications submitted, we just had to wait for news. It was a tense time for us. But Sarah had the bit between her teeth …

SS: We still had money to raise which was hardly a chore because we felt empowered through the positivity and the goodwill of so many people. Because we were a small team, I persuaded and cajoled friends to help us especially with the different events. Gilly Roberts was a great friend and had been involved in the very early days of Hall for Cornwall. She offered to help develop ideas for these events and came along on the day to help us. She had boundless energy and a total belief in the project, so no need to persuade her. She also helped with word of mouth about the Appeal, and her enthusiasm was infectious.

There were many, many ideas for events to raise money for the Appeal and because I had lots of personal contacts in the pub and restaurant industry, we were often offered help. The Pandora Inn at Restronguet put together a wonderful quiz which went down well; we had an offer from the Budock Vean for a murder mystery weekend, and Trengilly Wartha put on a wine festival at Trelissick. We had a lot of fun at these events – some were more successful financially than others, but they all helped us to achieve our goal.

CW: We organised some lovely fundraising events with performers who lived in Cornwall or originated from Cornwall and wanted to support us in our Appeal. Suzanne Manuel, Alan Opie and of course Ben Luxon all gave up their time to perform in different concerts. Other artists offered performances of their own shows, which we supported by booking and marketing. "Likely Lad" Rodney Bewes, performed his one-man show of *Three Men in a Boat* at the Falmouth Arts Centre in the May, and this was followed in June by a jazz night featuring the 100 Club All Stars with Campbell Burnap and Ritchie Bryant, at the Princess Pavilion, Falmouth. It was fun but pretty relentless, too.

SS: We decided we wanted to organise an enormous raffle with big prizes. We had heard of a fundraising success up country where a garage had donated a new car to be raffled. We thought this would be a great idea, particularly as so many people came into the hall on a weekly basis, either to go to the flea markets, commercial markets, the art exhibitions or events in the evening. Firstly, we had to find a garage owner who would help us. We contacted a number of local garages but most of them said that arrangements had changed between car dealers and manufacturers and so it was unlikely that a car would be donated. However, one dealer generously came up with an idea that was appealing. Mike Ward of Ward Vauxhall in Helston offered us a Vauxhall Corsa at cost price which I seem to remember was around £5k. We would need to sell enough raffle tickets to buy the car and then to make money on top. We decided to take the risk! The timing was right as we were not only building a lot of support but also receiving many, many donations.

We applied for a license to sell raffle tickets not only in City Hall but also at the Royal Cornwall Show, St Mawgan and Culdrose open days, and other events we were involved with, and managed to find a small team of volunteers to help us to sell them. We also gave out bundles of the raffle tickets to friends, family and businesses to sell on our behalf.

Through the generosity of three local businesses a raffle ticket could win:

First prize: Vauxhall Corsa
Second prize: £300 of holiday vouchers from Fox Travel
Third Prize: Dinner, Bed and Breakfast for two at the Roseland's Nare Hotel

We got permission to drive the Vauxhall Corsa into the Boscawen Street entrance of City Hall, where it remained on display for a few months.

The raffle tickets sold fast and we decided that we should organise an event at which we could announce the winning tickets. We arranged a Christmas Gala Performance on Saturday 9 December with Bodmin Town Band, the Climax Male Voice Choir, Mevagissey Male Voice Choir presented by Goff Richards. It was a sell-out! It was a great evening and the audience loved it. At the end of the concert we asked an audience member to pick one ticket from the hundreds and hundreds we had in the bucket. Unfortunately, Joyce Tobiason of Redruth was not in the hall when her ticket was drawn but I rang her soon afterwards to let her know. She was quite overcome and delighted that coincidentally she had won the car on her birthday. A few days later the keys were handed to her by Mike Ward who was also celebrating his first anniversary as a Vauxhall dealer. We more than covered the cost of the car and made over two thousand pounds for the appeal.

RH: A particular memory I have of the Hall for Cornwall raffle and Boscawen Street foyer was on the occasion of the visit of the then Chairman of the Arts Council England, Lord Gowrie. On entering the foyer, he was confronted by a Hall for Cornwall fundraiser, who, having no idea who he was, offered to sell him some raffle tickets. To which he readily agreed. She asked him his name, to which he replied "Gowrie". She then asked him for his first name, to which he replied "Lord".

SS: James Penrose, who owned Killiow Country Park and Golf Club, kindly offered to let us use his beautiful grounds just outside Truro for a fundraising event. We just had to come up with an idea that would make use of his facilities – and raise lots of money for Hall for Cornwall.

Killiow Country Park was perfect for a multi-disciplinary sports competition which would be about team building. We talked through ideas with a few friends who worked with different organisations locally, and who supported this approach. They gave us some great ideas and James fed in his thoughts, too. So we agreed The Hall for Cornwall Challenge would take place on Wednesday 20 September and then we put together a menu of sporting activities including target golf on the driving range as well as putting, archery, clay pigeon shooting, Land Rover driving tests, fly fishing, and a whiskey-tasting session. A packed day of activities! All the equipment for the day – from the Land Rovers to the fishing rods to the clay pigeon traps – were offered to us free of charge by Cornish companies.

Because the event would go on well into the evening and, with such a lot of competitive fun on offer, the participants were going to need refreshments. St Austell Brewery provided the beer and the Guinness and we provided lunch. We had a great response from local companies ranging from surveyors, a housing developer, solicitors, an engineering company, plus people from the car industry, a brewery and a zoo, who all promised to join in the competition.

On the day we had a very good turn-out with fifteen teams of four competing. We have listed these teams at the back of our book. The competition started in the morning with golf on the driving range and then whiskey tasting! The teams then moved on to clay pigeon shooting, followed by some impressive fly-fishing demonstrations, and the archery was pretty interesting, too. The driving was a serious challenge but the teams were able to have regular breaks between each discipline. James kindly allowed us to use Killiow House for refreshments and for the prize-giving. The Hall for Cornwall Challenge was a fantastic event that raised a significant amount for the Campaign and it also gave a number of businesses the opportunity for a get-together with some fun team building thrown in. As Roger Martin, then owner of Newquay Zoo and a team member of NG Associates summarized, "It was a great day that was superbly organised, never to be forgotten."

Here is our fundraising event calendar for the summer and autumn of 1995!

THE HALL FOR CORNWALL APPEAL

FUNDRAISING EVENTS

Sat 24 June Time 8pm Price - £7.50 each Princess Pavilion Falmouth	**The 100 Club All Stars** Featuring some of the top jazz musicians in the country
Fri 14 July Time 7.30pm Price £4 (students £2) Truro Cathedral Truro	**Cornwall Youth Wind Orchestra** Programme to include a wide range of works from the wind orchestral repertoire
Sat 15 July Time 7.30pm Price £4 (students £2) Carn Brea Camborne	**Cornwall Youth Orchestra** Programme: Symphony No.2 - Brahms Bright Blue Music - Torke 1812 Overture - Tchaikovsky
Mon 17 July	**Stithians Show**
Wed 19 July	**Street collection in Truro**
Sun 3 September Truro School Time 8pm Price £8 & £5	**An evening with Alan Opie** Pianist - Dick Taylor
Wed 6 September Trelissick Nr Truro Time 7.30pm Price £10	**Wine Festival at Trelissick - Evening** Organised in conjunction with Trengilly Wartha
Wed 20 September Killiow Park, Kea, Truro Time 9.30 - 3.30pm	**Hall for Cornwall Challenge at Killiow** organised Killiow Park in conjunction with James Penrose challenge for local businesses in 5 disciplines
Fri 29th September City Hall, Truro Time 8pm	**Hall for Cornwall Art & Craft Exhibition** Private view for Friends of the Hall and invited guests
Mon 2nd - Thur 12 October City Hall, Truro Time 10am - 4pm (closed Sunday)	**Hall for Cornwall Art & Craft Exhibition**
Thur 12 October City Hall, Truro Time 7pm	**Auction with David Lay** Hall for Cornwall Art & Craft exhibits
Fri 13 Oct - 15 October Budock Vean Hotel Mawnan Smith	**Murder Mystery week-end** A week-end of intrigue and fun in wonderful surroundings and atmosphere
Sunday 22nd October County Hall, Truro Time 7.30pm	**Cornwall Youth Jazz** In a class of their own
Sat 9 Dec City Hall, Truro Time 8pm	**Christmas Gala Performance** Bodmin Town Band - Climax Male Voice Choir - Mevagissey Male Voice Choir Presented by Goff Richards
Sat 9 Dec City Hall, Truro	**Finale to Grand Draw for car**

Please note that we shall be at the Shows in the County over the summer period.

lett25ma

CW: Another real success story was the response from the Cornish Societies all over the world. I knew about the diaspora both from my Piran Round days and more recently following an attempt to get a film made about Ben's grandparents, who had emigrated in the late 19th century and had dug their way across America from east to west, ending up in the lead mines in Bute, Montana. They had come back to Camborne in the thirties to sort an estate, dragging an unwilling sixteen-year-old daughter – later to become Ben's mother – who was horrified by what she saw as the primitive living conditions "at home". Years later when I met Ben's aunt, who had been old enough to stay behind, she spoke with a full-on American accent and an uncle became the keeper of the giraffes at the Golden Gate Zoo. Many people in Cornwall had relatives in other parts of the world and at Piran I had come to understand how important "home" was to this huge overseas community.

Claire Bowden-Dan, one of our trustees from the very early days, was also a pillar of the London Cornish Society. Claire put us in touch with an incredible number of societies all over the world who responded generously, as did towns and cities named by Cornish emigrants in memory of places they had left behind. Someone from one of the "other" Truro's even sent us his stamp collection. We celebrated the old joke that wherever in the world there was a hole in the ground you'd find a Cornishman with a shovel at the bottom of it.

SS: The model of the new Hall travelled miles as Chris and I took it to district and town councils throughout Cornwall, where we presented our plans and persuaded councillors to buy a seat as part of our Seat Appeal. We were by this time quite a double-act and always managed to enthuse our audiences, although we were often asked "What do you want to bother with a hall for? It's such hard work!" Well, we knew that, and used to patiently describe the benefits of having a hall in the middle of Cornwall.

On one occasion we settled into the Council chamber, I seem to remember in Launceston, and began our presentation, taking it in turns to speak. Chris set off, handed to me and there was a stony silence … Chris looked at me with eyes as large as saucers willing me to say something. I had dried! Thankfully, he knew what I should have said and managed to cover up the rather long pregnant pause. I have no idea to this day what happened to me; something distracted me and I completely lost my train of thought. That day gave me nightmares for years to come.

We took the model to the Royal Cornwall Show for three years running and we were lucky enough to share part of Cornwall County Council's stand, which was helpful as it gave our Campaign a sort of endorsement that we meant business! We also attended the annual shows at RNAS Culdrose and RAF St Mawgan. We attracted lots of attention and talked and talked about our plans and then held out our Hall for Cornwall tins for a donation. It was great fun, we had very little hostility and, though tiring, it was good to be able to talk to anybody and everybody about what we were doing and what we were going to deliver!

Nick Trefusis with Sarah at the Royal Cornwall Show – photograph by Cameracraft

Here I am at the Royal Cornwall Show in 1995 talking to Nick Trefusis about our plans for the future of City Hall using the model of the Hall for Cornwall. An essential tool!

CW: At one Royal Cornwall show, as well as taking our double decker bus which was painted all over with Tim Guy's slogans and artwork, we were supported by Dame Hilda Bracket. There was a marvellous moment when he/she was introduced to the Chairman of the Show, an impressive figure who wore a bowler hat. The poor man gallantly raised his bowler to the glamorous Dame only to realise mid doff that the Dame was a bloke. He blushed to his ears, crammed his hat back on and offered a hand. Dame Hilda took it and curtsied. The blush reached his hairline. "I say, look here! Who the hell are you?" demanded one of the Chairman's entourage. I had very long hair at that time and looked a bit like Billy Connolly, so, recognising "Billy", the astonished fellow gasped, "Are you – I mean, are you …?" "Och, aye, that I am," I replied graciously in my best Scots accent. Honour seemed to be satisfied and they went on their way chattering excitedly.

Chapter 18

City Hall Gigs

CW: To draw attention to the lack of a decent venue in Cornwall, Arts Centre Trust director Stef Brammar had embarked on some enterprising programming in unlikely venues. As well as bringing down the RSC to play in City Hall and then Truro School Sports Hall, she also began to programme a range of music, particularly modern and traditional jazz.

An early success was bringing Ronnie Scott to City Hall. When they arrived, you could see the band didn't think much of the venue and it was clear they thought that the all-female support band was a bit of a joke. When it came to the soundcheck, Ronnie and his mates sat at the back of the auditorium whispering and giggling. Until the girls started to play. The men's body language changed abruptly – it was as if they had been electrocuted! The reason? As a startled Ronnie put it, they were "bloody good!". The men did their soundcheck and, now on their mettle, let rip a couple of numbers. A chastened Ronnie departed to find a betting shop and a pint or two. It was a great evening which featured a fabulous two band jam session which was eventually brought to close in inimitable fashion by a knackered Ronnie announcing, "Thank you, thank you all, thank you ladies. We gotta call it a night – we don't know any more!"

Stef went on to programme other wonderful people – Larry Adler, Courtney Pine, and many, many others. An unlikely success was an American guy called Slim Gaillard, who was not so well known here. He sat on a tall stool downstage centre nursing an ancient acoustic guitar. Which he hardly played. Instead, he regaled us with tales of life in Chicago during the prohibition and how he had ended up as a driver for Al Capone. He was wonderful.

Stef was a genius at getting sponsorship and she developed a great working relationship with the owner of a certain Truro restaurant – The Bustopher Jones Jazz Band Ball soon became a fixture every New Year's Eve. She also programmed traditional jazz stalwarts including Humph, Chris Barber and Acker Bilk. They were great nights.

There were also some pretty strange events, as Bert Biscoe remembers.

BB: I always recall the Arts Centre Trust (under Simon Jutton) putting on David Icke. Every hobbit in Kernow was there. Icke had just finished a university tour and had a cassette (clearly recorded from Radio Luxembourg on a dodgy little Philips dictaphone) crammed with hits of the sixties, which he required to be played at high volume. One of the hobbits came over to the desk to say that if this awful noise was not removed at once the whole audience (the place was packed) had telepathically resolved to demand a refund and leave.

I went to the dressing room and Icke (ensconced between two statuesque and florally printed "wives"), said: "Do what you like!" I returned to the desk, searched my suitcase and discovered one tape – The Ukulele Orchestra of Great Britain. As the town clock struck 7.30 p.m. Icke descended the steps in his gold lame suit accompanied by The Ukulele Orchestra playing "I Can't Get No Satisfaction". Only the soundman laughed!

CW: Sarah and I very much wanted to build on Stef's earlier successes, and we chose to develop a wider music programme in City Hall in order to learn what worked and also to show the "Warner's Hall" merchants that the programme in the new Hall wouldn't be all classical music and opera.

It was a bit of a leap into the dark for both of us – we were going where we had not trod before! We needed male and female security people, a big bar, techies with the skills to handle full-on rock bands, jazz and folk, etc., etc. We put on some extraordinary events. Some flopped but generally they were crammed and often quite eventful.

Perhaps the strangest success was a Mongolian band with musicians who performed overtone singing – they were able to sing and play wind instruments continuously for several minutes without stopping to take a breath because they breathed in and out *while* they played or sang without a pause. They were amazing. Apparently they had buried all their instruments and costumes when a hostile regime tried to suppress their indigenous Mongolian culture, and then, decades later, when things became more relaxed, they had simply dug them all up again and carried on as before.

We had a Zulu band who were also seriously impressive. I often had to compere events and I asked a member of the band to give me some words of welcome in his own language. I learnt to say "Diabonga kikulu". I've always remembered it and have often wondered what, if anything, it actually meant. It could have been dreadfully rude, for all I knew. At the end of the evening, I asked one of the guys where he came from. I had meant whereabouts in Africa and was a bit startled when he replied in a booming voice, "Hull."

People came for a good night out. There was always energetic dancing, the consumption of large quantities of alcohol, and more often than not that unmistakeable smell of "certain substances" hung in the air. You could get high just by trying to breathe at some gigs – particularly when Al Docker's Ozric Tentacles were playing. That sweet smell would still be recognisable when the next morning's flea market opened, and early stallholders would sniff and wink knowingly.

BB: Whenever I look back over that period I always think of Al Docker. Al, if you recall, showed us all a market for music. He died very young, having spent his life living in the twilight world of risk-taking – Ozric Tentacles tended to produce queues.

CE: The mention of poor Al Docker reminds me of the Christmas gig he booked at the Hall when Theatre Techniques refused to do any work for it without payment up front. My husband Paul got me to take all our Christmas money out of the bank and give it to Al, who promised faithfully to pay it back. Luckily, he did, because it really was our entire Christmas at stake. I think I'd have killed the pair of them if he hadn't!

BB: It saddens me that, amongst the theatre and all the other stuff which swells programme after programme, the musical content adds up to a load of tribute bands. I once took my daughter Molly to a Queen tribute band – she was, and still is, a fan. She caused a stir in our neighbourhood of the stalls – where we were surrounded by waves of scarf-touting middle-aged Queenies singing along – by exclaiming, with a tone of serious (like "I want my money back!") shock that the Brian May lookandsoundalike (in his wig!) had hit three wrong notes in the big solo in "Bohemian Rhapsody". "It goes like this," she added loudly – and she sang it perfectly. I commiserated; and pined for the Ozrics!

CW: Perhaps the most bizarre occurrence was at a Young Farmers' event, when a young couple were discovered stark naked in a giant green wheelie bin. People at the gigs generally kept their clothes on – but they often got overexcited and emotional. The real problems, however, were always fuelled by alcohol, rather than cannabis. One night an objectionable drunken promoter tried to glass me with a pint mug and one of my fondest memories of City Hall was getting him by his collar and the seat of his pants and chucking him out onto Boscawen Street. It was straight out of a spaghetti western. And wonderfully satisfying.

Another evening I had a very different sort of surprise – it was my fiftieth birthday and my partner and I were going out to dinner at – you guessed it – Bustopher Jones. We were walking past the back of City Hall when I saw that one of the doors was not locked. I

Chris's 50th Birthday cake baked by Mandy Rolleston

started cursing and charged into the dark interior in a foul mood. Suddenly, the lights snapped on and a jazz band featuring a most attractive lady saxophonist started to play. The place was full of cheering and laughing people. Mandy then presented me with a birthday cake in the form of a naked female torso! What a night!

An artist who became very much worse for wear from the booze was Desmond Dekker. He was a well-known reggae singer, allegedly a mate of Bob Marley. He had languished while reggae was in the doldrums but was making something of a comeback with the reggae revival. When the support band finished no one could find Desmond, who should have been in the wings waiting to go on. The sell-out audience began to get restless and I began to get very worried. It was a bit unnerving so I sent Paul Enfissi, our Technical Manager, on a hunt for him, suggesting he scour the local pubs. Paul eventually dragged Desmond out of the Market Inn next door and hauled him up to his dressing room, where he said he couldn't go on. Even though he could hardly stand, I was determined that he would go on stage. He could make a fool of himself, but he wasn't going to make a fool of us. I slapped him around a bit, made him throw up in the dressing-room basin and then I chucked a lot of cold water over him. We lugged him downstairs and literally threw him on stage. The lights hit a drenched Dekker, and he paused, looking about as if to get his bearings. The crowd roared – and he gave the performance of a lifetime.

SS: We knew we had an audience for popular and rock music, which would prove to be really important to us during the fundraising campaign a couple of years later. But in the meantime we were experimenting and looking at opportunities to showcase different arts genres in the hope of discovering a range of audiences who would like theatre, dance, music and art.

The trouble was that backstage facilities for staging theatre and music were very limited. We cleaned up wherever we could and painted the dressing rooms to make them respectable for the artists, but it was still all pretty basic.

CW: Do you remember putting on Hawkwind, again to a sell-out audience? There were only three of them on stage and I have never heard three people make such a stupendous noise.

SS: Yes! that's so true. I remember popping into the Hall the afternoon before the concert with my mother and brother to see how the soundcheck was going. You could hear the noise halfway up Lemon Street! I have an image of my mum standing on her own in the middle of the Hall watching Hawkwind, seemingly completely oblivious to the noise they were making. As I dragged her away, she complained she was enjoying it.

Years later, an audiologist was discussing Chris's hearing loss. He asked him if he had been exposed to prolonged periods of gunfire. When Chris told me this, I replied that the cause was more likely Hawkwind and other bands in City Hall. They weren't all noisy, though. I remember one acoustic band that brought along a huge hollow log which was their percussion. They made beautiful melodic music.

CW: The hollow log was more like a tree trunk! We had other scoops – Chumbawumba played a few days after one of the band members had chucked a bucket of water over John Prescott's wife during a televised concert. But the best scoop of all was an unknown band which I had booked on spec for a very small fee. Completely out of the blue, they got picked up and were on Top of the Pops midweek and then played City Hall on the Saturday night. For the original miniscule fee. Very good for business! I remember standing at the back and yelling to my companion that the lead singer had real talent. The unknown band was called Radiohead.

SS: We had tried and tested City Hall many times, so as we moved into fundraising mode we started to look for bands who would support us. The Levellers came at the beginning of our appeal and we sold 650 tickets in about two hours. The band arrived during the day and Chris took them round the back of the building and showed them the first floor, which was dilapidated, full of pigeon droppings, dead pigeons and feathers. Mark Chadwick, the lead singer, was appalled by the condition of the building and said some great things in the press and to the audience that evening during a brilliant concert.

CW: Later in the appeal, Sarah managed to make contact with Roger Taylor's mum, who still lived in Truro. Roger, who was the drummer with Queen, was born and brought up in Truro, agreed to help us with a solo fundraising concert. Freddie Mercury had died in 1991 and Brian May and Roger were not performing together much over the following few years, but we knew Roger would give the appeal real profile – and ticket sales. He arrived with a small band, was charming and supportive. I have never seen so much kit – this diminutive blonde figure sat at the centre of a vast arc of percussion, which he proceeded to leather. A guy came up to me in the interval and said that the young band had driven him crazy by making such a racket when they rehearsed in Roger's mother's garage. "When they decided to call themselves Queen," he said, "I thought, wonderful, that's it, that's the end of them then."

SS: Debbie McCrory confessed years later that she had managed to trigger the alarm on Roger Taylor's drum kit, which was on stage, all set up. She thought she would sit in his seat for a moment before the concert started, but as she did loud alarm beeps went off and so she ran off stage and hid!

CW: The concert was a sell out and I will never forget that evening. Sarah and I spent some time up in the old projection box watching Roger and his band performing some of the old Queen songs. The audience was having such a good time. His was a rare gift, and we were very lucky to have been part of that special event.

SS: The last gig at City Hall was on 4 April 1996 when the Rhythm Doctors played to a packed house. It was a brilliant evening and the audience was having a ball but the evening was filled with such mixed emotions for the team. Standing on that stage to announce the closure of the hall at the end of the evening was very sad. It was the end of an era.

CW: And the dawn of a new one.

Chapter 19

1995 – What a Year!

SS: This is the year when everything came together. With the statutory consents for our plans for the new Hall achieved, we turned our attention to pushing on with fundraising.

We were in regular talks with Carrick District Council about our 125-year lease and also their offer to contribute £500,000 towards the cost of the refurbishment. Having attracted and appointed high-profile local trustees, turned HfC Ltd (which ran the City Hall operation) into a profit-making business which gave all its surplus to the Trust, secured the support of a fundraising consultant and developed the new plans for the Hall, which had received both planning permission and listed building consent, and raised the first £1m, we had kept our end of the bargain. We now needed Carrick's commitment and support in writing. This was finally achieved!

CW: I shall never forget the evening that Carrick finally agreed that we had met all their conditions. This meant that the lease could be signed, and this in turn meant that we could launch the Public Appeal from a solid base. No ifs, no buts, the people of Cornwall would know that if they supported the Appeal and raised the last bit of funding, the creation of the new Hall was a reality. It was a wonderful moment. As we walked down Lemon Street after the fateful Council meeting, we could see the old City Hall below us and we allowed ourselves to imagine its replacement. The Bustopher Jones dinner which followed never tasted so good. After a few drinks, one of our number dared to wonder if Carrick actually had the half million available, and we determined to ask for half the money up front lest there were other cynics abroad.

Much to my amusement Carrick did indeed have a problem with making good on their promise. An article in the West Briton dated 13 October 1994 with the headline 'Grant snag but hall appeal under way' recorded a council meeting at which it "emerged" that the promised £500,000 would only become available after the sale of some other asset!

But "after a few years" we had definitely not failed. And so it was that Carrick signed the 125-year lease at a peppercorn rent eventually handed over the first half of the £500,000 and promising the second half on practical completion.

SS: For some time we had been hoping that HRH The Duke of Cornwall would become the Patron of the Hall for Cornwall Appeal, and then in the spring of '95 we received news that he had agreed. He also agreed to write a letter of support which we could include in our fundraising folder. It took time to get the wording right but finally we received the letter of endorsement, which we sent to businesses, trusts, and individuals. Something that would make the people of Cornwall feel as proud as we all did at Hall for Cornwall. The doubters and waverers gradually began to give us their support. As did all five Cornish MPs – quite remarkable, as they had never all publicly agreed on anything!

ST. JAMES'S PALACE

The Hall for Cornwall campaign has persevered and prospered over the last few years and deserves the support of anyone with the interests of the Duchy at heart.

Cornwall really does need a properly equipped and up to date venue for the performing arts, conferences and trade fairs.

City Hall is an important Grade Two star building, which is sadly a shadow of its former self. The Hall for Cornwall project will both bring the semi-derelict Back Quay section elegantly back to life and provide the Duchy with the centre it deserves.

I hope that young people in particular will benefit from the wide range of activities offered by the new Hall - major tours will at last be attracted across the Tamar and there will no longer be the need to travel out of Cornwall in search of entertainment.

The new Hall will also create badly-needed jobs and will have a significant impact on the Cornish economy, especially the tourist industry.

As Patron of the Appeal, I commend the Trustees for their energetic efforts and I look forward to following the progress of the project.

Charles

CW: This was a key moment for the Hall for Cornwall Appeal. With the endorsement from The Duke of Cornwall as Patron together with his letter of support for the Appeal, we now had a serious profile. It was a great result and definitely a game- changing achievement for us.

SS: But we still had work to do!

CW: The media continued to provide regular progress reports; it was all very exciting and more and more new people came to see us at City Hall to learn about what we were planning and to discuss how they could help us. One day, a lovely man came in to chat to us – he said he lived in Fowey and knew Cornwall very well. He eventually revealed that he was Daphne du Maurier's son, Christian Browning, known as Kits. He was one of the literary executors of his mother's estate and was determined to preserve her memory. He was very interested and enthusiastic about our plans and explained that he was thinking about setting up an annual literary festival in Fowey in memory of Daphne du Maurier. We talked about whether we could develop links once the new Hall was opened, although the festival would be based in Fowey.

SS: Reluctantly we decided that we both needed to remain independent, and the first festival was a community initiative held in May 1997. The Daphne du Maurier Festival of Arts and Literature had the full support of the du Maurier / Browning family and was timed to celebrate the ninetieth anniversary of Daphne's birth. The festival has continued to grow since then. Held during May to include Daphne's birthday, it is now known as The Fowey Festival. Kits kept in touch and supported our seat appeal.

CW: Another visitor arrived in the office one sunny afternoon who would play a big part in Hall for Cornwall's future. Dennis Arbon, who lived in Maenporth, near Falmouth, popped in to learn about the project. He was an engineer and had been Managing Director of Caradon Mira Ltd until 1980. He was enthused with our ideas and offered to help us by providing all the sanitary ware for the new Hall and he added that he would love to get involved. I don't think he realised what he was letting himself in for, as it was not long before we asked whether he would be interested in becoming a trustee, not only because of his contacts for our capital project, but also because he was a "mover and shaker". Dennis, we felt, was someone we would need once the capital project had been completed and the new Hall opened. He was so supportive and generous with his time as well as financial help. An example of his generosity came in 2009 when he donated Upton Towans in Gwithian, to the Hall for Cornwall Trust. It was seventy-six acres of sandy beach, said to have inspired Virginia Woolf's *To The Lighthouse.* The beach was subsequently sold on behalf of HfC to a local buyer for £80,000. When Brian Mansell retired as Chair, Dennis took over and remained as Chair for many years, helping the organisation through some very rocky times.

SS: In the summer of 1995 we received news about our ERDF application. I remember the day well as I had been promoting the plans for the Hall at Stithians Show, which is a one-day agricultural show held annually since the early 1800s on the Feast Day of St. Stythians, the first Monday following 10th July. It is held on the Showground at Stithians and attracts thousands of visitors. We had our model of the new Hall positioned in a prominent place and spent a busy day sharing information about our plans. By this time, we were making good progress with our Public Appeal, so a couple of us were encouraging people to put money in our Appeal tins – every penny counts as we kept saying!

Towards the end of the day, I received a call to say that we had been awarded £2.2m from ERDF. Our application had been successful! It was fantastic news for the Appeal, and we received some great coverage from the media. More importantly, the award really helped our relationship with Cornwall County Council, which up till then had been slightly reticent about our campaign. Looking back, perhaps they were concerned that they would have to support the new Hall once the capital project had been completed.

The photograph opposite captures a delighted Brian Mansell, Chair of Hall for Cornwall with Sarah posing with lottery tickets and with the Hall for Cornwall model which had been such a vital prop for our fundraising campaign.

Lottery Success! Sarah and Brian Mansell – photograph by Cameracraft

CW: In the autumn of 1995, we received a very nice letter from the Arts Council England:

13 October 1995

Grant Reference: 9541

14 Great Peter Street
London SW1P 3NQ
Telephone
0171-333 0100
Facsimile
0171-973 6590
Minicom System
0171-973 6564

Chairman
Lord Gowrie PC
Secretary-General
Mary Allen

Chris Warner
Director
The Hall for Cornwall Trust
City Hall
Back Quay
Truro, Cornwall TR1 2LL

THE **ARTS COUNCIL** OF ENGLAND

Dear Mr Warner

National Lottery

The Arts Council of England has agreed to offer The Hall for Cornwall Trust a grant of up to £2,584,521 from the National Lottery Fund. This grant is towards the adaptation and conversion of City Hall, Truro into a flexible, high quality concert hall as detailed in the application for arts lottery funds.

This offer is subject to your organisation's acceptance of the enclosed Standard Conditions of Financial Assistance, together with such special conditions as relate to your specific application. Also enclosed is a schedule detailing the proposed grant payments.

If this offer is acceptable, please complete and **return to the National Lottery Director the enclosed copy of this letter**. The offer will lapse unless accepted within three months from the date on this letter. Please quote your grant reference number on all correspondence. If you have any queries, please contact your Lottery Officer.

Yours sincerely

Jeremy Newton
National Lottery Director

Lottery Switchboard: 0171-312 0123

SS: As we had hoped, we were one of the first sixty applications received by the National Lottery through Arts Council England. In those early days, some of the lottery awards were featured on a Saturday evening show televised on BBC when the weekly lottery results were drawn. We were lucky enough to be invited to take part in this programme and the BBC came down to Truro on a day when the Hall was filled to capacity with a flea market. There were masses of stalls, stallholders and people milling about, and the BBC team spent time filming the plans of the new Hall, filming the flea market, and then I had to announce the actual amount that had been awarded from the National Lottery, which was £2,584,521.

It was so difficult for the cameraman, as people passing by kept waving at the camera or standing behind me or walking in front of me. It was so noisy that few people were aware that this filming was taking place. The team was determined to capture the atmosphere in the Hall and the lively buzz, but it had its challenges and one of the challenges was me and my inability to announce the award fluently. It was one of the most embarrassing moments of my life as I stumbled over the numbers several times. My default in tricky situations is to start giggling. Not helpful. But the BBC team remained patient and hopeful that I would get my head together! In the end, the person interviewing me decided that we would write the figure down in large letters so that I could read it rather than memorise it. My "idiot card" looked like this:

Two million, five hundred and eighty-four thousand, five hundred and twenty-one pounds!

It was a massive figure to announce on national television, and quite a moment for us all at Hall for Cornwall.

Over a well-earned cuppa, we totted up our awards and grants:

£2,584,521	National Lottery through ACE
£2,206,557	European Regional Development Fund
£500,000	promised by Carrick District Council
£300,000	Foundation for Sports and The Arts
£50,000	Esmee Fairbairn Foundation
£30,000	Headley Trust (Sainsburys)
£20,000	Baring Foundation
£140,000	The public appeal including individual donations, trusts, events, seat appeal

Total so far: £5,831,078!

CW: It was all very well me and Ben having our dream of a Hall for Cornwall. But, in order to turn a dream into "bricks and mortar", sadly you need cash – lots of it in this case – and our dream, which came to be Cornwall's dream, would never have got to curtain up without Sarah's heroic fundraising efforts.

It was absolutely astonishing that our bids to those two huge funds should both be successful. Talk about jam today and jam tomorrow … and the day after! Buoyed up by our good luck, we continued with our events and one that we particularly enjoyed was our Art Auction.

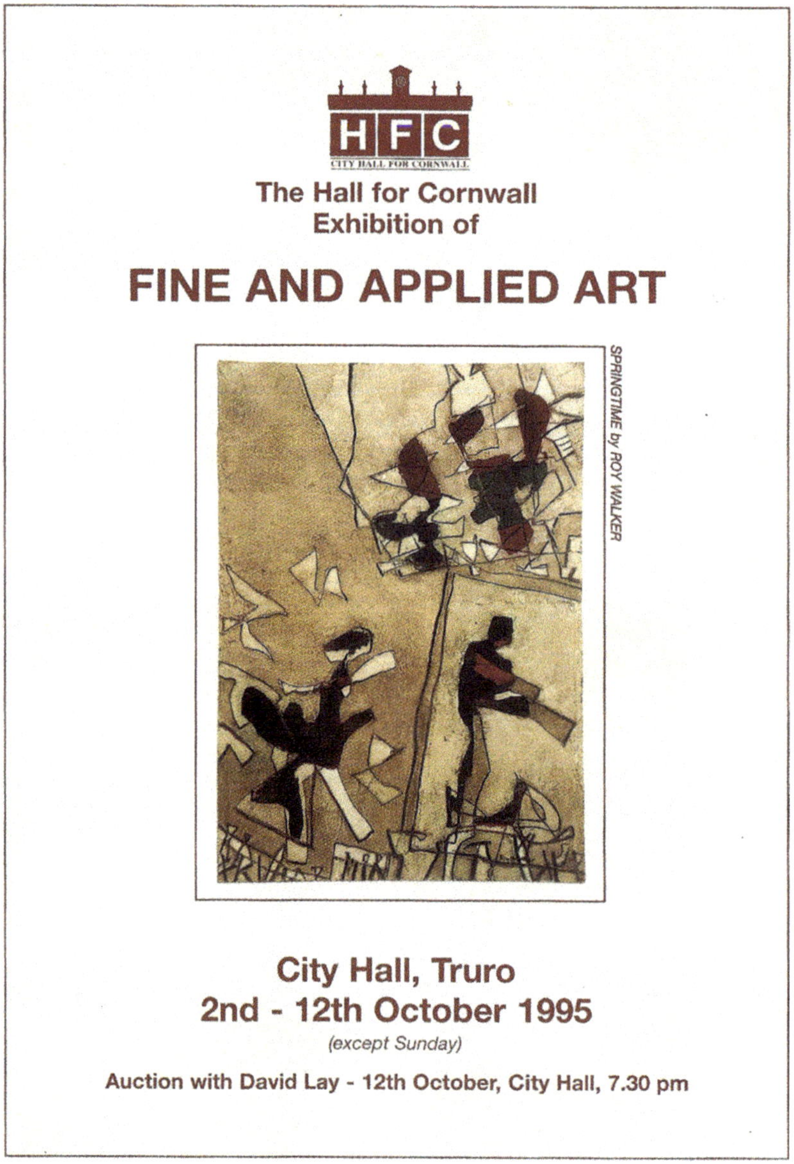

SS: With help from one of the development team from the Tate of St Ives, we put together a list of artists and artists' studios we planned to approach. We were not expecting artists to donate their pieces of artwork but asked them to give us their painting or sculpture or photograph for us to auction and then we would give them 25 per cent of the proceeds. We planned to put together a beautiful catalogue giving information about each artist and the artwork. We had a great response from eighty-one artists from all over Cornwall. We were so lucky to receive contributions and some from really well-known artists – John Miller, Bryan Pearce, Vivien Prideaux, Sally Wills, Felicity Robertson, Roy Walker, Michael Strang, Martin Lanyon, Theresa Gilder and many other "names".

CW: Once more we used the Annexe in City Hall as a temporary gallery to hang the artwork, and we borrowed plinths and tables to display the sculptures, fabrics and jewellery. Our in-house techies also re-rigged the lighting which we had used for Roy Walker's art exhibition a couple of years earlier. Once again, we had a wonderful art gallery which did justice to some fabulous work.

Chris and Sarah waiting for David Lay, the auctioneer to start the Art Auction

We had to employ a security man during the viewing day when people came in to look at all these gorgeous pieces!

David Lay FSVA, a well-known professional auctioneer from the Penzance Auction House, agreed to conduct the auction on our behalf. David was a serious player in the wider art world and had once achieved the record-breaking price of £230,000 for an 18th-century mahogany bookcase. Thanks to him as well as our distinguished contributors, we generated a lot of publicity leading up to the event.

SS: We sent out loads of invitations to the evening auction and we had a good response. On the night, a goodly number of local people came along to support us, but the best news was that others arrived who we did not recognise. We investigated. It turned out that there were a couple of pieces of art that national dealers were interested in …

Debbie McCrory feeling the pressure on the evening of the Art Auction

The auction went very well and we sold nearly everything and raised about £40,000. The following week was spent working out the exact amount we needed to give to all those artists who had supported our appeal. I remember Mary Sheppard (our Accounts Officer) was particularly happy with her purchase!

MS: I overheard Vivien Prideaux saying how disappointed she was that her fabric picture didn't sell for more; I didn't dare tell her that I was pleased to have bought it.

Chapter 20

The Balancing Act!

SS: In January 1996, the trustees, now confident in our ability to raise the remaining funding, decided to invite tenders for the building contract, as by then we had raised £5.5m towards the Hall for Cornwall project. Their aim was to close City Hall in April, when we would move out so that the contractors could start work.

The trustees and design team, including Chris, sat through the interviews of those contractors who were shortlisted. A unanimous decision was reached to appoint Tilbury Douglas, who had worked in the South West and who Brian Mansell, our Chair, and Peter Fazakerly, Project Coordinator, felt confident would deliver our plans for the new Hall.

We were heading towards the end of an era for the City Hall with a mixture of excitement and sadness. A terrific team achievement which inevitably would create uncertainty for all the staff, flea-market regulars and local people who popped in to see us on a daily basis.

CW: About to be homeless, we were now under pressure to find both an office for our much-reduced team and a temporary space for the flea markets. We needed to generate income whilst the City Hall was closed and to make sure that the stallholders would follow us into the new Hall. Carrick was unable to help us so we set out to find a benevolent local businessperson who might take us in for a while. We soon found office space in Lemon Street at a vastly reduced rent, and then, following a couple of meetings, local property developer Denis Angilley offered us the old bus station in Truro. We had found our temporary flea-market space. It was located behind Lemon Quay and had a large open space and some warehouses with roofing but no sides.

The land has since been redeveloped and now houses Marks & Spencer and a car park. Denis agreed that we could move our flea market there for a low rent until the new Hall opened. Ann Jennings and the stallholders were relieved to find a temporary home and Mandy and co. established a limited catering operation there. It had its challenges, particularly as it was pretty cold and damp during the winter months.

SS: Whilst we settled into our new temporary home, Chris and I were preoccupied with whether we had the right structure in place in respect of our charity and our trading company. We had set up Hall for Cornwall Trust, which was responsible for developing the plans for the new hall, fundraising for the costs for developing, and delivering the capital project. This did not include running the City Hall which was a predominantly commercial operation.

CW: Trading – which can include fundraising (from merchandise to events) – is a risk activity. If it is to be undertaken by a charity, the safest option is to create a wholly owned charitable trading company. There are several advantages. If the trading company becomes insolvent, its bankruptcy will not be a drain on the parent charity's resources. Donors can therefore feel safe in the knowledge that their donations will not get frittered away on failed trading activities. Additionally, the charitable trading company, provided that it covenants its profits to the parent charity, will not be liable for corporation tax. But it has to hand over those profits on a specified date each year. We had therefore formed Hall For Cornwall Ltd (HfC Ltd) which operated independently with Sarah and I as the Directors and was the company which ran City Hall. Through it, we had the freedom to employ people, run a catering operation, and book events without much reference to the trustees. Bliss! The original Hall for Cornwall Trust remained responsible for fundraising and, ultimately, for the construction of the new Hall, and the plan was for HfC Ltd to take on the new Hall's trading operations. So far, so good.

But a heavy-duty problem had emerged which could well have scuppered the project – it became clear that, even though we were a registered charity, VAT would be applicable to the building contract. This came as a bit of a shock to both of us and there was a moment of horror when we realised that we needed to raise circa £6m plus VAT. At 15 per cent I make that £900,000. It seemed iniquitous that public money from the Lottery and the ERDF and all the other awards and donations should be taxed in this way. We just didn't have that extra money, and besides, who on earth would want to fund the VAT? That just isn't sexy!

It was the subject of most of the discussions that Sarah and I had at the time, with both of us seeking advice, reading up about similar projects and talking to our cost consultant. I don't know where it was published but I accidentally – yet another serendipity? – read an article about how developers of retail premises were getting round the problem. They had found a loophole and it goes like this: the developer builds the shell, which is leased to the retailer, who fits out the shell to their requirements. The only VAT payable is based on the rent.

Now, trustees tend to be a cautious lot and they also tend to be painfully aware of concepts like "fiduciary duty" and "financial probity", and they certainly tend to fret about the potential for their personal liability if things go belly-up, because they are after all Directors within the meaning of the 1988 Act. I remember on a very rainy day sitting having a sandwich lunch in a barn with trustee Jim Beeching. Somewhat to his amazement, we were both guests on the same Roseland shoot. As we ate our croust (crib), I tried to persuade him of the benefits of using the Foundation for Sport and the Arts' £300,000 to develop the Back Quay building as a restaurant and viewing platform overlooking the building site. He was definitely not up for it because his very real worry was that, if the project failed to go ahead, he – they, the trustees – might have to pay that money back.

Persuading the trustees that my proposal to create a second trust to lease the shell from the original trust in order to save the VAT on the construction costs had legs was therefore clearly going to be a bit of an uphill struggle. After all, how on earth could this long-haired "creative" with a reputation for spending money, who had never held down a "proper" job, and who, in Brian Mansell's words, might very well not be "sound", possibly know anything about VAT? But the idea had legs and eventually some poor soul – probably Sarah – had to approach HM Customs and Excise and enquire whether this cunning plan was actually legal. The answer – eventually – was "yes"! Bravo the VAT man! The new trust was called The Hall for Cornwall Property Trust… interestingly with the same Trustees as the main Trust!

SS: Another big conundrum was about cashflowing our building works. The terms and conditions of ERDF and the Lottery Fund through Arts Council England, our biggest grant funders, stipulated that the funding would be released upon submission of receipted invoices for works carried out. In other words, we would have to pay the contractor and the professional team before receiving their funding. We had approximately £1m in our bank account, but that would soon disappear, so we needed an overdraft or a bank loan.

Off I went to our bank manager to explain that we needed some support to help us cashflow the works. He was the local bank manager, young, clearly ambitious and being fast-tracked for greater things, but even he was somewhat taken aback when he asked me how much I would need. I told him that £1million would do it. He said he would review our cashflow for the building works and talk to his regional directors, who would have the final say – but he was not optimistic.

Just after that meeting, I went over to France to visit great friends of ours. Michelle, who is Irish, and Andrew, had invited friends and family to Castelnau-de-Montmiral for a long weekend of celebrations and parties. A large contingent came over from Ireland and boy did we party! Michelle and Andrew had organized a menu of activities and visits to different places over that weekend. On the first evening we took part in a wine tasting that was held on a rose farm. Our host was a Danish rose grower who was breeding new roses for lots of supermarket chains including Marks & Spencer. It was a perfect event for us to get to know the family and friends who had gathered for the weekend. One family member I met that evening was Michelle's uncle James Deeny, who was a senior member of a well-known bank in Dublin. I kept thinking of the likely cashflow issue that we would face once building works started at Hall for Cornwall and hoped that James might be able to guide and advise me. The evening was well underway, it was a warm and beautiful evening and we were surrounded by acres and acres of stunning roses. I will never forget the sunset or the intoxicating scent of the roses. The wine tasting was not quite the same as those I had been to in the past and it was not long before the party was in full swing, with our Irish friends leading the way. I thought better than to talk business with James that evening.

The following day, we met up for lunch and, as luck would have it, I found myself sitting next to James. I decided that now was as good as time as any to talk about the Hall's cashflow issue. He was absolutely charming and listened politely as I explained about the Hall for Cornwall and that we were starting on site but in due course would find it difficult to cashflow the capital works even though we had secure offers of funding in place. As I explained our position, I watched as his face relaxed and with a twinkle in his eye he said that this would not be a problem for banks in Ireland. He went on to explain that Ireland had made the most of being in the European Union and had applied for and received numerous ERDF grants which were transforming Ireland's infrastructure as well as numerous buildings. He said that it was common practice for banks to bridge finance against approved grants in Ireland. This meant that the projects could begin work and he did not think that this should pose too much of a problem for the banks in Cornwall either. Cornwall had not received much funding from ERDF at that time, and those projects that had been successful were most likely to have been awarded to Cornwall County Council, which would be in a position to cashflow a project. Therefore, I needed to thoroughly understand what I would need to do to persuade the bank to help us. The next few days included further conversations with James and some note-taking, after which I felt well briefed and confident of the task ahead.

As soon as I returned to Cornwall, I arranged a follow-up meeting with our bank manager and then set about explaining in more detail how the bank could help with bridging finance against the approved grants from ERDF and ACE. I provided him with copies of the contracts and examples of how other projects had been supported by banks in Ireland. Following some toing and froing, our request for a bridging loan rather than an overdraft was approved … what a relief! I could look the contractors in the face and tell them they would be paid on time.

CW: April arrived and it was time to move out of City Hall. Before handing over the keys, I had a last look round. It was an odd feeling – the poor old place looked tattier than ever but we knew that in eighteen months a pretty spectacular phoenix would have risen from the ashes. We agreed to pose for one final photo in City Hall with the stage as our backdrop.

Here are most of the team members – trustees and staff - who worked their socks off during our time in City Hall. From left to right:

Back Row: Chris Warner and Ian Clarkson
Middle Row: Yvonne Allis, Ben Luxon, Jane Lofthouse, Martin Schute, Jim Beeching, Peter Fazakerly, Brian Mansell, John Worlledge and Mary Sheppard
Front Row: Jackie Pound, Lizzie Barradell, Mandy Rolleston, Caroline Enfissi, Sarah Smith, Ann Jennings, Debbie McCrory and Beverly Skilton

Hall for Cornwall Trustees and Staff in City Hall – April 1996. Photograph by Cameracraft

CW: Time to think about programming the first season … but priority number one was to focus on the impending demolition and rebuild.

I quickly developed a good working relationship with the contractor and regularly attended site and sub-contractors' meetings. I bought my own hard hat, making sure it was a different colour to everyone else's, and was soon made welcome on the site when necessary. And quite often when it wasn't …

SS: It was never going to be easy because, as the contractors revealed more and more about the building and its issues, additional costs slowly started mounting. Every day we seemed to hear about another problem. Chris was determined to stay at the table and I totally agreed. The design team and contractors worked well together but tensions were inevitable and Peter wasn't always around to find solutions. Thankfully, Chris just turned up on site most days.

CW: With most capital refurbishments and redevelopments of old buildings there are always many unknowns, and soon our contingency fund was being eaten away by what came to light as the contractors got to work. While we were determined to make sure that we did everything we could to avoid endangering the ability of the new Hall to deliver on the programme promises we had made, inevitably Peter Fazakerly's first priority was the budget. Unfortunately, he quickly became enemy number one because of his relentless pursuit of savings which would compromise the technical viability the Hall. At one point, Brian too went so far as to advocate, in order to save the cost of buying the stage lighting, that we should hire in all the lanterns when we needed them. I asked him how often he used his car and suggested that he could save some money by hiring the wheels when he needed them. He was not amused.

A good example of this cat-and-mouse game was the ongoing conflict over the pianos. The thing is, if you want to attract top international pianists like Vladimir Ashkenazy, you have to provide an instrument which they will enjoy playing. After all, they're not short of invitations. We needed a piano which was so excellent that word would get round that it was worth the trip to Truro just to have the pleasure of playing it. More concerned about expense than excellence, the trustees were continually on the lookout for savings – as if Cornwall and the Hall somehow did not deserve the best. I was concerned that if I was forced to accept a duff piano, the words "Don't go to Truro because the piano is awful" would echo round the international circuit faster than a particle in the Hadron Collider. The only possible choice was a Steinway. And a Steinway cost £50,000 in the middle nineties. And Vladimir and friends would need to warm up before the concert on a second, merely good, piano. A Yamaha C would cut the mustard for just £25,000. Peter just didn't get it, and Brian even went so far as to have a serious row with our piano adviser, who travelled the world as András Schiff's tuner. The row concerned Brian's view that to bend the piano wires through ninety degrees when they were under such tension was structurally unsound (no pun intended), and anyway he simply could not see the need for a such an expensive grand piano. He just didn't understand why a Steinway would be such an attraction for top-flight pianists. I tried to explain that the Arts Council was paying for the piano and that cutting it would not produce a saving because ACE would simply reduce the grant. Luckily, Ben, Claire and Jane stuck up for me.

SS: At the time, Peter Fazakerly was Captain of Truro Golf Club, which by all accounts was quite a big commitment, so I think what with the golf and trying to reason with both the contractors and the client, he was run ragged and pretty exasperated by the time we completed the contract.

The Stage Manager later chose "Mr Fazakerly is in the building" as the coded announcement on the backstage Tannoy which warned staff of a problem. Never underestimate a techie!

CW: Remembering the conflict over the pianos puts me in mind of a conversation between Ben and the House Manager at Lanhydrock after we'd given an concert in the Long Gallery. In an attempt to make conversation, the unfortunate guy from the National Trust had asked Ben how we had got on with the piano. After a brief pause, Ben replied with an absolutely straight face that the Trust could make quite a lot of money if they used it for a piano-smashing competition!

SS: Anyone who has been involved with a refurbishment of an existing building will know that although the design team tries to plan for all the possible pitfalls. While the quantity surveyors estimate the provisional costs which feed into the project budget, it is inevitable that things won't always go as planned. Although demolition of the central areas of the existing City Hall went well and costs remained pretty much as projected, it was not long before the contractors uncovered that beautiful granite cantilevered staircase, which sadly did not work with our design for the new Hall. It cost us in both time and money, as there was a significant delay whilst we negotiated with English Heritage. Those sorts of discoveries can cost a project dear, and the staircase did.

As we started eating through our contingency fund, we had many conversations about what we could lose from our list of the equipment which was required to make the Hall state-of-the-art. It was a difficult balance, as at the same time we had to satisfy the two main stakeholders – ACE and ERDF – who, after all, had funded well over half of the cost of the project. We couldn't just leave out the technical lighting or the seats.

CW: Or the pianos.

SS: It took a number of sometimes heated discussions to persuade the trustees, Peter Fazakerly and the contractors that we had to build and fit out the Hall as we had planned.

CW: Inevitably, all eyes turned to Sarah – we needed some more money.

Chapter 21

Finishing the Fundraising

CW: Even though the building work had started, we were still very keen that the Public Appeal should not be just about raising money; we wanted to create a sense of ownership for the new Hall with as many people as possible. The very diverse programme proposed for HfC meant that a correspondingly diverse range of fundraising activities could reach out to a very wide audience who we hoped – out of curiosity if nothing else – would become the actual audience for the new Hall. We wanted to build on our "A Space for You" slogan and to encourage the people of Cornwall to feel it was truly their Hall. Lots of people got on with a myriad of small events at schools, WIs, Rotary and Round Table clubs, and kindly gave us the donations.

SS: I had read about an initiative for raising funds from the public by offering the opportunity to name a seat for an amount of money. We had 1,000 seats planned in our auditorium! I knew this could be a really popular way of raising funds. However, around this time there had been a court case where HMRC were claiming that VAT had to be paid on the donation. It would be important to demonstrate that our donors had no rights to the seats and would not benefit from the gift in any way. The solution was to make sure that the plaque with inscription – rather than the seat itself – was what was being donated. Our accountants agreed, and we had a debate as to who might provide, ideally at no cost to HfC, the plaques and the inscriptions.

Mallett & Son Ltd was an independent hardware store located in Victoria Square in Truro, a stone's throw from City Hall. Robert Mallett was the Managing Director and both Chris and I knew him well. Robert had been interested in the plans for the Hall for Cornwall and we had kept him updated with our progress. Our philosophy was that it is always worth asking! We set about meeting up with Robert to see if he might be interested in donating 1,000 (hopefully) brass plaques, which would need to be inscribed. He agreed to our proposition, but with the proviso that there could only be a set number of letters or numbers inscribed on each plaque. We now had a plan and knew we could really push on with the Seat Appeal.

CW: Tim Guy designed an excellent leaflet for us with the strapline: "A Seat for You" and the Seat Appeal became our main focus once work started on the building.

We persuaded the manufacturers to give us an example of a new Hall seat so that people could try it. We decided to place it outside Truro Cathedral, a busy part of town, and we asked passers-by to sit in it for a moment. Those that were willing to do so would be photographed and appear in the new leaflet. It was a great idea and we had plenty of people keen to test out the seat, which then spent most of its time exhibited in the Boscawen Street entrance to City Hall.

A SEAT FOR YOU

Work on the Hall for Cornwall has started, it's time to get involved

The dream of a well equipped centre for the performing and visual arts in Cornwall is soon to be a reality.

Work has now begun on a £5.7m scheme to convert the City Hall in Truro into a brand new multi purpose hall with a flexible auditorium offering 950, 800, 600 or 400 seats or 2200 standing for pop concerts.

The hall will serve the whole of Cornwall and will provide space for:

antique fairs • ballet
bands • banquets
balls • cabaret
concerts • conferences
choirs • dance
drama • exhibitions
fashion • lectures
meetings • markets
opera • orchestras
pets • recitals
rock • theatre
tours • trade shows

The Hall for Cornwall will be **a space for you**, bringing the best to Cornwall and presenting the best from Cornwall.

We need to raise just £90 000 to complete our funding.

Take part in **A seat for you** by making a donation of £100 to help us reach our final target and your name will be recorded on one of the seats in the new Hall.

"BUY" YOUR SEAT NOW

300 NAMED ALREADY

HFC

HALL FOR CORNWALL APPEAL

A SEAT FOR YOU

Name
Address

Postcode

Please tick the boxes:

- I would like to "buy" a seat in the main auditorium with a brass plaque on the back of the seat for £100. I would like the name recorded on my seat to be:
- I would like to support the Hall for Cornwall, and I enclose a donation of £
- I would like to join the Friends of the Hall and I enclose £25 as my first annual subscription
- I would like to make a gift by:
  - Gift Aid
  - Deed of Covenant
  - Credit Card *(Barclaycard / Access)*
- I would like my name recorded in the specially bound book to be displayed in the new hall

Please send this slip to

Sarah Smith
Appeal Director
Hall for Cornwall Trust
City Hall, Back Quay
Truro, Cornwall, TR1 2LL
Tel: 01872 262465

People were very sceptical about the level of comfort that a folding seat could afford. The real bonus of having a demonstration seat – aimed primarily at persuading people to sponsor "their" named seat – was that the people who sat in it discovered that it was actually really comfortable.

SS: We distributed the Seat Appeal leaflets as widely as we could because "work on the Hall for Cornwall has STARTED" signalled that the project was actually happening. The response was better than we ever imagined – families bought blocks of seats, there were seats named after relatives, pets and famous people like Freddie Mercury. It was lovely to read through the lists of names – and yes, we had names on 1,000 seats by the time we opened the new Hall. An elderly lady who was one of our staunchest supporters "bought" ten seats and the ten plaques spelt WELLWISHER.

We also felt very humbled and proud to learn from trustee Jane Lofthouse that the Cornish Gorsedd wanted to sponsor a seat in the new hall. Jane, a bard of the Gorsedd, said that the Gorsedd's decision was an endorsement of the Campaign and that the seat plaque should read "'Gorsedd Kernow".

I loved this leaflet that Timothy Guy Designs created because of the little box saying "Open Autumn 1997"! This image has been restored twenty-four years later by Matt Grocutt.

CW: Once we had the big ERDF and Lottery awards in the bag and the ink was dry on the lease, people really believed the Hall was going to happen and that sponsoring a seat would help to get us past the finishing post.

As soon as the last seat had been "sold", Robert Mallett and his trusted team started inscribing the 1,000 brass plaques. These were works of art and must have taken hours. They were carefully placed in numerous boxes ready for the moment when our technicians and carpenters were allowed to start fixing them on the back of the seats in the auditorium.

Timing was of the essence, as we could not just waltz into the Hall with our plaques and screwdrivers until the contractors had finished. Meanwhile, we set about planning where each inscription would go. Thankfully we had avoided giving our generous donors the opportunity to say where they wanted their seat in the hall so we just had to mark up on the plan of the auditorium to show our staff where each of the thousand brass plaques would be placed. Then we would have to make sure that every seat had its correct brass plaque fixed before the Gala Night. What could possibly go wrong?

SS: Alongside the Seat Appeal, I was still scouting for funding opportunities. I was having some success with trust fund applications and securing donations from individuals, but we needed a windfall from somewhere to make sure we had enough for the increased capital costs. We also needed to create a financial safety net for the programme for the first six months. There were two possibilities – English Partnerships, and another lottery pot called the Heritage Lottery Fund. Chris and I thought we could make a case, but it would not be easy.

We managed to find a contact who could help us get to the right people at English Partnerships, and discussions commenced. An application followed, and after some weeks we received the good news that we had been awarded a grant which would make a significant difference to our emptying funding pot.

Chris and I did have one area in the building that we really wanted to change. We had accepted that Truro City Council were resistant about us using the Boscawen Street "front" entrance as the main access to the Hall, and we had designed the whole building so that artists, audience and staff entered from the "back" of the building on Back Quay. The Boscawen Street entrance remained unattractive. It was vast, draughty and dark, and often attracted drunks, dossers and people in need of a late-night loo …

A corner of the dismal "front" entrance to City Hall – 1995 – photograph by Martin Howse

We felt it would be wonderful to use this large area as more than just a grubby fire exit. We naïvely thought we would be able to persuade Truro City Council to review both their lease and their thoughts about this part of the building – after all, we weren't asking to take over the first floor, which included the courtroom and their council offices.

We believed we could make a case to the Heritage Lottery Fund (HLF) for some additional work in this area, not least because we had not used this part of the building in any other grant applications and also because it had remained untouched by the contractor. In 1996 the HLF was still a relatively new funding body and unfortunately it would not fund a project that was already being funded by the Arts Council England Lottery. That was a problem for us because of course the Arts Council England was one of our main funders. I contacted HLF and they agreed to come and visit City Hall and have a tour.

After putting on hard hats and showing the HLF Case Officer all the work that was currently underway in the rest of the building, we showed her the Boscawen Street foyer. We were open with our explanations about why we had not been able to include the main entrance, and having already spoken to Cllr John Christie, Mayor at the time, we felt that we could come to an arrangement with the City Council regarding their lease. We were convinced that if we could demonstrate that we had potential offers of funding in place, we could have meaningful discussions with both City and Carrick councils and that we would eventually be able to take responsibility for the foyer.

CW: I wanted to buy out the shops which blocked two of the three grand granite archways facing Boscawen Street, partly because Roger and I had discovered that there was a hidden granite staircase which was the mirror image of the existing granite staircase to the City Council premises on the opposite side of the Boscawen Street foyer. The hidden staircase stopped abruptly on the ceiling of the café, which had once been the city rent office and which still retained an enormous walk-in safe. Some pantry! I saw an opportunity to restore the foyer to its former glory. Sarah, however, saw a funding opportunity!

SS: A few weeks before the meeting with HLF, we had approached Truro City Council to see if we could have access to their entrance area to the right of the foyer and we also had had chats with the café owners who were leasing the shop front on the left. There was some reluctance, but we reckoned that if we offered the right price, we could obtain those areas as well, which would make a substantial difference to this end of the building by opening it up to the street. We were pleased with our meeting with the HLF officer and following that visit we were invited to submit an application. It was not a simple application, but we went ahead and put together what we thought was an interesting case for support. We were optimistic mainly because we were on such a roll of good luck at the time!

Sadly, three months later we received a “thank you but no” letter from HLF, which, with hindsight, was probably for the best, as we got no further with the Truro City councillors, who were still quite cynical about the future of the new Hall. The café next door, while having more faith, was also very relieved because they were sure that the new Hall would generate more business for them.

We had hoped for a big chunk of funding from HLF which would not only help in doing up what used to be the main entrance but would also help to fund the telling of some stories about the history of City Hall. Twenty-two years later, Julien Boast, Director of Hall for Cornwall, has been successful with a National Lottery Heritage Fund bid. This will help fund changes to the Boscawen Street main entrance and will help to celebrate the complex history of the City Hall and the people who used and loved it.

CW: Hey-ho!

Chapter 22

Demolition and Discoveries

CW: During our brief tenure of City Hall, among other challenges, we survived two attempts to sue us, one in the High Court, no less. The High Court writ alleged theft of intellectual copyright regarding Sarah's caricature map. We felt that our adversaries were trying it on, so Sarah persuaded Peter Dexter, our solicitor, to answer the writ by depositing £5,000 with the court and writing a jolly note saying how much we were looking forward to seeing them before M'luds. They backed down pretty sharpish and we got our money back!

The other legal challenge was from the lady who used to do rather well by running the flea markets. She alleged we'd stolen her living. But anyone could book the hall and put on an event. Indeed, it still annoys me that for years Carrick allowed her profits to leave the building rather than operating the markets in house and using the considerable income from the stall rents to maintain the poor old hall. Conclusions on a postcard, perleees!

The dilapidated City Hall had however served us really well as a research and development enterprise which Sarah, confounding the doubters, had made do better than break even. It had been both an invaluable, highly visible base and a brilliant PR and research tool from which we could launch the fundraising campaign for the new Hall and from which our phoenix would soon emerge.

It had been our home. And ironically, we had become quite fond of the old place …

And then, almost before we knew it, the demolition people were knocking on the door. However excited we were to be finally making a start on the construction, I think we were all quite sad to say goodbye.

While the start of the demolition contract was a cause for celebration and brought employment to the men in hard hats and reinforced work boots, the arrival of the diggers resulted in unemployment for many dedicated, loyal and incredibly hard-working people who had given their all to the project. With an eighteen-month build period ahead of us, there was simply no way to fund salaries and wages in the down time. Nor was there any guarantee that they would get their jobs back in the new Hall. Because the HfC board had made it very clear that new appointments would be made after an open and fair recruitment process. Even the people who stayed on to run the temporary flea markets which occupied premises on the other side of the square knew that their jobs were not due to altruism but rather to economic imperatives – we were very concerned that someone would kidnap the stallholders (much as we had done) by offering them a nice warm shed elsewhere. The truth was we needed their stall rents in the new Hall in order to balance the books, and we also needed to keep faith with all the people who had repeatedly made me promise, in public, that the markets would continue in the new HfC.

To those who felt bitter and betrayed when City Hall closed, all we can say is we were so sorry at the time and we remain sorry now. Thank you once again for your "all", which you gave so generously, and which made such a very real difference.

SS: For understandable reasons, the demolition site was out of bounds. The following photos show the stripping out which was done at tremendous speed.

Commencement of demolition - photograph by Mike Godfrey & Martin Payne (Tilbury Douglas)

Old inner entrance to the hall from Back Quay – photograph by Mike Godfrey and Martin Payne (Tilbury Douglas)

The old roof slates and battens being removed from City Hall – photograph by Mike Godfrey and Martin Payne (Tilbury Douglas)

The demolition people however did all right out of City Hall because they worked on a fixed price and could keep whatever they found. The most exciting discovery was a vast slate floor under the wooden floorboards of the roller-skating rink. The slabs were about six foot by four, and really thick. They were worth a fortune.

CW: Oh, how I wanted some for my kitchen!

But thanks to the trustees I did manage to come away with some trophies most of which I have kept! I still have the large Wells Fargo-type safe which had graced Mr Ashby's office for many years. It is made of four-inch-thick steel and it needs four people to move it. After a short sojourn at my house in Cornwall it now resides under my stairs in Suffolk. Like many safes, there's not much in it, but I'm very fond of it. I had also been given permission (in the Bill of Quantities) to take the cast iron spiral staircase which gave access to the former cinema projection box in City Hall. It was a thing of wonder because the stairs located with a stud into a central iron pillar and theoretically it could have been extended without limit if you had enough bits. A real stairway to heaven … My last trophy was a large, galvanised watering can which had been used by the old City Hall caretaker to flush out the urinals with a heady brew of Jeyes Fluid. Mark and I never saw eye to eye when I rented the old hall for productions because, like all caretakers, he had an uncanny knack of jangling his keys at sensitive moments towards the end of a rehearsal. He sensibly took the opportunity to retire as soon as we took over City Hall. His watering can, still reeking of Jeyes Fluid, ended up in my garden and had a forced early retirement caused by a falling tree which, with possibly supernatural accuracy, squished it into a thin disc. Think Coke can and a descending Monty Python boot. It had made me smile as I watered my garden and I still mourn its loss. Mark, did you do that?

SS: Talking of strange happenings.. during this period one thing that I don't believe ever got reported by the media was the demolition guys' nervousness about being in the Hall towards the end of the day. They were convinced it was haunted, with some saying they had seen a Victorian man walking around in the area where the old office and dressing rooms were. Most thought it was very creepy, and these great big burley demolition guys were definitely not hanging around after dusk. However, once the building had been stripped out, and the main contractors arrived on site, there were no further sightings reported. Maybe, Mr Brown, the Victorian gentleman, decided the building would be fine in the end.

CW: Next up it was the turn on the archaeologists who confirmed that an open-air market had taken place on the rectangle of open ground bounded by the two grand façades of Boscawen Street and Back Quay. The early market stalls, which backed onto the long sides of the rectangle, gradually became permanent, and the annexe on one side and the dressing rooms and corridor on the other had the same footprint as these early stalls. Then at some point the central open-air bit between the two now permanent rows of stalls was roofed over. Before we got hold of the keys, this rather idiosyncratic and much loved building served the citizens of Truro as, among other things, a roller-skating rink, a rifle range, a venue for wartime dances, a cinema, the Fat Stock Show, and, with the addition of a stage, as an occasional theatre. It held many memories for all sorts people, like the old lady who asked me if she could have a specific annexe pillar when we knocked the old hall down. When I asked her why, she replied that her future husband had proposed to her by the pillar at a dance in 1942. Others shared less romantic memories, mainly to do with getting completely plastered at the beer festival, or stoned out of their brains at various gigs.

SS: The dig was much more fun than the demolition because we were allowed to visit the site from time to time and because it was a slow process similar to peeling an onion. The City Hall had gone through several incarnations over the years before we moved in, and the ground plan of the old hall reflected its earlier functions. Details are set out in the 1997 archaeological report of City Hall Truro by Cornwall Archaeological Unit.

CW: Gradually the site gave us glimpses of mid 18th-century life next to the Truro River. The archaeologists found that before the quays were built, the riverbank was a long slope up which high tide would have crept past the Back Quay building and nearly to the middle of the old Hall – which of course was not even a twinkle in anyone's eye at that stage. They found cobbles such as you might expect on a slipway, the foundations of a small building with evidence of a furnace, loads of broken clay tobacco pipes, and lots of mug-sized cracked crucibles.

Mug-sized crucibles– photograph by Cornwall Archaeological Unit

As a creative with an over-active imagination, I saw in my mind's eye the owners of the crucibles getting really annoyed every time they cracked, bellowing a very rude word in Cornish, and then hurling the offending red-hot articles into the river, where they would have hissed as they slowly sank. Not so. Every good Cornish schoolchild knows that the people on the bank were assaying samples of tin, and that each crucible was deliberately broken in order to prevent the contamination of the next sample to be assayed. The colossal granite structures facing Boscawen Street and Back Quay remain a testament to the wealth that tin had brought to the Duchy since the time of King Arthur. Why these people broke so many of their clay pipes remains a mystery.

SS: The closure of City Hall for the start of the building works had generated much publicity from local radio, television and the ever-popular West Briton, which was a weekly newspaper published each Thursday. The aim of our HfC campaign was to ensure that we generated something newsworthy each week – a school that had raised money through the children's endeavours, progress of the demolition of the mid-section of the Hall, what the archaeologists had found buried, fundraising progress, bite-sized chunks of anything newsworthy. We also managed to attract the West Country TV news and Radio Cornwall regularly. It was so important to keep that momentum going so that we could continue to "sell" our seats!

CW: I can't remember what I had been doing in the City Council offices, but I know I was just leaving when the Clerk stuck his head round his door and called, "Hey, Chris, come and look at this!"

I suspect I had been to see the Mayor, Cllr John Christie. The Mayor's Parlour was a haven of peace and John was a sympathetic supporter who did what he could to ease his Council's path through the trauma experienced by many City councillors regarding the whole HfC project. It could not have been an easy task. Councillors not only tend to love the sound of their own voices, but they also tend to feel it's safer to oppose change rather than support it. Their glasses were neither half full nor half empty – more like a meagre quarter pint in a pint glass, which they feared might very well get spilt if someone were to jog their elbow. Perhaps they would have been happier with smaller glasses. Most of them had fought a valiant rear-guard action in a doomed attempt to prevent the loss of "their" beloved City Hall, and John had stuck his neck out as one of the few who had supported the proposals for their new upstart neighbour. Perhaps it would be too unkind to say that there were shades of Northern Ireland politics in many councillors' entrenched positions, but there certainly were moments of the kind of rampant political opportunism which had prompted the Rev Ian Paisley to loudly point out that Mrs Thatcher's broken finger was attached "to the hand that signed the Northern Ireland Agreement". I felt for John – Council meetings were lively enough without the inflammatory issue of Hf C – although they were occasionally leavened by conspiratorial moments of Pythonesque hilarity: for example, when Cllr Pie-in-the-Sky accidentally voted against his own amendment.

Anyway, the Clerk called and I trotted obediently along the corridor. It would have been churlish not to. Without a word – which was quite unusual for the Clerk – he beckoned me to follow him. We walked in silence along the corridor and suddenly he stopped at a tiny door which I had never noticed. He unlocked it and led the way up a steep narrow wooden staircase. Eventually we came out behind the clock, which faces Boscawen Street. It was whirring and clunking impressively. I dutifully stopped to admire it, for I mistakenly thought the clock was the reason for our climb. Not a bit of it. A peremptory crooked finger encouraged me to follow him up another stair, which was really little more than a ladder. When we got to the top, the Clerk opened a trap door and we stepped out onto the roof. He guided me across to a parapet. For a moment I wondered if he was the secret hitman for the Truro Mafia – but no, we stopped just short of the drop. I looked down, experiencing a mixture of fear and fascination. I mean, you can't help looking down, can you? However often you've been told not to. In the movies, the victim – and the camera – always look down. So I looked down and what I saw took my breath away.

I was standing on the rear wall of the City Council's monumental granite building. We were probably fifty or sixty feet up and we were looking across a vast and largely empty rectangle of ground towards the inner wall of the Back Quay building. When the City Hall had been meeting its nemesis at the hands of the demolition crew, there had been piles of this and that and "whatnot" – as Alan Bennett would say – all over the site. No longer. The good fairies had donned their Marigolds and cleaned the site to within an inch of its life. Nothing remained – not a hint of what had been there before. Just mud.

Back in the sixties, my then partner and I used to work fit-ups at the weekly rep in Guildford. The theatre was very limited and very tatty and there was a real clamour in the town for a new building that would be fit for purpose. But as long as the old rep stayed upright, the Council wouldn't budge. Then one morning we came to work, opened the auditorium fire doors and there was the sky instead of the ceiling. It had burnt down in the night. The logs were no longer jammed, and plans for the new Yvonne Arnaud Theatre progressed apace … Thirty years later, we got the same shock when were allowed to see what the demolition crew had been up to. We opened the doors from Back Quay – and saw the sky. Whoops! There she was, gone.

Site cleared and levelled looking towards Boscawen Street – photograph by Mike Godfrey and Martin Payne (Tilbury Douglas)

In quick succession I thought: OMG, it looks huge, then I wished to hell the trustees had allowed me to use the Foundation for Sport and the Arts money to open a restaurant with a picture window on the second floor in Back Quay. Diners could have gazed down and watched our phoenix rising. What a PR gift that would have been! Next, I noticed the excavated orchestra pit and I just fell about laughing with joy. Even though the site was all bare earth, I could see where the stage would go, behind the oval hole which was the orchestra pit, and it was easy to imagine the auditorium filled with row upon row of blue seats, each with its unique brass name plaque. All our ideas, all our ideals, all our hopes and dreams had somehow survived. I looked at the Clerk and grinned helplessly. And then I collapsed into gales of hysterical laughter that any fellow Crazy would have recognised. Anyone who has won the Lottery would probably know what it felt like.

The two photos opposite show what happens when you dig very large holes near a river!

As I looked down on that vast space which had so recently been the City Hall, I thought there's no stopping us now. Wrong. Again. I had no idea that we would soon discover a spectacular cantilevered granite staircase in Back Quay, or that one of the subcontractors would go into administration. The granite staircase, which was hidden under an easily removed wooden staircase, unfortunately turned the opposite way to its planned replacement. This would be serious stuff because none of the new landings would work and it would be very iffy to secure listed building consent in order to remove it. The Back Quay part of the site was forced to shut down while we negotiated, and Brian Mansell, our Chair, went into overdrive because of the dire cost implications. But trying to influence the nice Conservation Officer wouldn't work because she held all the cards. Brian argued the case forcefully, threatening to go to appeal, but she calmly reminded him that involving English Heritage would simply cause further delays. She also reminded him that if we didn't get permission to replace the staircase, the whole interior of Back Quay would have to be redesigned and the new design would require new planning and listed building consents. I thought Brian was going to explode but he had to give in. In the end we lost about three months, but it could have been much, much worse.

It was not just the cost of the site delay which ate into our contingency fund – the removal of the cantilevered staircase was in itself both another challenge and an extra expense. Granite weighs a hundredweight per cubic foot, and the huge granite steps had been built into the wall as the wall was being constructed, so we couldn't just pull them out like extracting giant teeth. In the end they were cut off by a specialist team using diamond-tipped cutting equipment. The stumps were left in the wall.

High Tide in the orchestra pit – photograph by Hall for Cornwall

Excavating the under stage basement – photograph by Mike Godfrey and Martin Payne (Tilbury Douglas)

Looking back, I remember how we had to plan for the challenges of running the site. Basically, anything which couldn't fit through the central arch of Back Quay had to be craned in. We thought that even the crane that would do the craning would have to be hoisted from the street over the roof of what was still a Grade II* listed building. Not so. It emerged that if the big crane breathed in and held its breath it could just squeeze through the central door of the Back Quay façade. Once the big crane was safely on site and working, big diggers, other large plant and all the huge steel girders which would span the auditorium and stage would all dangle like children's toys as they disappeared behind the granite façade. Once the steels were inside assembling them proved to be quite a challenge – as Ian Hick, (IH) the Structural Engineer recalls.

IH: One event which sticks out was that I needed to halt the crane lift of the principal roof frames due to issues with how this was to happen on site. Because of the size of the frames, two cranes were required, producing a tandem lift, which in itself needed careful coordination. We had previously specified the points from which the frames were to be lifted in order to ensure that the whole truss remained stable. When on site, however, it was apparent that the steel erector had changed the lifting points, such that if the lifting continued there was a risk of the frames buckling. After a heated discussion, the decision was taken for us all to review the design in our office where we were able to prove that the frame would indeed have become unstable if lifted. It was then safe to say that a new steel erector was provided on site, and the lift continued without incident.

CW: What seemed like years ago, the then Mayor, the one who'd asked me to keep receipts, had enquired how people would know we had made a start. I had foolishly replied we couldn't decide whether to wrap the façade in silver foil or to paint the granite pink. The look on her face was wonderful. As it turned out, the traffic grief every day on Back Quay was a most satisfactory visible sign that HfC was on the case.

It was a new experience working with a large construction team. All my life I'd mostly worked with people who didn't particularly care if they got paid and for whom creative excellence was the driver rather than keeping to a budget. I was invited to attend the contractor's regular team meetings and there I was introduced to the real world of business, risk and reward. Fascinating! Have you ever noticed how football players maintain a deadpan expression on the pitch, glazed eyes averted, particularly if they've just made a terrible mistake? The same as poker players? The subcontractors were masters of that art of facial neutrality.

The first of many early morning structural steel deliveries to Back Quay – photograph by Roger Quew (Tilbury Douglas)

Making the contract run smoothly was a real challenge for the main contractor because there wasn't much room to store stuff on site. Normally, builders store materials and vehicles around the edges of the actual construction site. Here, there was no such luxury. So it was vital that the subcontractors kept to a tight schedule. If there was a hold-up for some reason – materials late or dumped in the wrong place, or like the discovery of the granite stair – everyone was potentially affected. I guessed no one wanted to be blamed for anything, but, like schoolboys before the Head, they all looked as guilty as hell at those meetings! Gradually, everyone relaxed and things became more friendly. I think they even began to enjoy working on something which wasn't your average construction project. And perhaps the client was a bit more fun than usual …

SS: Yes, Chris, I suspect that was the case, but this was definitely not a normal everyday construction job and we did have to deal with many challenges along the way which involved our stakeholders, contractors, design team and trustees.

CW: An unexpected consequence of the successful Lottery Fund bid was the requirement set out in the conditions of grant regarding commissioning artists to deliver a range of artworks for the new building. The trustees did not find this easy, particularly when money was tight. It was a bit like the piano saga all over again. No savings could be made by cutting what some saw as an unnecessary expense and something of little value.

The Arts Council England for years had a policy of making sure that living artists should benefit from the capital projects which ACE funded. It was a case of he who pays the piper gets to choose the tune. The board found themselves having to call for presentations from artists and then make some choices. It was an uneasy time for them, but I found it a most enjoyable process …

I had great fun dreaming up my own arty projects, and my absolute favourite would have celebrated the history of Back Quay by using holograms to recreate the river, the wharves and the sailing ships which docked there. Sadly holograms proved too expensive. Through researching this idea, I had discovered a "light artist", and we hatched another lovely plan using rope lights – very cutting edge at that time – to pick out the architectural features of the Back Quay façade in a range of colours. Rope lights were to be inserted into the arches of the great doors and windows which faced the car park. Unfortunately, that also proved too expensive. But happily, we ended up with "the twinklies", which were inserted into the large blank surfaces of the proscenium arch which faced the seats. A projector with rotating filters diverted multicoloured light along fibre optic cables in a random sequence, delivering ever-changing star-like twinkles for the audience to enjoy each night before curtain-up. Very Zen. Usually they were the last thing to go out when the house lights dimmed, having a moment all to themselves before fading as the curtain rose.

Another project which came out well was the iron balustrade which stopped people falling into the Back Quay foyer from the first-floor balcony. I'm afraid there were probably others which I have forgotten, but I will always remember the work commissioned from Vivien Prideaux, who is a well-known Cornish textile artist who works all over the world. Floor to ceiling panels of specially dyed silk were installed in the Back Quay foyer and were cut to echo the stone piers and vaulting of a church. Thus, the silk appeared to hold up the ceiling. Vivien called the work "Warner's Dream".

We announced the opening date and the contractors knew that I was booking the first season. I regularly focused their minds by keeping them posted on what shows I had signed up to appear in our hole in the ground.

Chapter 23

A New Regime

CW: Looking back, I should have walked away at curtain-up. Or better still, the construction-orientated members of the board should have walked away in triumph – building job done, on time and to budget. Cue applause. Brian and John particularly had brought enormous experience and expertise in managing large construction contracts, which was something the rest of us simply couldn't begin to wave our hands at. The problem was that those two could not wave their hands at running an arts venue. They should have handed the hall over to a new board which had the relevant expertise and experience to run a middle-scale concert hall and theatre. But hindsight is wonderful and people rarely know what they don't know. They didn't resign at curtain-up and neither did I because I was afraid everything that we had worked so hard for over the last ten years would be at risk if we were unable to develop a programme for the new Hall in line with what we had promised to all those people who had supported us.

When Brian and John joined the board, I don't think they had grasped that building the Hall was just a means to an end rather than an end in itself. Their vital expertise was to realise the bricks and mortar of the new Hall and neither Sarah nor I had thought that they would want to stay on after the Hall was opened. They didn't leave; so, like an unhappy couple, Brian and I were stuck with each other.

SS: Brian was an extremely strong character and had been used to running the Highways Department, so being faced with Chris and I, who were determined to ensure that our dream was not compromised, must have frustrated him. He had his moments with Chris, and just before we were about to close the old City Hall and go on site, he said, "There's no way you are going to be Clerk of the Works." Luckily, that was not on Chris's bucket list and we had all thought that one of the design team would take it on. Chris wasn't interested in managing the contract and all the nitty-gritty stuff – such as door furniture – that made up the Bill of Quantities. Brian thankfully appointed Brian Hardman who had worked with him at County Hall. Brian was a great addition to the team.

CW: Brian Mansell did eventually succeed in clipping my wings and this time it was far more challenging, more successful, more unpleasant and much longer lasting. The efforts to raise enough funding, to make sure we had the right designs, to get as many people on side and keep them on side, as well as making sure that we put a positive spin on every item of interest and news relating to HfC had been fun but exhausting. Sarah, who had been so vital to the project since 1992, had hinted to me on more than one occasion that she was not sure she wanted to be the General Manager of the new Hall once the capital works had been completed. She felt that she was a firefighter, a fixer who thrived on a challenge, and she wasn't sure that the new Hall would do it for her. In addition, some of her family had recently moved to Bristol so she was thinking of being a Bristolian again. In other words, she might like to move back home.

I couldn't quite get my head around her thinking and I imagined that as time went by she would not be able to resist running the new Hall with me for at least a couple of years.... After all, it would be state-of-the-art and such a change from running a dilapidated building within which we had been unable to be truly adventurous with our programming. We had worked in partnership on every aspect of the vision, the plans and what we would be able to present in our new Hall. But I think Sarah thought she had done her bit, and with a change in her family circumstances she seemed convinced that the Hall needed "new blood". Someone with energy and enthusiasm, who would run the Hall with me and fulfil our vision; and the vision would be safe because we had put it all down in writing.

One board meeting soon after the old hall's closure, when the trustees were discussing the running of the new hall once it had opened, Sarah announced that she would be standing down. At first the trustees ignored her – not unusual! Then, aware that we would need to get on with looking for a replacement, Sarah faced the board and said that she had decided to leave us. We couldn't quite believe it, but it was agreed that we would talk to South West Arts and start the recruitment process. Although Sarah and I had always been equal partners, the trustees, egged on by Brian, who was a firm believer in hierarchies, decided that they were going to appoint a CEO.

It was not going to be a particularly easy task either; the board would be looking for someone to move to Cornwall, to start up a brand new Hall, to attract a brand new audience that Sarah and I were convinced was out there, someone who would be prepared, with no previous form to go on, to put on an eclectic programme. The good news was that we had planned for this leap into the unknown and Sarah, by her usual magic, had raised about £250k as a safety net. What could possibly go wrong?

We had a surprisingly good response to our advertisement, which was placed in a number of national newspapers. Sarah, a couple of trustees and I were tasked with shortlisting the applicants and after some debate selected a shortlist of five or six – all male! The trustees decided that they would invite all those shortlisted down to meet us informally on the evening before the interviews. It wasn't, however, the most relaxed of evenings! It was in fact rather strained and certainly strange for us as we looked at all these newcomers who were clearly surprised to end up together in the same room experiencing "death by sherry" and making small talk.

SS: The following day was long and arduous and neither Chris or I were on the interview panel. Instead, we were charged with looking after those waiting to be interviewed. I seem to remember that Chris and I picked out someone who we thought would fit in well and hoped that the interview panel would agree. But it was not to be.

Keith Garrow was appointed Chief Executive of the Hall for Cornwall and joined us in early 1997, giving him time to familiarise himself with the plans for the new Hall, get to know the existing staff, appoint new people and get to know Cornwall before we opened in November that year. Keith and Chris had to take isometric tests to assess their compatibility, and predictably it emerged that Keith was a detail man while Chris was a broad-brush person. In gardening terms, Keith worked in the greenhouse while Chris preferred to wield a chainsaw. Chalk and cheese can work in some marriages, but theirs was to be a stormy one.

An added humiliation was Chris being made to renegotiate a new contract with this Chief Executive. Chris was to remain Artistic Director but was also given responsibility for Operations. Chris was clearly being both harnessed and shoehorned into a job that really wasn't right for him. Half his job would now be in the greenhouse. Not quite where he was best suited! Oh, the joy of interpreting isometric tests…

I left Cornwall in November 1996 but still worked at HfC for the next twelve months until the new Hall officially opened and would drive from Bristol each week and spend two and a half days continuing with fundraising and helping Chris make sure that the contractors delivered what we had promised.

I also watched with concern as Keith started to make his mark and influence the programme choices towards what he thought the people of Cornwall wanted. Keith did have real skills and experience; he hailed from somewhere north of the Wash, was very down to earth and had experience of running venues which had to make a living without grants to support their programmes. He had a range of commercial entertainment contacts that I never even knew existed. Bums on seats was what drove him and he didn't really care who the bums belonged to or what their owners were watching as long as they had bought a ticket. He wasn't interested in all the "arty-farty" stuff that Chris cared so much about and which had played such an important part in the Lottery bid and the Public Appeal.

Keith had his own ideas and really wanted to make up his own mind on what was best for the people of Cornwall. He had a different approach to the staff, and by all accounts when someone arrived late to the office he would look up from his desk and endearingly shout, "You're late, lad – I'm not paying you to take your bloody coat off."

You could, however, be forgiven for feeling quite sorry for him. I don't know if the trustees actually gave him much support. They wanted two things from him – to get Chris off their backs and to make the books balance. Just before he was due to join us, the poor man asked for help with his re-location expenses and an advance on his salary to help get him through to his first pay day at the end of the month. The trustees declined. Not a great welcome. And I don't think he had any experience of Cornwall, not even on holiday. And here he was, pitched head first into a very tight-knit group of people, many of whom cared very passionately about "their" Hall. Bearing in mind that it's supposed to take thirty years to be fully accepted as a paid-up member of Cornish society, he found it difficult to relate quickly to people with such a stout sense of their own culture and personal identity, let alone register those arcane and invisible rhizomes of heritage and family relationships which link Cornish people together all over the world.

I don't think the board ever gave Keith much of a steer about the kind of programme they wanted. Mind you, I'm not sure they knew what they wanted, but "luckily" we had Boyden's business plan, which had set out in detail what the programme should contain. That was the programming road map. To begin with, Keith wouldn't have much room to manoeuvre.

CW: For some time, while the contractor raced to deliver a finished Hall on time, rumours that the board was proposing to appoint a "General Manager" had swirled through the Lemon Street office like October fog on the Fal. I remember one unkind person who worked in the office even took great pleasure in saying to me as often as possible, "You won't get away with that when the GM arrives." But surprise, surprise, while all eyes were on the demolition, the dig and our new building rising from the rubble of the old – and well before Keith sat at his desk – I was left in peace to book a cracking, balanced, à la Boyden, programme for the first quarter.

First-class musicians and orchestras required at least twelve months lead-in, which meant going to "pencils" and then "heavy pencils" at least eighteen months before the opening night – in other words the moment the building contract was signed – because time to extract the marketing material from the artists, time to design and print the brochure and then allow three months for people to book tickets all had to be factored in. Add in helping visiting performers to fix up dates at other venues before and after our booking, keeping an eye on the building, still making sure there was actually going to be a suitable piano for Vladimir, and involvement in the appointment of new staff, all meant that this really was a busy old time.

Meanwhile, Keith got stuck into the preoccupation that afflicts so many new CEOs – after nearly a decade of much the same graphics, he decided HfC needed a rebrand. While it kept him out of my hair to some extent, it was both extremely annoying on a personal level and very concerning that he should feel the need to do this so close to our opening. He just didn't get why it was called the Hall for Cornwall and he even made a half-hearted stab at a name change.

BL: What else could it have been called? Theatre, Arts centre, Community centre, just Centre, Concert Hall? Any of those would have either antagonised or frightened the wits out of most people in Cornwall. You gotta knaw the Cornish, boy!

We also knew that whatever transpired it had to be multi-functional, something simple, something for everyone, and that its name should be able to convey this - in other words - a Hall - for meetings, concerts, theatre, dance, exhibitions, markets, etc. Take your pick.

Adding "for Cornwall" was the simple rallying call – the Hall would be for everybody.

CW: Remember that in the early days we had absolutely no intention of building it ourselves. "A Hall for Cornwall" was simply our early battle cry which morphed into "The Hall for Cornwall Campaign." We just felt that it was disgraceful that a whole county did not have a decent venue and we wanted to prod someone into doing something about it…

BL: And of course, "A Hall for Cornwall" suggested the glaring need for and the lack of such a commodity. The name needed to be more embracing than specific - like St. Johns Hall or Truro City Hall or even possibly The Warner or The Athenaeum or…

SS: But it was not only Keith who wanted a name change; once the lease was signed and when it became clear that the project was a reality, people did begin to ask what we were going to call the new building. There was much discussion, sometimes heated. Chris favoured "Plen an Gwarry" but we thought that was a bit esoteric. "Playing Place" was proposed but was rejected on the grounds that there would be confusion with a certain village near Truro.

After ten years or so the HfC brand name was so familiar to thousands through constant exposure in the media and later through the appeal that it proved impossible to settle on an alternative.

HfC new logo 1997

Tim Guy with the new Hall for Cornwall graphics 1997

CW: People in Cornwall were familiar with the concept of a 'all – a multi-purpose space belonging to and serving its community, and which was capable of hosting a very wide range of events. We decided to stick with it. When the battle cry "A Hall for Cornwall" was no longer relevant, we simply changed the name to The Hall for Cornwall. Which is what it was.

I attended Keith's meetings with Tim Guy and fought a largely unsuccessful rear-guard action against a new logo which I felt was pretty meaningless even if it was more dynamic than our sturdy old HFC.

SS: The final outcome was certainly very different and clearly signalled the next part of Hall for Cornwall's journey. I was glad not to be part of those discussions because although I had great faith in Tim's designing ideas and skills, it marked the end of an era for us and for me in particular, as by now I spent half my time working at Hall for Cornwall and half at Bristol Old Vic. Once the new Hall opened, I would completely leave Cornwall. Naturally my emotions were mixed!

CW: A far more pressing matter for me was making sure that the details for every event in the first season's brochure were triple-checked for accuracy and that the brochure was designed and printed and ready to flop through Cornish letterboxes by mid-August – three months before the Gala. It would therefore need to be designed by mid-June and at the printers by mid-July. However rigorously I checked it – and it was not easy to get much peace amidst the frenetic preparations for the opening – I still dreaded the possibility of opening the first box and immediately spotting a mistake. But all was well and I think we were all very proud of it. In that first programme was, everything we had promised and worked towards - in colour, with a seating plan and ticket prices.

There was a note in that first season's brochure which went like this: "One of the primary aims of the Hall for Cornwall Campaign was to provide the Duchy with a concert hall that would do justice to the artists already performing in Cornwall but that would also serve to attract the best musicians across the Tamar." And we had done just that. The great unknown was how many tickets would be bought. Talk about a leap of faith! I think that St Aquinas would have been proud of us.

Keith was later moved to write in the introduction to the second programme brochure: "During the period between opening in November and the end of 1997, an average of over 5,000 people a week attended shows and concerts at the Hall, a great success by any standards."

Someone (possibly Ben) once said to me that, after a while, the very qualities that attracted you to a new lover would probably be the cause of your break-up. And so it was that as time went by, some people on the staff felt that Keith's much needed attention to detail had morphed into fiddling while Rome burned.

The West Briton

Established 1810

THE WEST BRITON is still the *highest selling weekly paper in the UK

*Source – Audit Bureau of Circulations (January-June 1997)

FREE THIS WEEK

A 24-page guide to the Hall For Cornwall – its facilities and its shows.

50p — TRURO & MID CORNWALL EDITION — Thursday, November 13, 1997

Hall For Cornwall ready

By Lee Trewhela

IT IS up to the people of the county to ensure that the Hall For Cornwall – which opens on Saturday – is a success, according to the chairman of trustees Brian Mansell.

Although there have been previews throughout this week, the [illegible] the public for an invitation-only gala concert on Saturday night.

Even though the hall has a full programme until April, Mr Mansell says it is up to the people of Cornwall to ensure that there is a full and varied bill for evermore.

"This truly is a hall for Cornwall, and it is up to the people of the county to attend and tell us what they want to see," he said. "We are going to have to pay our own way, now that we have spent all our funds on refurbishing the building," added Mr Mansell.

"We have achieved our first objective, and now it is up to all of us to achieve the next stage of making the hall a success."

The venue will be opened with a brass fanfare on Saturday, followed by a varied concert featuring internationally-renowned pianists Nettle and Markham and a performance of Carl Orff's *Carmina Burana*, featuring the Bournemouth Sinfonietta.

Chief executive Keith Garrow said that the black-tie gala evening was a "once in a lifetime" event.

● Keith Garrow, Chief Executive of the Hall For Cornwall.

The headline on the front page of The West Briton – 13 November 1997

Chapter 24

The Contractor's Memorable Moments

CW: The guys from Tilbury Douglas were quite special. Always cheerful, always able to see each new heart-stopping problem as a solution opportunity, they had a particularly intimate relationship with that rather difficult old lady we knew as Truro City Hall.

Like an aging aunt, she was full of surprises and she only revealed her darker secrets as the guys in hard hats got deep down and personal with her. In return, these guys underpinned her dodgy foundations, made her watertight again and gave her a proud new life. Martin Payne (MP) was the Senior Engineer, and Roger Quew (RQ) was the Project Manager.

MP: Soon after the start of our contract works and following the completion of the demolition works, when carrying out the underpinning operation to the old medieval wall that divided the Hall from the adjacent Woolworths Store, lots of sweets started trickling over the foundations. When we cleared back the soil it became apparent there was a false wall between the Hall and Woolworths' Pick & Mix station, and the accumulation of years of sweets rolling underneath was migrating into the new excavation.

Excavating boundary wall to start underpinning the existing structure – photograph by Mike Godfrey and Martin Payne (Tilbury Douglas)

In another discovery during excavation works, we unearthed a lot of empty bullet cases in one area while removing the floor. We later found from historic records that the Hall in the Victorian era had been used as an indoor rifle range for the public and for military reservists.

RQ: I was instructed to head for Truro and take over managing the Hall for Cornwall contract, as the current Project Manager Mike Godfrey was leaving for major heart surgery; I hasten to add, nothing to do with the contract! I had arrived as work was reaching the stage of foundations for the steel frame and the under-stage pit concrete walls being cast.

Our Senior Engineer, Martin Payne, gave me a tour of the construction site to get me up to speed. As part of that tour, we were on the roof of the adjacent building Woolworths when the fire alarm went off. I asked the obvious question: "What is that?" It transpired that we had taken down the scaffold for the demolition works the day before and all sorts of measures had been put in place to avoid setting off the alarms, and we thought that operation had been completed. An apologetic scaffolder emerged from the side door explaining that he had only popped in to retrieve a fitting and had broken an alarm glass. I asked Martin what we should do; to which his hilarious reply was, "Take your hard hat off and mingle with the customers leaving the store!" The manager of Woolworths later informed us that when they replayed the CCTV all the people who left the store with items had returned to pay for them … Only in Cornwall.

During this tour I noticed a thirty-tonne crane set up in the centre of the site (well, I suspect you all would – they are quite large) and I asked how it got there. The answer was, through the arched doorway on Back Quay. This I could not believe until the day, months later, it was time for it to go. Have you ever seen a thirty-tonne crane breathe in? It went through the opening very carefully with one inch each side to spare and not a scratch on crane or walls. Magic.

30 tonne crane on site erecting the steel frame of the building. Note the doorway it came through in the background! photograph by Mike Godfrey and Martin Payne (Tilbury Douglas)

The site offices had been set up in the former hat shop on the mezzanine floor over the Boscawen Street entrance/foyer, which was fine apart from the deep pile carpet – not a normal site office floor finish and not ideal for muddy boots, etc., from the site works. The carpet was fine when wet, but when dry it created a dust storm; we all suffered with dry sore throats and the site coffee consumption went up!

Talking of dry throats, there was another remedy, "Ye Old Ale House", which became our alternative meeting room-cum-R&R for our team, and I can confirm that the contract's success was down to many pints of Doom Bar! And a lot of deep discussion on the day's issues.

Another aid to the team's wellbeing was Ann's Coffee Shop next door on Boscawen Street, which sold the most delicious doughnuts – these helped the team spirit but not my waistline.

A "Topping Out Ceremony" was arranged for when we had completed the roof decking, and this was set up on the roof, with press invited, and was to be carried out by Lady Mary Holborow, The Lord Lieutenant for Cornwall. Everyone assembled for the photoshoot. A barrel of Doom Bar had been set up and Lady Mary was given a pint to christen the roof, but her throwing skills were a bit off and instead of wetting the roof she soaked Brian Hardman, the site Clerk of Works. The construction team thought this was quite appropriate as he did like Doom Bar; then it was pasties all round for guests and the whole works team – and the barrel did get emptied.

The 'Topping Out Ceremony' carried out by Lady Mary Holborow with Peter Fazakerly, Mike Godfrey, Roger Quew, Chris, Keith Garrow – photograph by Brian Hardman

The regular evening site visits and tours of the works progress by the HfC trustees were always interesting and got more exciting as the construction took shape and both laymen and contract workers could start to see the beginnings of a theatre. To the laymen, it remained far too long as a shell before we reached the finishing stages and all the shiny bits.

As you have previously read, there were a lot of planning issues and these did have an effect on our programmed works. I can recall one particular site meeting where I was frantically chasing details to enable progressing the works, and stressing we were falling behind the programme, only for it to be announced by the client's Project Coordinator, Peter Fazakerley, at the end of that meeting that HRH The Duke of Cornwall would be attending the official opening of the theatre on the 11th November 1997 and this was top secret. I nearly went for heart surgery as well!! All I could see in my mind's eye were the headlines in the local press: "ROYAL VISIT CANCELLED: contractor fails to complete contract, local community devastated." Somehow, with a great deal of effort by all, we managed to achieve that date.

The input from English Heritage for the listed buildings section of the works did cause us a number of challenges, for example having to keep the chimney in the Back Quay building at roof level and remove all existing support below and install new support within the roof void. Our suggestion, to replicate the chimney in fibreglass, did not go down very well at all, but would have saved a mountain of work and money.

Trustee Site Visit – Chris, Jane Lofthouse, Debbie and Claire Bowden-Dan – photograph by HfC

Lady Mary Holborow and VIPs on a site tour – photograph by HfC

Later in the contract, when the works were underway inside the Back Quay building, i.e. getting to the finishings, we found the inside of this building was near derelict, with plaster hanging off the walls and rotten flooring, we even had to evict the pigeons before we could commence work. We had a visit from the English Heritage inspector and a question was raised referencing the lath and plaster partitions. With large areas of lime plaster hanging off the walls and most missing altogether, we were instructed to screw the plaster back to the laths. This was attempted with little success, so plasterboard and skim were used and the rooms duly took shape.

Another problem arose late in the contract while excavating out the old floor slabs of Back Quay foyer to lay a new concrete floor at the required level. We uncovered the foundations of the main support column for the building which turned out to be just a pile of rubble. Work was stopped while Ian Hick, the Structural Engineer, designed the necessary piling and underpinning. We then sited a mini piling rig in the foyer and work recommenced driving piles, diamond-core drilling to the column, and inserting steel beams to carry the load. This was challenging at a time when we should have been installing the café and box office, but again it all got completed and you can't see any of the essential work that were carried out.

Back Quay the major work required to support the chimney with nothing beneath it – photograph by Roger Quew (Tilbury Douglas)

Underpinning works to main support column in Back Quay – Photograph by Roger Quew (Tilbury Douglas)

After this, we started work to the granite arched entrance from Boscawen Street which involved grit-blasting all the granite columns and arches. This was organised to be carried out over a weekend, when the building would be empty, all planned to the last inch, everything ready for the early start on Saturday morning. It was also my weekend off and I was away camping for the whole weekend. The grit-blasting went well, with all paint and stains etc. accumulated over the years removed, it looked brand new and was completed in one day. But – and this was a big but – the cleaners for the Council offices arrived to clean the Council chamber above the foyer on Sunday morning to find the chamber completely covered in dust and grit. Unbeknown to us, there were vent ducts running from the chamber to Boscawen Foyer to let fresh air into the room. A frantic clean-up operation was set in motion by my Construction Manager, Colin Crabb, mobilising everyone he could get hold of, and all was cleaned up for their Monday council meeting. I arrived on Monday morning and got the full story of the weekend. They did well - the foyer looked a picture and my camping weekend was peaceful and relaxing!

There was one particular day I clearly remember as the moment I first got the feeling of a theatre and not a construction site. On a Saturday we arranged for waste skips to be run all day to site, and with a crew of men we set about clearing all packaging waste etc. from the building. The scaffolding had just been dismantled, and by the end of that day you could see an auditorium (minus the seating). It looked a huge space, a very satisfying moment.

Just when you think you're there, something has to shatter your confidence. On 10th November '97, the eve of His Royal Highness's visit to the new Hall, I drove around Lemon Quay on my way into the site and saw a crowd of workmen in the street outside the site entrance all staring down at the road. I pulled up to find out why, only to see water hosing out of the road surface. A South West Water Inspector was already on site in his nice clean blue uniform and cap. He said the water main was fractured. We had planed the road surface that morning ready to relay the area – this had been our only site compound area for the whole works – and the vibration from planing the road surface had cracked the old cast iron main. I said it must be repaired as we were resurfacing the road in two hours. His reply was alarming: "I have no operatives, they are all on a safety course today." My response was that HRH The Duke of Cornwall was due on this spot tomorrow at 10.00 a.m. "Do you want to tell him?" In true Cornish spirit, he shot off in his van and was back on site within half an hour, off with jacket, on with boots, and into the muddy water to fix it himself – a real star.

Boscawen Street Foyer refurbished

We resurfaced the road as we had planned but were unable to apply the yellow lines until the following morning, so when The Duke of Cornwall arrived, we were relieved when he did not step on the wet yellow lines, as we knew he loved his old shoes. Then we were all presented to him and he toured the whole of the new Hall in its pristine glory ready for the Gala Night on Saturday 15th November 1997.

The Gala Night was special and went well, with Chris giving a passionate speech from the new stage, which left no one unaware of his satisfaction in achieving his dream. The site team and their wives had a great time, but we had assumed, wrongly, that there would be some food and had not eaten, so after the performance, and too late to get into any restaurant, we all walked down to Burger King in our tuxes and with the ladies in their long dresses, looking somewhat out of place ordering our cheeseburgers etc. – but who cared.

A few days later I overheard Danny La Rue complaining about his dressing room not being up to his expected standard. The dressing rooms and green room were formed within part of the old Boscawen listed building, which meant that the original stone walls were just painted white.

...You can never please everyone.

Chapter 25

Planning and Programming the new Hall

Duchy Opera's marketing material for Die Fledermaus

CW: In the spring of 1997, the contractors were still going hell for leather because the opening date was set come what may. But alarm bells were ringing because they were still building and installing things which needed our attention. For example, one afternoon someone from Tilbury Douglas rang through and asked me to mark up the entire backstage plans with every 13 amp socket required. By teatime, please. Ooh! and could I just confirm where I wanted the mirrors in the dressing rooms? And did they need lights around them? Stuff seemed to just keep on arriving. Seats, lights, curtains, cable, crockery, ovens …To add to all that, Duchy Opera was winding itself up for its first production in the new Hall in March 1998. In spite of an unkind person once calling our baby the Hall for Warner, Ben and I were not deterred from co-directing *Die Fledermaus* – how could we resist? The big chorus number "Champagne! Champagne!" seemed particularly appropriate. We also had sets to design, rights to secure, musicians to book, singers to audition, in order to have everything settled before the final rush to the opening and be ready to go into rehearsals after the panto.

The biggest job of all was finalising the HfC programme covering the opening in November through to March, designing and distributing the brochure and getting the tickets on sale. While at the same time pencilling events for the second season …

The hole-in-the-ground syndrome had improved because the hole now had not only a roof but an impressive auditorium. While that definitely made a trip to Truro seem more attractive, the elephant in the Hall turned out to be geographical.

When I was young and on tour, we just chucked everything and everyone into the back of a battered Ford Transit and then took turns to drive through the night to our next venue. The more established artists who we were trying to attract to the new Hall had moved on from that sort of caper. However, while they were keen on getting a good night's sleep in a comfy bed, they were also keen on maximising their weekly earnings. Most thought that Cornwall started just after Bristol and that when they got to Exeter it would be but a short hop to Truro. The reality was that to do one show in the Hall would knock out the better part of three days of a visiting company's week. It was therefore uneconomic. It soon became clear to me that either the price we paid performers would have to increase or I'd have to find them a gig on the way down to Cornwall and a gig on the way back. I set about establishing a network of venues which were far enough away from Truro not to poach our audience but close enough to allow time for a get-in before a performance after a day's drive. Places like Exeter, Taunton, Street, Ilfracombe and Barnstaple were all prepared to play ball because it was win–win for everyone. For example, Humph or even the Bournemouth Sinfonietta could play Bristol, Taunton, Truro, Street and then perhaps somewhere on the South Coast. The model worked well for cabaret, classical music ensembles, comedians, folk, talks, etc., etc. The venues got a more keenly priced show because the artists got a better return from a week on the road.

There was another unintended consequence occasioned by the concern expressed by the small-scale arts centres in Cornwall that the new Hall would put them out of business. It was similar to the unfounded fear, expressed some years later, that life as they knew it for the smaller established gardens in Cornwall would come to an end once Eden opened. I worked hard to persuade the arts centres that actually the smaller gardens would thrive on the back of the increased number of garden visitors coming to the county. The Hall would be bringing down artists which no 100-seat venue could afford but there would be potential audience development opportunities for the smaller venues. They could host the education programmes offered by large, Arts Council-funded companies in surroundings more suitable for workshops, and these workshops, which, spread across the whole of Cornwall, would generate new audiences for not only the main event in the Hall but would also bring young people into the arts centres. An added benefit for the Hall was that we could programme a market or another fit up the day after the show.

SS: 1997 was certainly a busy year for all of us, spinning numerous plates in a hailstorm! By contrast, Debbie McCrory who was the Box Office Manager remembers those times with great affection:

DMc: We started selling seats for the first Christmas Panto in the summer of 1997. They sold like hot cakes. When all the seats in the auditorium were set, I used to wander around looking out at this huge space, thinking, my God, it's going to be full soon. The fire brigade came one morning to inspect the entrances and exits and the seating plan. Their visit was going well until we came to the row of seats at the top of the front stalls, where there was a wide walkway before the upper block of raised seating. The decision was made that one row of seats had to come out because there was not enough disabled access. That was a huge stress for the team, but especially for me and the box office, now having to tell up to thirty-nine people on every performance that their seats did not exist anymore. Very distressing, but we managed to rearrange everyone. Phew!!

CW: Most theatres are in use for about twenty-four hours a week. That is a very poor use of expensive plant. We had always been determined that the new Hall should be open as much as possible during the day so that people who might not normally come to a performance could get to know the new building, find out where the loos were, have a cuppa and feel comfortable in it. We'd had a bit of practice running daytime flea markets in the City Hall, and they were financially so important to us that had we moved them into a temporary home on the other side of Back Quay during the build period. And yet, at public meetings people would still try and catch me out by demanding an assurance that the markets would be included in the new Hall programme. It was an easy promise to make – how many theatres do you know that can make £1,000 a day with minimal effort? When things were tough financially in City Hall, I used to pray for a nice wet summer so we could run extra markets for the bedraggled tourists.

Of course, nothing is for nothing, and programming a daytime market restricts the type of show which can be safely programmed for the same evening. The amount of time needed to change from flat floor to seating is one critical component, and the amount of time required to get in, light and tech the incoming performance is the other. Bert Biscoe, in his memories, talked about his first-hand experience of lugging 500 folding chairs from the cramped store underneath the stage, then linking them together in straight rows with appropriate space for escape routes. Some brave souls would try to number them. If the chairs were pre-numbered that meant setting them out in the correct order, which took more time and which, more often than not, went wrong, leading to frantic wrenching apart of the chairs in order to reset them in the correct order, probably as the audience was starting to arrive. The seat numbers were painted on the back of the seats, making it impossible for the workers who were placing them to see from the front whether the seats were set in the right order. Some promoters would try to attach paper seat numbers to the fronts of the chairs after they were set. Quite often these flimsy sheets of paper, held in place by Sellotape, would be dislodged by members of the audience as they sidled down the rows looking for their seats. For either method to be successful, the seats had to be laid out to a predetermined plan. Not for the faint-hearted, it was chaotic, noisy and stressful, and the laying out of the auditorium quickly and correctly required several strong and even-tempered people who could cope with bashing their heads on the low under-stage joists. Oh, and don't forget that the letter which identified each row had to be fixed to the floor in some way. Most promoters gave up; just didn't even attempt to use numbered seating. Particularly as it was a flat-floor auditorium, this meant that audiences would come early in order to "bag" the best seats – usually before the layout was complete. It was time-consuming and labour-intensive – and the end result was not a quality experience for the audience's eyes, ears or posteriors.

Ben and I had noticed that all this kerfuffle did not occur very often in Bracknell because the turn round was not practical. It took too long, was too labour intensive and too expensive. We were determined that "our" seats could be set and removed as fast and economically as possible with as few staff as possible. The new Hall's tiered seating would be contained in giant wheeled chests of drawers which would slide out or withdraw at the command of one operative holding the controls for the motors which powered their movement. The seats were stored in situ and automatically popped up or folded down depending on which direction the drawers were moving. It was brilliant – once we'd worked out how to stop the "drawers" jamming!

Even so, even with the magic chests of drawers, the ideal show to follow a market was one which had minimal staging requirements. Dave Allen, with his single stool, his one glass of gin and two pre-rigged lights would have been perfect.

Please forgive me for mentioning a much later problem, which eventually became a perfectly formed solution opportunity of which I was very proud. The small venues did a good job of nurturing emerging modern dance companies which, having developed very fast, were soon knocking on HfC's door because, with its eighteen-metre-wide proscenium, the new Hall made a fabulous dance house which presented the likes of Random, Motionhouse, Ballet Rambert and the Royal Ballet. The arts centres felt it was unfair that they had taken the early risks with unknown contemporary dance companies only to lose them to the Hall when those emerging companies became established. Anthony Waller from the Cornwall Dance Agency and I devised a scheme which gave a payback to the venues which had taken the early risks. We would pay a percentage of the Hall's box office takings from newly established big dance companies like Random. We went to the Arts Council to discuss funding for it. It was such a novel idea that we had to explain it three times before they understood our plan – but they eventually gave us a substantial grant. Sadly, it made the Hall's bean counters very unhappy. They just didn't get it.

SS: In the first season of the new Hall, we programmed a wide range of "one night only" small-scale shows – cabaret, comedians, jazz, small bands and classical music ensembles. These included Danny La Rue, Fascinating Aida, Bjorn Again, Humph 'n' Helen, Jethro, Chris Bonington, Kathakali, Acker Bilk, Patrick Moore, the bands of the Coldstream Guards and the Royal Marines, the Musically Mobile benefit concert, That'll Be The Day, Fabulous Fats, the Roy Wood Big Band, TAODS Carolaire, Bash Street Theatre, Rootjoose, Cornwall Youth Orchestra, Fairport Convention, Jactito's Macbeth (for two nights), the BBC Big Band and Boys of the Lough, John Harle, Miracle Theatre's Robin Hood, and the Fusion Guitar Duo.

CW: Classical music included a Piano Subscription Series with Leslie Howard (who had helped to choose the Steinway), Vladimir Ashkenazy and John Lill. The Suites and Serenades Series included The Guildhall Strings, Zephyrus, and the Haffner Wind Ensemble. There was a four-part orchestral series with three Bournemouth Sinfonietta concerts, and one with the Academy of St Martin in the Fields. And a lovely lunchtime series called Brahms with Bang & Olufsen.

Larger shows which played for a week included Middle Ground's The Holly and the Ivy, Whirligig Theatre's Babe the Sheep Pig, Rambert Dance Company, Duchy Opera's Die Fledermaus with Ben, and Wallace and Gromit in A Grand Night Out.

Added to all that, there were to be occasional lunchtime concerts, plus the fairs, and the flea markets. And of course, there was Basil Critchley's Snow White and the Seven Dwarfs, presented by Albermarle Montrose Productions.

SS: Chris programmed in this way because we had to find audiences for different products in order to work out who our audiences were and what they were interested in. We had discussed this when we were putting together our business plan with Peter Boyden. He advised us to raise extra funds to put into a "programme pot" to enable us to experiment and which would allow us to fail with some things that might not attract an audience. We took Peter's advice on board and although we did not end up with the amount we had hoped to put in our "programme pot", we did have enough to give Chris a degree of flexibility – as you can see from the wide variety he programmed in that first season. It was, as they say, trial and error, but the number of tickets sold in that first season was so impressive. It was clear that there were audiences hungry for theatre, comedy, music and dance. Some generated income for the Hall but some did not. Chris had to work out and balance the programme so that we could provide an eclectic range of work that would generate enough income to keep the Hall going.

CW: All in the preparation, as they say but first, we needed to make sure that the contractors met the deadline of the hall's grand opening!

Chapter 26

A Tale of Two Openings

CW: In a final coup, our two indefatigable ladies – Sarah and Lady Mary – persuaded HRH The Duke of Cornwall to not only attend the opening night but to give the cue to the backstage staff to raise the curtain. The scary bit was that we therefore had to agree a date for this special curtain-up. And stick to it.

There was still masses to do – lanterns to hang, cables to be run, house tabs and masking to be flown, lighting to be rigged, sound and comms systems to be checked, bars and fridges to be stocked, ovens to be fired up, glasses and crockery to be washed and volunteer stewards to be trained.

The new restaurant– photograph by Roger Quew (Tilbury Douglas)

There had been some hairy moments along the way, not least the exhaustive proving of the smoke integrity of various sections of the building. I don't know how many fire doors there were, but it seemed like hundreds and every door had smoke seals which were tested with real smoke by the fire brigade. Every smoke sensor had to pass a similar test. The water pressure in the sprinkler system had to be checked and signed off. The lifts had to be proved. Every exit sign and corridor light had to be checked to make sure that, if there was a power cut, the battery system would automatically take over. The magnetic locking system on every door had to be checked to make sure that in the event of a fire all doors would automatically unlock. And so it went on, from basement to fly tower. The snagging list seemed worryingly long as the opening night loomed and failures which had been rectified failed again, had to be fixed again and then retested. There could be no Entertainment Licence until every bit of kit was signed off. And without the licence, we would not be allowed to open. It was a bit nerve-wracking!

While the contractors were racing to deal with the "snagging", the skeleton HfC staff, working out of our temporary office in Lemon Street – ironically, just a few doors down from the old Arts Centre Trust office – started to interview people for the senior management posts in the new Hall. The trustees, against all advice, saw fit to appoint a Marketing Manager who everyone thought would be quite hopeless. Luckily, on taking up references, it emerged that this guy had never worked in one of the theatres listed in his CV. What a relief! Once these Heads of Marketing, Catering, Technical, Front of House, etc., had been appointed, they in turn set about recruiting the staff who would support our seven-day-a-week operation. There was a real sense of excitement for both old and new staff when we eventually moved into the new building. Although it had never been "beyond our wildest dreams", but it was pretty exciting.

Before the grand opening night when The Duke of Cornwall, would cue the house curtain to rise for the first time, we needed to check that everything and everyone worked safely and efficiently. We decided to have some previews – just like a West End theatre! And we realised that they would be a splendid way of thanking the huge number of supporters who had kept faith from the early days. It would have been lovely to have invited them all to the grand opening, but sadly, major donors and the great and the good had to be given priority.

We decided to run a series of private "dress rehearsals" for invited audiences in each of the five auditorium formats. It would allow us to test all things technical, including the acoustics, and would also give as many as possible of the 120 brand new volunteer front of house staff a chance to practise their training. We soon learnt that the old adage "if anything can go wrong it definitely will, probably at the worst possible moment" also applies to the theatre.

The 120 volunteers were a particular challenge. Although volunteers, they would, along with the box office staff, be the main point of contact with our customers. They would also be responsible for important matters of safety, such as evacuation in case of a fire or a bomb scare. They would have to know the building inside out and be capable of fielding people who felt ill or who had had some sort of accident. They were a wonderful gang but they were a bit high-maintenance – volunteers often feel they are a cut above some other employees because they are giving their time. Their motives for volunteering are often quite varied. They may want access to free tickets, or at least to watch the shows while on duty – which they were not supposed to do because they needed to keep an eye on the audience in the same way as stewards at a football match have their backs to the pitch. Some volunteers were there for social reasons. I often felt I was running a sort of upmarket cultural dating agency … What they all had in common, however, was that they cared passionately about the Hall and they generously gave their time.

The first preview (in 900-seat mode) was also the first time that the new lanterns had been on for any length of time. Before LED bulbs, big theatre lanterns got very hot. After about half an hour the incredibly sensitive smoke sensors picked up the vapour from the paint on the hot lanterns. The sensors set off the fire alarms and the system automatically alerted the fire brigade. The 900 people in the first audience had just settled into the first ever performance in the so eagerly anticipated new Hall when they were required to evacuate. As the last of the audience was leaving the building, they were met by firemen in full kit, lugging hosepipes and urgently looking for a fire that no one could find. Luckily, it wasn't raining. We felt that the evacuation of so many people had all gone rather well, although some suspected that I'd done it on purpose. However, when it happened on the following two evenings, the fire brigade – like Queen Victoria – were not amused.

After that, I had to make a little pre-show speech reminding people that they were at a dress rehearsal and that things would probably go wrong. I think it added a certain frisson to the proceedings. Anyway, that week was thrilling for everyone concerned. After nearly ten years of rolling the HfC boulder uphill with the help of so many different people, it was absolutely the bees' knees for anyone who had been involved to see the performances

Back Quay foyer – photograph by Roger Quew (Tilbury Douglas)

in the finished spaces. Having begun life in our imaginations many years previously they had then morphed into drawing after amended drawing on the Hocking and Newton CAD (Computer-Aided Design) system. And now, here these imagined spaces were, for real! We had in effect built at least five different auditoria. And people were now actually sitting in each of them, laughing, listening, watching and applauding. For the first time they were also able to experience some of the other beautiful public spaces which had been created by Roger Hocking and Paul Newton. And of course, they could try out all the new loos and get served promptly with a drink in the interval……And we could see if the new signage worked for people not yet familiar with the new building.

An added bonus came just before opening, when Councillor Pie-in-the-Sky rang me to ask if I could find a job in the new Hall for his grandson …

There was quite a lot of public excitement about The Duke of Cornwall's proposed visit, which was to include a walkabout on Lemon Quay and after which he would come out of the front entrance into Boscawen Street to greet the crowds gathered there. The issue of

The Trelawney Bar – photograph by Roger Quew (Tilbury Douglas)

Auditorium completed with seating and lighting – photograph by Roger Quew (Tilbury Douglas)

who would pay for the crowd barriers and the police costs became a problem which nearly scuppered the whole affair. HfC didn't have a budget for this, and to this day I don't know who actually did pay. The royal visit had to be planned in the minutest detail – who His Royal Highness would meet, who would host his visit, what the Cornish police required and what the close protection officers demanded. I remember a dedicated loo had to be set aside, searched by the anti-terrorist people and then sealed and guarded in case it was needed.

A special opening night brochure was designed with a foreword written and signed by The Duke of Cornwall. Tickets were by invitation only and had to be strictly rationed because the 1,000 available were nowhere near enough. His Royal Highness was to sit in the front row of the upper part of the auditorium, and particular care had to be taken with the allocation of the seats closest to him. The names and addresses of everyone sitting close enough to pose a threat had to submitted to the security people.

Just as there weren't enough tickets to satisfy the demand, so there was not enough time in one evening to include all the proposals for the programme because everyone wanted to showcase the full range of Cornwall's performing arts. There had to be a choir, the youth orchestra should play, Ben should sing, Duchy Opera should do a number, there should be theatre, dance and ballet. The wish list was so long, I worked out that the performance would last at least four hours. Eventually, it got whittled down to a programme which still tested to the full the comfort levels of the new seating.

Helped enormously by the media, which kept everyone updated weekly, expectation was steadily growing. The week that we were due to open, the West Briton published a guide to the Hall, its facilities and its shows. Everything that we had hoped for was happening!

After all the preparations, after all the previews, after all the efforts of so many people to translate that twinkle in Uncle Benjamin's blue eye into a £6.5m reality. Back Quay was filled with excited onlookers (safely behind the aforementioned crowd barriers) who cheered HRH The Duke of Cornwall as he walked by on his way to open the new Hall. We had lift-off …

Everyone had to be seated before The Duke of Cornwall came into the auditorium. When he did enter, everyone stood until his close protection officer had placed his personal cushion on his seat. I knew that he'd been having back trouble, but I did wonder if he'd heard rumours about the length of the programme. When His Royal Highness was finally installed in what would have been the centre of the front row of the balcony in a conventional theatre, the audience sat expectantly. There was a subdued buzz. Conscious of 1,000 pairs of eyes upon us, I had to make conversation through the inevitable delay before we got the signal that The Duke of Cornwall should press his cue button. He was

INSIDE: Your guide to the hall, its facilities and its shows

The Hall for Cornwall

Your guide to Cornwall's exciting new entertainment venue

Free with the West Briton, Cornishman and Cornish Guardian

an easy person to talk to, but then I guess he's had a fair bit of practice. I remember thinking of all the things which could go wrong at the worst possible moment. I was finding it hard to concentrate when His Royal Highness asked me what I did. I replied that I was the Artistic Director. "Oh, good," he said, "Thank God they've got one."

Eventually, the house lights dimmed. The audience hushed. The deep crimson house tabs remained lit. The twinklies dimmed. A spot then picked out the Button, and the Royal Hand which pressed it. And the curtain slid silently upwards to reveal a packed stage ...

SS: Chris was always a bit of a dreamer! His account makes a great tale and I'm sure what he has described is what he would have wanted. The fact is that The Duke of Cornwall wasn't actually there at the Gala Opening on the 15th November. He had agreed to come and "raise the curtain" but we had to change the date a few times because of delays to the completion of the hall. Unfortunately, His Royal Highness was unable to attend the Gala but he did agree to come to open the Hall for Cornwall officially a few days before. Chris is right about the sniffer dogs and the other security arrangements.

The Duke of Cornwall came into the box office from Back Quay to meet a small number of us, who were both excited and very nervous! There was a very large crowd outside, who were kept away from the entrance with help from police and the barriers. His Royal Highness was a popular and regular visitor to Cornwall, so always attracted a crowd. However, on this day it was more significant than usual because, apart from the opening of the new Hall, it was one of the first public appearances that The Duke of Cornwall had made since the untimely death of Diana, Princess of Wales at the end of August.

RH: I particularly remember the day of the official opening. We were all arranged in a partial circle in a clockwise direction in order of "importance" in the Assembly Room, such that The Duke of Cornwall would meet the trustees first, followed by the HfC management team, the design consultants, the contractor, etc. On entering the room, His Royal Highness did his own thing and went around the ensemble in reverse direction. When he got to me, he admired my tie, one of a limited edition in satin silk, purpose made for HfC by local artist Vivien Prideaux, who had also designed the "Warner's Dream" silk artwork hung in the Back Quay foyer.

SS: We then escorted him up to the front row of the balcony through a door into the main auditorium. He was very relaxed, and more than put us at our ease. As we approached the door it opened, and I asked him to walk in first – straight into a blacked-out auditorium! He walked confidently along the front row of the balcony to his seat and sat between Chris and I. We only had trustees, a few members of staff, the design team, the contractor and security people in the audience. On stage a large group of schoolchildren sang a number of songs including a couple of Cornish favourites. When they sang "Trelawny", The Duke of Cornwall turned to me and asked what this particular song was. I explained that it was a very popular Cornish anthem which all Cornish people sang whenever possible!

HRH The Duke of Cornwall being presented with a bouquet – photograph by Cameracraft

At the end of the performance, we left the auditorium and congregated in Boscawen Street entrance where Chris's six-year-old daughter presented His Royal Highness with a bouquet of flowers. She was smiling in her Polwhele House School blazer, and I still have that photograph, which always looks a little strange as I am wearing the same colour suit as The Duke of Cornwall!

CW: Ah! Yes. Well! Thank you. Ahem. I think I got a bit confused. Your account explains the fact that you and I strode out holding hands onto the stage on the 15th and thanked all the people who had helped us from the beginning. I can't remember The Duke of Cornwall being part of that.

SS: No, he wasn't, Chris, but instead we had well over 250 people on stage at any one time, either singing in one of the choirs or playing in one of the orchestras or brass bands. It was a real spectacle and such a beautifully organised evening.

CW: Now I think about it, I recall that, at the end of the Gala, we did the old gag of having a huge drum roll, which caused everyone to stand up expecting the National Anthem and then the drum roll morphed into Trelawny. I'm sure you wouldn't have allowed us to do such a thing with the heir to the throne in the audience. Nevertheless, we did get some cracking publicity out of his visit!

Chris and Sarah on stage – Gala Night Opening – photograph by Nigel Greenhalgh

SS: The auditorium was absolutely packed, and we were so pleased that many of those who helped to realise this dream were there on Gala Night to witness the first official performance at Hall for Cornwall. There wasn't a spare seat and the auditorium looked spectacular as everyone waited for the evening to begin. Some of those who joined us were members of the design and construction team who had worked tirelessly to deliver the Hall for Cornwall.

RH: It was a proud moment for us all, and it should be said that the successful completion of the project was complemented by an excellent working relationship between Chris, Sarah, the trustees, the design team, the Clerk of Works, the Project Co-ordinator and the contractor's site management team.

Members of the design and construction teams for Hall for Cornwall

SS: We did all get on well together. The whole team wanted to be at that wonderful Gala evening, where the atmosphere throughout was electric. We felt a great sense of occasion. We were full of excitement as the curtain went up. And I bet most of us breathed a sigh of relief when it finally came back down again!

CW: But what could possibly have gone wrong?

BL: For me, I think the evening went by in a haze of euphoria looking out into that beautiful space crowded with people, and at the same time disbelief that it was really happening and that we'd actually done it. A strange, rather dream-like memory, now – and I have no idea what was in the programme!

Choirs and orchestra on stage – Gala Night Opening 15th November 1997 – photograph by Nigel Greenhalgh

33. Twenty years or so later, both Chris and I met The Duke of Cornwall at a reception in the Royal Cornwall Museum. We had time for a real conversation and we told him what a difference his early patronage had made to the Campaign. He seemed rather surprised.

Chapter 27

PS

SS: From a standing start, between Sunday 16th November and Saturday 6th December (so not including the panto), Chris's records show we sold roughly 15,000 tickets. And we'd kept our promises.

CW: Audiences see a full house and naturally assume the venue is making a bomb. It doesn't work like that. The problem is, in the game of chance played by the venue and the companies which it books, the odds are nearly always stacked against the venue because the standard deal is a 70/30 split of the gross box office take – in favour of the performer. If the venue sells 15,000 tickets at an average of £12 – that's £180,000 – the performers get £126,000 and the venue gets just £54,000 to pay all its running costs. Occasionally the venue can drive a better deal, say 60/40, but sometimes top comedians will demand 90/10. Some performers demand a guarantee – they get paid even if the show flops. And everyone wants their money on the night. It's hard for any venue to break even, let alone save money in order to subsidise community rents …Especially when you've just lost a whole row of you best seats, costing the Hall about £50,000 a year - for ever.

SS: It's fair to say it is a struggle. I have been involved with theatres since those days at the Hall for Cornwall and know how difficult it is to get the programme right. It is a balance to make sure that visiting companies or individuals cover all their costs and more, but also important for the venue not to make a loss on a show. Over the years, I and many others have experimented with different ways of making it fair for each party and, whichever way, there is not often a win–win outcome. Venues make provision for losses in their budgets by ensuring that at least once a year there is a "cash cow", which, historically, is the Christmas show or pantomime. The income generated from these popular shows can see a theatre or venue through leaner times, offsetting those shows that don't make money and enabling programmers to take a few risks along the way. As well as this, programming new theatre productions is often not an instant success as it takes time to build audiences. Those audiences need to build trust in a venue - after all they are paying for tickets and want an enjoyable or a thought-provoking experience. Once the audience trusts an organisation, it can be more confident when taking a risk – but not too often, as this can result in losing an audience. It is a fine balance. There are some wonderful production companies and theatre out there which deserve to be programmed and shared with audiences. That is why it is so important for a venue to know and understand its audience. It's a challenging world to be part of, but a lot of fun and so rewarding.

CW: I agree! Running a venue is a bit like running a restaurant – it's personal: you need to be there to greet the punters and to talk to them again in the foyer after curtain-down. As Crispin Raymond observed, you need to know who is occupying your seats and you should also try to get to know them. And sometimes you say, "Hey, trust me, try this, I'm sure you'll like it." But if you let people down, the effect is akin to them having a bad meal in your restaurant. You will have to work incredibly hard to rebuild trust and to get them to come back. My mantra to the staff used to go like this: if a customer has a good experience, they will tell five others – if they have a bad experience, they will tell thirty.

I will always be grateful to Mike Alfreds for agreeing to bring his new company, Method and Madness, to Truro when the Hall was still a hole in the ground. Mike was a very distinguished director who had a glittering career all over the world. In the UK he had directed for the RSC and the Globe, and his agreement to a three-year relationship was a significant endorsement for HfC. The word was that he was in receipt of an eye-watering three-year grant from Arts Council England, which may well have encouraged him to take the risk. Nevertheless, with Method and Madness in the HfC diary, others soon had the courage to follow his lead.

Remember Jethro? After a sell-out show on a Saturday night, I was standing in the wings while he waited to go back on for his curtain calls. He'd had a full house in stitches for the whole evening and there were going to be many people with sore ribs in the morning. The audience was going wild, demanding more. Jethro sidled up to me in the gloom and said something which was drowned out by the applause. "What?" I bellowed. "Us is free Monday, boy," he shouted back. I didn't understand. "Us is free Monday. You get on out there and tell 'em. Go on!" So I did. I asked if everyone in the house would tell others that there was to be another gig the day after tomorrow. There were roars of approval. "Promise?" I asked. More roars. Jethro came out and the audience lifted the roof. The box office opened on Monday morning and on Monday night, purely by word of mouth, us had another full house.

DMc: Jasper Carrot came to play HfC - the nicest man ever - all he wanted on his rider was a bottle of mineral water and a salad sandwich. Not like Van Morrison, who was in a bad mood from the moment he stepped into the building. He hated his dressing room, I had to run and find a portable TV so he could watch Neighbours! then he went on stage for only twenty odd minutes and left. As you can imagine, the crowd was really miffed, we all tried to explain that Van had appeared and there would be no refunds. We had to call the Police because most of the audience did a sit in!! Not a great memory.

CW: I remember that night too. For most of his twenty minutes Van sang with his back to the audience. People were very angry. In those days you usually had to pay performers in cash on the night so immediately after curtain-up my job was to work out the "contras". These are supplies and services requested by the artists e.g. food and drink and extra stage hands which were deducted from a performer's share of the ticket sales, which in the case of Van Morrison's 70/30 split worked out at around £10,000. His belligerent company manager accused us of stealing one tea towel and he wouldn't back down. He might have counted his tea towels, but he hadn't counted the stagehands. He didn't realise that in revenge I had charged him for an extra man.

DMc: One of my funniest memories is "The Chippendales". I was backstage, while they set up all afternoon and the guys used a temporary workout gym set up in the Assembly Room. They all ate a lot of pasta for their dinner! I have never seen so many screaming women, it was a bit scary. I helped backstage, as in one scene three Chippendales were in a shower cubicle, which meant I was in the dark behind the shower pumping water from a container into the shower head! I had to struggle not to laugh, as they really were butt naked!! My other job was to rub baby oil on two blow up pink chairs!! Don't ask …

Paul Daniels and the lovely Debbie McGee appeared one night, and the tickets just were not selling very well, we had around 290 people coming to a 900 seat capacity. Paul came to the box office asking how many people were coming, I said sorry it's not a great audience – Paul said "but it will be". He had his gold Rolls Royce parked outside the box office doors, and he went out and stuck his flyers all over it. Then he and Debbie went all over Truro shaking hands and asking people to come to the show for a discount price. Needless to say, he played to an almost full auditorium, what a great guy.

Ken Dodd – well all I can say is that the staff were exhausted, and basically had to push him off stage at 1.30am !! after two shows that day…

Danny La Rue – came to the star dressing room, which was a "wet room" no carpet, he took one look from the doorway and said – "I want carpet, never have I had concrete under my feet before a show." I had to run to Hardy Carpets who kindly gave me an off cut in a cream colour, got back and laid it out; he liked it BUT then he said, "It's terribly dull in here, can you get some flowers or something?" Off I went again, this time to Casa Fina, who loaned me big silk flowers and a vase.

Danny was happy and did a fantastic show. I went in the next morning to take back the carpet and vase – but the vase had gone. A note said that Danny loved it and had taken it home!!! HfC paid Casa Fina for the flowers and the vase.

SS: It's not just about the shows though, what fascinates me is that Hall for Cornwall has become a social hub for so many people – audiences, staff and volunteers. Over the years I have heard so many stories about the fun people have had at the Hall. One of my favourites, is from an ex-member of staff, Phill Wills who explains:

Back in 1989 I performed in the Entertainer at Truro 6th Form (now Sainsbury's) then I was picked up at 9pm and whisked down to City Hall to perform with the Nimrod's Marching Band in the finale of The Music Man. We marched down through the aisles of City Hall playing 76 Trombones!

Several years later in 2002 I began working at the box office at the HfC. I met many wonderful people, both customers and performers including Susannah York, Dawn French, Dionne Warwick, Linda Robson, Ken Dodd, who I accompanied around Truro and looked after his Dog (who I'm sure was called Diddy!)

I met my wife Gill at HfC when she worked in the catering department. We married in 2011 in Truro Cathedral and have two children, Elliott and Marnie. Thanks to our jobs at HfC they are here in the world.

CW: When Wild Works took Woolf Child to Fellbrigg Hall in Norfolk, the late Bill Mitchell and Sue Hill gave my daughter the chance to work on the production as a trainee director. After the show one night I heard a tremendous yell, "Chris, Chris!" and this guy rushed over to me and gave me a bear hug. I had no idea who he was or why he was so excited to see me! It emerged that his wayward life had changed after he was taken on by HfC as a stage hand. A few years later he was the Stage Manager on Woolf Child and was a tour manager taking bands and shows all over the world.

BB: Over the past twenty-five years, the Hall has not only established itself as a major Cornish venue, and developed a programme of great variety. It has also done what we said it would and has been a major influence in shaping modern Truro. I must say that I was incensed when Chris Warner was made redundant. He had poured his heart and soul into the project and delivered it. I am glad to see that he was welcomed back to mount events for the Cornwall Youth Music Action Zone (CYMAZ) and for Duchy Opera until he eventually left Cornwall. He also became a valued, honest and straight-talking member of Carrick DC who did not suffer fools. We all owe Chris a huge debt for his courage, creativity and humility.

It's particularly fitting that Chris and Sarah Smith should be writing this book at this time because it coincides with a major reconfiguration of the auditorium and other areas – "their" hall was so popular that we've wore it out in just over 20 years. Reopening will not be easy but the acute business sense developed under the present leadership, will bring it quickly back to life.

Each morning I wake up and look at the time on the Town Clock. When I do it's not simply to check the time but also to make sure the buggers ain't knocked her down, nor never will!

SS: Well that's us done.

CW: So long!

Oh, and thanks for all the fish!

SS: But before we go, we want to thank all those who helped us, our amazing staff team who often went above and beyond the call of duty. Our Trustees who were our ambassadors, fundraisers and who often had to fight on our behalf. Sadly, Brian, John and Jim are no longer with us, but we have hopefully painted an image of how hard they and the rest of the Trustees worked.

CW: Brian's wife, Mavis, told Sarah that her family always referred to Brian, John and Jim as the three Muppets as they used to grumble and mutter together like the old guys on The Muppet Show.

SS: We can't put our pens down without thanking the Design Team, Peter Fazarkerly, Brian Hardman and the Contractors who made it happen and of course the Arts Council England, ERDF, Carrick District Council, the Foundation for Sports and the Arts, Esmee Fairburn Foundation, Headley Trust (Sainsbury's), Baring Foundation, English Partnerships, other trusts and companies not forgetting the hundreds and hundreds of people, not for their fish, but because they believed in the project, encouraged us, helped to raise our profile, took part in our fundraising events and gave us their time and their cash. Incidentally, the total cost of the project was £6.5m in 1997 which would be worth as near as dammit £10.5m in 2020. Worth every penny I'd say!

CW: You all know who you are! You bump started our HfC juggernaut and it set off down the yellow 'n' black road until it arrived a bit out of breath at that opening night in November 1997 when HRH The Duke of Cornwall didn't actually raise the curtain but at which the orchestra played Trelawny with such a mighty opening drum roll that the audience was on its feet because they thought it was the start of the National Anthem. Which of course it was.

SS: Lastly we should never forget Ben Luxon CBE who opened doors for us, gave his time when he didn't have very much of it, who inspired us, who sang for us, gave his love, his humour and unwavering commitment, from coffee table to curtain up, along with everyone else who pushed and shoved to get the monster over the line. Pie in the sky?

CW: Who says?

SS: Please can we put our pens down now? Please? And say goodbye? Please?

CW: OK...........You first.....

SS: No you first.......

SS & CW: Goodbye and......

If we shadows have offended,
Think but this, and all is mended,
That you have but slumber'd here
While these visions did appear.
And this weak and idle theme,
No more yielding but a dream,
Gentles, do not reprehend:
if you pardon, we will mend:
And, as I am an honest Puck,
If we have unearned luck
Now to 'scape the serpent's tongue,
We will make amends ere long;
Else the Puck a liar call;
So, good night unto you all.
Give me your hands, if we be friends,
And Robin shall restore amends

A Midsummer Night's dream: Act V, Scene 1

Acknowledgements

Inspiration

Julien Boast, Chief Executive & Creative Director, Hall for Cornwall who suggested that we write our story and explain why we made certain decisions. He has been a constant source of support and encouragement throughout this process. Thank you, Julien – Chris and I have really enjoyed going back over those years again and contacting people who we haven't been in touch with for too long.

Royal approval

HRH the Duke of Cornwall for his support as our Patron.
Jeff Johnson from HRH the Duke of Cornwall's Royal Household for assisting with royal approval of those chapters telling the story of The Duke of Cornwall's involvement as Patron of The Hall for Cornwall campaign.

Encouragement

Patrice Fellowes at Pernice Press who got us started by for offering to publish and then encouraging us to publish it ourselves.

Judith Forde for reading various versions, finding tons of typos and for her independent encouragement to keep going.

Production

Roger Bacon of Mustard Creative for the book design.
Printed by CPI.

Photographs & Images

Julian Essam for his shot of the HFC auditorium which was the centrefold in the 1997 Gala programme and is our book cover.
Matt Grocutt – Designer who refreshed all the original designs by Tim Guy.
Martin Howse of Truro Camera Club for photographs of City Hall in all its glory.
Nick Toyne for his fifty-year-old photographs of Piran Round and the Northcott Theatre.
Cameracraft, Truro for photographs of the Hall for Cornwall appeal.
Caroline Walker, Project Archivist, University of Exeter.
Cornwall Archaeological Unit for the photograph of the crucibles.
Hartley Boats for the photograph of a Wayfarer.
Press cuttings from West Briton Newspapers.

Memories

Bert Biscoe add Independent Cornwall councillor, Truro City councillor and Mayor of Truro (2020-2021).
Claire Bowden-Dan – Trustee.
Stef Brammar.
Tim Guy, also for the photographs of the fundraising literature.
Ian Hick – Structural Engineer.
Roger Hocking, also for his architectural drawings and photographs.
Benjamin Luxon CBE – founder and president.
Mavis Mansell for sharing stories told by Brian Mansell.
Martin Payne – Senior Engineer, Tilbury Douglas for his photographs of the construction site and the finished building.
Roger Quew - Project Manager, Tilbury Douglas, also for his photographs of the construction site and the finished building.
Wendy Shier.
James Williams - Trustee.
Phill Wills – HfC staff member 2002-2012.

Memories from the City Hall Staff Team

Mary Sheppard
Mandy Rolleston
Caroline Enfissi
Debbie McCrory
Jacqui Pound

Those whose involvement with Hall for Cornwall we have shared

Denis Angilley
Dennis Arbon
Jenny Arquati
Peter Boyden
James Deeny
Tina Evans
Stephen Hybs
Robert Mallett
Peter Mansell
Roger Martin
James Penrose
Vivien Prideaux
Michelle Pugh
Derek and Wendy Reid
Gilly Roberts
Tim Smit
Smith and Reed
Nick Trefusis
Kate Wild

Current Hall for Cornwall Staff team

Julie Caplin Grey
Charlotte Somers
Helen Tiplady
Lucy Innes Williams

Vice Presidents

Thank you to those who lent their names as Vice Presidents in the nineties

The Bishop of Truro
David Bellamy
Rodney Bewes
Sir Richard Carew Pole
Cllr John E H Christie, OBE
Sebastian Coe OBE
Sir Alan Dalton CBE DL
David Harris MP
Justin Hayward
Robert Hicks MP
George Hoare
Lady Mary Holborow
Jan Leeming
Ben Maile
Lucy Penrose
Lord St Levan
Peter Sissons
Matthew Taylor MP
Robin Teverson MEP
EV Thompson
Roy Walker
Sarah Williams

Hall for Cornwall Challenge at Killiow Country Park – September 1995

Devoran Joinery
Vickery Holman
Robinson Reed Layton
Midland Bank
Barclays Bank
AC Systems
Jay Mineral Services
Nalder & Sons
Robert Hartley
NG Associates
Hall for Cornwall Team
The Lark Group
St. Austell Brewery
Alverton Manor

Hall for Cornwall Campaign – A Seat for You Appeal 1995

We would like to thank and acknowledge all those who raised money through our seat appeal. We wanted to publish all your names but unfortunately, because of data protection regulations, we are no longer able to share the list. You know who you are and thank you so much for your support.

Funders and Donors

We have listed most of the grants and have recognised the help we had in securing them but we have not mentioned every individual. Thank you to all those people who put their shoulder to the wheel.